THE SOCIAL THEORY OF CLAUDE LÉVI-STRAUSS

THE SOCIAL THEORY OF CLAUDE LÉVI-STRAUSS

ALAN JENKINS

Lecturer in Social and Political Philosophy
The Polytechnic of Wales

First published 1979 by
THE MACMILLAN PRESS LTD
London and Basingstoke
Associated companies in Delhi
Dublin Hong Kong Johannesburg Lagos
Melbourne New York Singapore Tokyo

Printed in Great Britain by offset lithography by
Billing & Sons Ltd, Guildford, London and Worcester

British Library Cataloguing in Publication Data

Jenkins, Alan
  The social theory of Claude Lévi-Strauss
  1. Lévi-Strauss, Claude   2. Structural
  anthropology
  I. Title
  301.2′092′4   GN316

  ISBN 0–333–23527–4

This book is sold subject
to the standard conditions
of the Net Book Agreement

Contents

Acknowledgements   vi

INTRODUCTION   1

PART ONE   *Anthropology as a Semiology: Lévi-Strauss's Methodological Protocols*   4
    I   The Nature of the Social as an Object of Knowledge   9
    II   The Epistemological Justification of structural Method   21
    III   Conclusion   37

PART TWO   *Structural Anthropology, Primitive Social Organisation and History*   39
    I   Lévi-Strauss's Concept of 'Society' and of 'Primitive' Societies   41
    II   The Structures, Mechanisms and Functions of the Kinship 'Level'   44
    III   An Integrated Critique   74
    IV   Conclusion: Society and History   88

PART THREE   *Ideology and 'Mythic Thought': The Structural Interpretation of Symbolic Representations*   94
    I   The Structural Interpretation of Ideological Systems: Totemism and Mythology   96
    II   The 'Science of the Concrete' and the Unity of Ideology   148
    III   Conclusion   154

CONCLUSION   156

Notes   163

Bibliography   175

Index   189

Acknowledgments

I should like to record my gratitude to a number of individuals who have given me help and encouragement over the period in which this book was written. For intellectual encouragement I am indebted to the late Dr J. B. O'Malley, to Professor J. D. Y. Peel and to Dr B. Hindess of the University of Liverpool. For enormous personal support I am grateful to Lesley, Ian, Elspeth and my parents.

I and Macmillans are also grateful to Jonathan Cape Ltd and Harper and Row, Publishers, Inc., for permission to reproduce the extracts from *The Raw and the Cooked*, translated by John and Doreen Weightman, and to George Weidenfeld & Nicolson Ltd and The University of Chicago Press for permission to reproduce the extracts and figures from *The Savage Mind* (1966). We have made every effort to contact all copyright holders but if any have inadvertently been overlooked we will be pleased to make any necessary arrangements at the first opportunity.

Introduction

Conceived as a work in social theory, this book conducts an examination of the rigour of the concepts and categories which one particular author – Claude Lévi-Strauss – constructs and sets to work in three particular areas: first, in the philosophy and methodology of the social sciences; second, in the general understanding of the nature and constitution of societies as totalities and of the constituent structures of a particular type of society; and, third, in the conception of specific symbolic and ideological practices within societies.

As such the approach is wholly theoretical and it must be stated at the outset that it tries to overcome the arbitrary distinction of issues as 'philosophical', 'sociological' or 'anthropological' which seems to be prevalent in much social thought. It is not really possible to write an adequate piece of work on Lévi-Strauss without involving oneself in all of these areas, and I have tackled the detail of both anthropology and philosophy precisely because this was essential to give a properly rigorous consideration to his contribution to each of the above three areas. Other texts published on 'structuralism' and on Lévi-Strauss have cut corners on both exposition and criticism but I have tried to avoid this as much as possible. Indeed, the justification for the present work lies in the contention that many of the host of 'general overviews' and 'introductions to structuralism' which abound now that the Anglo-American world has assimilated 'semiologically' orientated concepts (whether in literary criticism[1] or in social anthropology),[2] and which interminably repeat the same simple formulae about the 'linguistic analogy', generally pay more attention to the inessential, the superficial, and far less to what is *theoretically* crucial about the discourses and theories to which they make reference.

What I try to do in this book is to confront Lévi-Strauss 'head-on', as it were, and question *the adequacy of his concepts*. Involved in this is the rejection of a conventional view that what is really at stake in the analysis of theories is the general situating of an author's work within intellectual history using techniques from 'the history of ideas'. This latter consensus tends to generate a mode of analysis of theoretical

1

discourse which concerns itself with what are supposed to be the set of 'factors' which together produced the forms of conceptualisation and analysis being examined: it is held that only by considering these 'factors' can the latter be really comprehended in their originality. Recognisable here, for example, are those attempts to piece together Lévi-Strauss's work as the result of a specific intellectual-historical milieu imposing certain 'influences' on the author, which suggest that it can only be fully understood once the extent of the traces of these influences has been ascertained. Certain texts of Sahlins, Leach, Harris, Hughes and Badcock exemplify this general approach,[3] but it is perhaps Scholte and Rossi who are the best examplars.[4] While the latter for example seeks to reconstruct the historical antecedents of a particular concept of Lévi-Strauss's discourse (the unconscious), the former brings together and assesses the effectivity of a whole barrage of 'influences': not only specific authors (Rousseau, Durkheim, Mauss, Kant, Marx, Freud, Lowie, etc.), but whole discourses (linguistics, mathematics, cybernetics and information theory) in an antiquarian *tour de force*.

However, whatever the 'influences' selected, whatever similarities proclaimed and however exhaustive and at what level the search for telltale traces, all such approaches usually commonly fail to elaborate on *why* this particular strategy for the analysis of the theory at hand should be adopted in the first place and why the object considered should be the product of the 'factors' and influences mentioned. On the one hand we are rarely given an explicit justification for the mode of approach (it is implicitly assumed to be correct), while on the other equally rarely are we furnished with a demonstration of the causal connection maintained: far too often recourse is had to Lévi-Strauss's own reflection on his 'influences' as 'evidence' – he need only, for example, state a personal intellectual debt to Marx, Freud and geology (in *Tristes Tropiques* for example) for commentators to produce putative correspondences of his concepts with those of the latter.[5]

In the first part of the text, in discussing the analysis of 'methodologies', the insuperable problems for the analysis of theory generated by the 'influence' approach – stemming from the difficulties entailed in the establishment of the kinds of causal relation it wishes to maintain – are mentioned, and it is in the avoidance of these dilemma and in the establishment and execution of a more adequate interpretation of what is essential to Lévi-Strauss's work that the present work hopes to achieve some originality in each of its consecutive sections.

At the outset it must be stated that it is not a series of putative productive 'factors' grouped around a theoretical discourse – the condition of its supposed 'origin' — which constitutes its essential feature but the conceptual structure of the discourse considered as a whole, as a result. This structure or theoretical 'problematic', as it has been called, exists as the proper object of all interpreters and commentators, but it cannot be simply regarded as openly given to inspection. On the contrary, it consists in a real complexity of concepts, categories and classifications referring to specific objects in theory ('language', 'the state', a specific type of economic system, for example) whose mode of arrangement and interdependency has to be reconstructed according to a strategy (a theory of theory or of discourse)[6] implicit or explicit. This arrangement and interdependency of categories and concepts bequeaths to the theory considered its modes of causality and of explanation and if it is accepted that these are the root phenomena in social thought with which all ought to be concerned then it follows that it is to this immanence of theory, this internality of its constituent categories, and not to relative externalities such as the experiences of the author, his subjective influences, his intellectual milieu or whatever, that adequate analysis and criticism has to turn.

It is hoped that in this book this approach will be made more explicit and pushed to further conclusions than in other assessments of structural anthropology, but it cannot be claimed that what is set forth below is a full realisation of this mode of analysis of theory. Much in the 'theory of discourse' remains tentative and vague as yet, and Lévi-Strauss's work, because of its notorious opacity and imprecision, is a far from ideal object for its analyses.[7] Because of this there will be in places an inevitable degree of vagueness in my characterisation of Lévi-Strauss's system of concepts as a whole, as can be seen where I have used the term 'problematic'[8] rather loosely to designate a putative unity of classifications and modes of explanation at the basis of his whole 'oeuvre' at the same time as attempting to specify the nature of the structural discontinuities within the different *regions* of this work. However, hope remains that together the three major sections which make up this book demonstrate two important points: first, that despite a thirty-year development 'structural anthropology' can be regarded as a conceptual unity; and, second, that this unity, organised as it is with respect to three different analytical objectives, can be criticised at many points for its conceptual level and specification, for its classificatory adequacy and explanatory efficacy in such a way as to demonstrate what is both philosophically and anthropologically acceptable and non-acceptable within its social theory.

PART ONE
Anthropology as a Semiology: Lévi-Strauss's Methodological Protocols

INTRODUCTION

In the past decades there have been a number of authors within the social sciences who have subscribed with considerable optimism to the view that a conceptual unification of these sciences around a central methodological programme would bring revolutionary social scientific developments. The content of such a programme has of course been the subject of endless debate but a very common view has been that all the social sciences have similar objects – types of *communication* – and that prescriptive techniques for dealing with these different objects ought to be derived from an examination of disciplines such as cybernetics, systems and information theory and linguistics, which appear to attain high levels of rigour in their analyses of communicational processes.[1] The ideal of a 'master science' which somehow respects the disparity between diversity and unity, universality and particularity, is constantly in mind.

Mention of linguistics is particularly important, for its contemporary developments have led to renewed interest in the possibility (favoured originally by Locke and C. S. Pierce, followed by de Saussure) of a general 'science of signs' or 'semiotics'. Developments in structural linguistics have led to literally hundreds of methodological proposals for structural/semiotic analyses of domains other than natural language in the hope of reproducing the levels of scientificity assumed to be achieved by the former discipline.[2] Not unnaturally, these proposals are not homogeneous in content: there is a wealth of variation in the way different positions conceive of the possibility (and necessity) of such a theory. While for some authors (e.g. U. Eco) the existence of quasi-

4

linguistic sign-systems other than language, as objects, seems almost self-evident, for others (in particular Hjelmslev) semiology is a theoretical necessity deriving from the nature of the structure of linguistic theory.

Now this is not the place to attempt to consider all the convergences and divergences of the various methodological invocations for a comparative semiotics: this would constitute a book in itself. Here we are directly concerned with the 'protocols' for the semiotic foundation of anthropology which are present in the work of Lévi-Strauss. We shall be concerned with the latter's attempts to reformulate the basis of social anthropology as a semiology through the provision of a structural methodology. In what follows the discussion will attempt to provide a thorough and clear-cut critique of this methodology by isolating 'strategic levels' at which criticism of the protocols may be formulated so as to be most effective in an examination of the concepts which make up that methodology.

This mention of 'strategic levels' at which criticism is to be pitched is most important because it is a basic contention here that any analysis of any theoretical methodology in social theory is an enterprise which is immediately confronted with theoretical problems itself which derive from the problem of working out a strategy of analysis with respect to the work at hand. It cannot be upheld that this formulation of strategy is an unimportant or arbitrary matter: on the contrary, discussions of theory and of discourses consisting of concepts, classifications and categories are *themselves* implicitly theoretical and entail therefore specific forms of conceptualisation. It is a matter that is to say, of a *theory of theory or of discourse*.[3]

THE ANALYSIS OF A 'METHODOLOGY'

Now, having mentioned the importance of a theory of theory or of theoretical discourse it should not be thought that there exists a closely argued and commonly accepted set of ideas within this area. Far from it, the theory of discourse is a relatively undeveloped area within social theory although advances have to a certain extent been made by contemporary French philosophers in sketching some of the important issues within this area. Thus, Althusser, Foucault and Derrida among others raise fundamental problems connected with the whole practice of 'reading' theoretical texts, and following on from their work other authors have attempted to state the main features of the central problems of concern.

However, this is not the place to give a detailed discussion of developments within the theory of discourse – it will suffice here to state a *strategy to be adopted* in looking at a set of methodological statements and to defend that strategy in a concise manner. It seems to the author that the analysis of any methodology in the texts of any theorist must at least maintain a schematic two-fold distinction. First, methodological statements or protocols can be conceived as being composed of two conceptual elements which are usually juxtaposed in any discussions, but which are really distinct. Very schematically these are, on the one hand, *substantive* concepts which demarcate the general nature of the 'objects' or 'phenomena' (*internal* to theory) under consideration, and on the other hand *epistemological* formulations which specify the scientific status of various techniques of investigation which are supposed to be adequate to those phenomena under consideration. These elements are always effectively combined in those discourses or systems of concepts whose main concern is methodology. Indeed methodology *per se* is a conjunction of these two elements in some form.

Second, each of these particular elements ('substantive' and 'epistemological') of the methodology may in itself be sub-divisible and subject to internal connections between discrete concepts. This internal nature of the two elements will vary from theory to theory and its character depends ultimately on relations of dependancy and interconnection of a *logical* nature between the concepts which form the bulk of the discourse as a whole. Thus, depending on the discourse, the set of statements which make up the epistemological element may contain the traces of a theory of knowledge and of science which can vary across a whole spectrum of philosophical positions (it may be 'neo-positivist', Kantian, etc., etc.). Likewise, and importantly, 'substantive' elements may contain general concepts of the nature of the object or potential phenomenon of theory under investigation which 'articulate', with a definite type of dependence, with other concepts which have a logical place within the discourse as a whole but which figure primarily and mainly in the actual analyses which the discourse undertakes and constructs *more or less independently* of statements of methodology. In general, then, a distinction is maintained between *the formulation of a task in methodological terms* (composed of substantive *and* epistemological theses) and *the concepts constructed in a body of theory which are supposed to realise this task substantively*. These are two *levels* of a discourse, and each has distinct conditions of existence irreducible to the other: the substantive specifications of the different concepts constructed in social theories are *not* reducible to simple realisations or manifestations of a methodological programme 'in action', as it were.[4]

It follows that in my analysis of Lévi-Strauss's problematic I attempt to maintain where possible a two-fold strategic distinction which does have a theoretical justification at its basis. In many modes of analysis of Lévi-Strauss's work no such justification for treating the different levels of conceptualisation in a certain manner is provided – the non-problematic character of 'reading' and the legitimacy of a certain approach is tacitly and somewhat dogmatically assumed beforehand.[5] Two approaches exemplify these points. First, we have the widespread reading which sees his work as the realisation or effect of a set of historical and intellectual influences.[6] Here Lévi-Strauss's concepts are examined less for their distinctive content and logical interdependency than for their manifestation of the 'traces' of the concepts of others: in the latter's case usually for Marx, Freud and structural linguistics. This *presupposes* a number of dubious things – first, that any problematic can be made up from an *ad hoc* conglomeration of concepts from widely different problematics (with widely different objects), and second that these concepts (the 'Marxian', the 'Freudian') which are held to be the 'building blocks' of the problematic in question can themselves be 'recognised' in a simple and essentially straightforward fashion. Both these propositions must however be treated with extreme caution – the first relies upon the second and the second itself regards the practice of the isolation of distinct types of concepts (of Marx, of Freud) as unproblematic, which it indeed surely is not. Consider the furore of theoretical debate in the first case over the 'correct' Marx or the 'correct' Freud! We are being offered a 'correct' Lévi-Strauss which presupposes a 'correct' reading of the concepts which are his component influences or 'historical/intellectual antecedents'. The theory of discourse is both rendered doubly necessary and doubly settled in an essentially arbitrary way.

A second type of reading consists in the reduction of Lévi-Strauss's whole system of concepts to a 'methodology in operation'. Here Lévi-Strauss's substantive analyses of whatever domain of the social are conceived as the simple results of the methodology of structuralism being applied to an object independent of theory. Structural Anthropology, it follows, is in essentials the *structural method*. It suffices to say that the very great danger of this reading is that once the reduction of the whole discourse to a methodology-in-operation is effected, the task of establishing the nature of the dependancy and connection between the concepts which are constructed to analyse a particular feature of the social (for example a particular kinship formation) becomes almost impossible in any coherent fashion.

It is hoped that the difficulties accompanying such modes of analysis will be overcome here to a certain extent by utilising the distinctions – admittedly somewhat crude ones – which have been emphasised above. Accordingly, most of the analysis which follows attempts to devote separate and detailed consideration to each type in itself and tries to provide an account of the logical dependencies between the major concepts of each part.

The first part of the chapter will be devoted to the predominantly substantive proportion of Lévi-Strauss's methodological concepts and here consideration will be directed to the latter's *concept of the object of anthropology* – that is, to the general concept of *the nature of the social* upon which structural anthropology relies and is based. It is how social or socio-cultural 'facts' *per se* are conceived as the objects of theory that will be at issue, and my discussion will give an exposition of the essentials of Lévi-Strauss's position and then go on to establish definite theoretical shortcomings within the overall conceptualisation. Following this, in the *second* part of the chapter I shall turn to the distinctly epistemological element of the methodological formulations and consider Lévi-Strauss's conception of those methods which are proposed to produce a scientific knowledge of the 'objects' previously demarcated. We shall see that there are a number of different aspects of these formulations but I shall concentrate on the overall conception of scientificity in the social sciences (and the concomitant ideas on the nature of the production of knowledge within these sciences) which 'structural anthropology' advocates. Section II thus raises a quite different (although connected) set of issues to those examined in the first part of the chapter.

We shall see that the unity of Lévi-Strauss's 'structural' methodology derives from the conjunction of substantive ideas on the *structured* nature of the objects of anthropology (this structure being part of their essential constitution) with epistemological formulations on the correct scientific means to be adopted in order to abstract or reconstruct this fundamental order: in the last analysis, a theory of the abstraction of the basic essential form of an object by the construction of a model or formal calculus of that object revealing its structure. The unity is therefore centred upon the ambiguous concept of 'structure', which is used *both* substantively *and* epistemologically. On the one hand the essence of the objects of anthropology is their *structure*, in the sense of their constitutive internal organisation. On the other hand science or a scientific social theory abstracts the 'essences' from its objects by revealing their essential underlying structures.[7]

1 The Nature of the Social as an Object of Knowledge

It can be stated at the outset that for Lévi-Strauss, the 'socio-cultural' is a domain of symbolisms or significations in which disparate ideas and 'meanings' are realised and expressed through symbolic action. As a whole, this domain must be considered as divided into a set of discrete semantic spaces, each organised as a distinct mode of signification or 'semiosis'. Thus

> Toute culture peut être considerée comme une ensemble de systèmes symboliques au premier rang desquels se placent le langage, les règles matrimoniales, les rapports économiques, l'art, la science, la religion. Tous les systèmes visent à exprimer certains aspects de la réalité physique et de la réalité sociale, et plus encore, les relations que ces deux types de realité entretiennent entre eux et que les systèmes symboliques eux-mêmes entretiennent les uns avec les autres. [Any culture can be considered as a totality of symbolic systems, the most important of which are language, rules of alliance, economic relations, art, science, religion. All the systems seek to express certain aspects of physical reality and of social reality and, furthermore, the relations between these two types of reality and between the symbolic systems themselves.] ['Introduction à l'oeuvre de M. Mauss', p. xix]

These systems or cultural formations are in fact totalities of 'collective representations' elaborated within societies at a supra-individual level. Lévi-Strauss has this much in common with Durkheim in that objects of social thought are conceived of as systems of objectified ideas and meanings generated socially and cohering according to definite logical relations.

Lévi-Strauss departs from Durkheim (and Mauss), however, in the specific way in which he understands (a) the mechanisms and principles which underlie the 'architecture' of systems of collective representation and generate their symbolic quality, and (b) the objective foundation and origin of these mechanisms. First, Lévi-Strauss asserts – by an often metaphorical recourse to linguistics, systems theory and cybernetics – a set of theses on the mechanics of social representation; and, second, he roots the possibility of this mechanics in a supra-individual psychic mechanism – the unconscious. Let us consider this 'mechanics' to begin with.

Of the types of metaphorical representation of the symbolic nature of cultural configurations by far the most important are those which employ references to the nature and constitution of language.[8] While metaphorical use is made from time to time of systems and information theory[9] this is nearly always restricted and vague and the theoretical function of the metaphor (which *is* its most important aspect, above all) is minimal: it may be for instance to simply characterise the overall function of a class of phenomena being considered rather than to provide theoretical guidelines to the analytical compositions of these phenomena. On the other hand, references to language and to linguistics play a primary theoretical and methodological role: here the metaphors and analogies used have a crucial methodological function within Lévi-Strauss's problematic, a role both epistemological and substantive. This is so because for Lévi-Strauss linguistics is conceived as the paradigm of a science of the cultural and the natural reference point for a scientific 'semiotics' of different cultural configurations to which anthropology is to contribute. As early as 1945 linguistics was conceived as the means through which a scientific knowledge of the cultural would be attained and despite a series of reservations and qualifications this position is still more or less advocated.

It is important to bear in mind two points, not always made distinct, which make plain the theoretical essentials of Lévi-Strauss's appeal to linguistics. First, there are epistemological reasons for Lévi-Strauss's conception of the primacy of linguistics and language within the social sciences. The 'privileged' nature of linguistics is an effect of the fact that it is held that, in treating its object in a certain manner, for the first time a truly scientific knowledge of a social object had been constituted by a discourse. If this is accepted then the question arises as to whether the other social sciences may achieve scientificity by, in like manner, evolving and refining similar methodological procedures to those involved in linguistics in the treatment of *its* objects of investigation.

Second, Lévi-Strauss proposes substantive reasons for why such a development of comparable methodological techniques ought to be possible. These derive from putative 'substantial similarities' between the object of linguistics and what is presumed to be the object of anthropology. For Lévi-Strauss what makes the 'structural' methodological project *viable* is not only the epistemological virtues of linguistics but certain comparabilities and specific correspondences between the configurations of 'collective representations' (the objects of the anthropologist) and natural language, as organised totalities.

As I have said, for the moment I want to concern myself with these *second* 'substantive' assertions within Lévi-Strauss's discourse which I have just mentioned. These raise the whole question of the kind of relationship which Lévi-Strauss posits between language and other 'cultural domains' and between language and 'culture-in-general'. We *can* suggest that there are *two* basic levels where a substantive 'link' is posited between language on the one hand and the cultural configurations or systems of collective representations on the other:

(1) To begin with, at a relatively high level of generality and prior to the analysis of cultural domains, both are conceived as *a priori* manifestations, expressions or results of the action and effectivity of an implicit collective mental mechanism called 'the unconscious', which forms the locus or origin of the form of their structures and internal modes of organisation. Both are indeed, phenomenal expressions of the same 'essence'.

(2) Second, specific cultural configurations are presumed by Lévi-Strauss to be represented by his analyses as having internal structures, modes of reality and types of signification basically comparable to those of language. In the substantive analyses of kinship, totemism and myth Lévi-Strauss characterises these objects as 'semantic spaces' of a quasi-linguistic constitution; i.e. as 'semiological' systems.

It must be borne in mind above all here that these two levels are directly interconnected, although they are *not* reducible to each other. While at the second level the culture of a society is asserted as being composed of *discrete spaces of phenomena* each of which has an essential internal basis which forms the key to the mechanism by which they signify, function and reproduce themselves, for Lévi-Strauss these essences/bases (in fact 'structures') of the phenomena are existent only as the products of the unconscious mind and its mode of action (bringing us to the first point). The essential structures of various cultural phenomena are nearly always conceived as the products of this mental faculty or mechanism which underlies them, making them possible, and acting so as to carve out these structures within distinct spaces of the 'real'.[10] Furthermore these 'essential structures' of the various cultural systems can always be expected to present direct similarities among themselves precisely because of the mode of action of the unconscious in organising the material at its disposal according to definite modalities.

In this manner we can see the manifest importance of the concept of the 'unconscious' in Lévi-Strauss's idea of the nature of his objects and consequently in his substantive arguments in favour of a quasi-linguistic methodological approach in anthropology. *If the 'source' of the type of order manifested by language is also at the basis of the type of order present in the rest of culture and if this 'source' has a constant mode of effectivity, then we are justified in investigating culture as a whole with methods which have been so successful in linguistics, as we can expect both language and other sectors of culture to be similarly structured.* Such is Lévi-Strauss's implicit reasoning. It will follow that if an order is indeed demarcated in non-linguistic aspects of culture using an empirical method which is a 'modification' of linguistic techniques then this will tend to reinforce the thesis that all culture is structured after the fashion of language. The unity and substantive justification of a 'structural approach' to the objects of anthropology in the last analysis derives from the theory (in Lévi-Strauss's case, but also in the work of his disciples, e.g. Lucien Sebag) that these are *phenomena whose essence or 'source' is the same as that of language*: the structural nature of language is held to be an effect of the 'praxis' of the unconscious, this praxis underlies all cultural forms, *ergo* all cultural forms have a structured nature like language, which is also given by the mode of action of the unconscious. In this way the constancy of the effectivity of the unconscious, as Lévi-Strauss conceives it, is a lynch pin of the substantive justification for advocacy of a structuralist methodology.

However, can this conception provide structural anthropology with the support it requires by furnishing a theoretical justification for the application of quasi-linguistic approaches to systems of collective representations? In order to determine this the concept of the 'unconscious' (and its place within various areas of Lévi-Strauss's work) must be looked at in more detail. We shall see in what follows, however, that a negative answer must be given to the above question: *in themselves the assertions of the existence and operation of the 'unconscious' are insufficient to found a semi-homologous relationship between language and other cultural sectors which would justify the advocacy of structural methods for the treatment of the latter domains.*

THE CONCEPT OF THE 'UNCONSCIOUS'

Lévi-Strauss's conception of the 'unconscious', as we have said, is that of a locus or substratum of all symbolisms: the condition of the existence of the cultural domain as the fusion of both natural and 'ideal' factors. As such, the 'unconscious' (and its 'embodiment in the symbolic function') underlines all systems of ideas and furnishes the origin of their order – its importance for social thought is thus paramount, as it promises to be the key to the diversity and unity of empirical cultures. Naturally, given this importance it follows that *the nature of its specification is absolutely essential* and because of this we must examine the arguments Lévi-Strauss gives for the existence and operation of the mechanism, in order to (i) formulate the exact function of the concept in his methodology, and (ii) provide a fully adequate criticism of the postulates it supports.

Now in virtually every one of Lévi-Strauss's major texts written to date some conception of the 'mind' or the 'unconscious' or the 'symbolic function' (these are often used interchangeably) is proposed as having a distinct kind of determinacy as a 'structuring force' or 'capacity' constituted supra-individually, and operating at the basis of all culture. Indeed this conception is represented in so many ways that there is a danger that one might be tempted to see it as devoid of substantive function. This would be a dangerous error, however – the conception *does* have a central theoretical role in Lévi-Strauss's discourse, as we shall demonstrate shortly. Note, however, that the arguments which Lévi-Strauss gives for qualifying the existence, nature and effectivity of the 'unconscious' draw upon work already done in linguistics, psychology, philosophy and cybernetics for support, and the results of his own work are seen as *reinforcing* the thesis of its ubiquity. In the following discussion *three* aspects are important:

(1) a detailed account of Lévi-Strauss's representation of the 'unconscious' is given;

(2) it is shown that the nature of this *representation* (its vagueness, etc., etc.) derives from the fact that Lévi-Strauss is theoretically unable to specify (for good reasons) the mechanisms of operation and modes of existence of the 'unconscious' beyond a few schematic assertions (which cannot use as 'evidence' results attained by the other disciplines cited above), despite its overwhelming importance in his problematic;

(3) the lack or failure of specification is related to the theoretical role of the 'unconscious' as a concept [11] – in structural anthropology we shall see that it has the function of a 'constitutive essence' whose nature by definition is to act as an 'origin' but whose modes of action and constitution can never, *because of this*, be specified in any adequate manner within the limits of the problematic; the concept is theoretically necessary to Lévi-Strauss but its weakness

only signifies the failure of the latter's position to come to terms with its internal difficulties.

THE OVERALL CHARACTERISATION OF THE UNCONSCIOUS

We are never ever really given a concise, detailed elaboration of this entity: what we are given by Lévi-Strauss is at most three types of assertion about it.

First, the 'unconscious' is represented as a 'form' or an apparatus or aggregate of forms empty of, and prior to, mental 'contents' which acts by structuring and organising, according to certain modalities, these contents. Thus, in an attempt to differentiate his own concept from what he takes to be Freud's, Lévi-Strauss asserts in *Structural Anthropology* that

> The unconscious ceases to be the ultimate haven of individual peculiarities – the repository of a unique history which makes each of us an irreplaceable being. It is reducible to a *function*, the symbolic function, which is no doubt specifically human and which is carried out according to the same laws among all men, and actually corresponds to the aggregate of these laws[12] [p. 202–3]

and in particular

> The unconscious . . . is always empty – or more accurately it is akin to mental images as the stomach is to the food which passes through it. As the organ of a specific function the unconscious merely imposes structural laws upon inarticulated elements which originate elsewhere . . . [ibid., p. 203].

In such passages and elsewhere we are left in no doubt that the entity being posited is the locus of 'permanent and logical structures' of the mind whose effectivity is a structuration of material and ideational elements placed at its disposal.

The second feature of this entity is its dominantly *intellectual* or *cognitive* orientation, and its *conceptual* or *logical* constraint and influence on the material 'given' to it. This primacy of intellection or cognition at the root of the unconscious and within the symbolic function, as a consequence, is brought out most clearly in the discussions of its effectivity at the basis of the generation of totemic classifications and mythic representations.[13] The structural analysis of myth is, for example,

> a matter of the transportation of the *Kantian* enquiry into the ethnological domain, with this difference . . . that I move to the limit: by investigating what there might be in common between the humanity which seems so remote to us and the way our own minds work; by trying to disengage the basic and constraining properties of all mind, whever it may be [*Confrontation over Myths*, p. 59; my emphasis].

The reply to P. Ricouer's charge (in this text) that this work is a 'Kantianism without a transcendental subject' is that this is an inevitable philosophical consequence of the ethnographic approach adopted. The very reality of myths in particular as collective representations manifests the operation of a universal apparatus of intellection as their fundamental dynamic. This is reaffirmed in the final volume of the *Mythologiques* (*L'Homme nu*) where we are told once more that [14]

> An apparatus of oppositions built into the understanding functions whenever recurrent experiences, be they of biological, technological, economic, sociological or other origin, take control much like those innate forms of conduct that we attribute to animals and whose phases succeed one another automatically whenever an appropriate combination of circumstances triggers them off. Similarly elicited by such empirical combinations, the conceptual machinery is set in motion *ceaselessly extracting meaning from every concrete situation however complex and turning it into an object of thought by adaptation to the imperative demands of a formal organisation* [p. 539; my emphasis].

A third type of assertion about the 'unconscious apparatus' may be briefly mentioned. In a number of places Lévi-Strauss tries to relate this 'system of mental constraints' which he posits and which compose the 'unconscious' to a *natural* foundation in the brain and in 'cerebral structures'. The structure of the brain is vaguely homologous with the structure of the mind: their conjoint action, by governing symbolic action, is responsible for setting up formal relations of contrast and opposition between material and ideal elements within a culture and so generating ordered systems of representations. If the latter, as it is suggested, can be shown to be built up by mechanisms of binary opposition (as can certain levels of *language*) then this is only because of the *prior* existence of a pre-given mental and cerebral *binary* mechanism which is the capacity to generate oppositional relations.[15]

This attempt to give the system of mental constraints a natural foundation is perhaps clearest in the paper 'Structuralism and Ecology' (1972) where Lévi-Strauss explicitly refers to two basic determinisms of action – one deriving from the constraints of natural conditions upon man and the other from stable 'mental constraints' (that is, from the requirement that actions conform to the determination of the ideal realm) – and attempts to interrelate them on a natural substratum. Here emphasis is placed on a putative physiological basis to perceptual processes which interlock with the 'higher intellectual activities of the mind'. We are told that we must dismiss an 'outmoded dualism' because

> when the mind processes the empirical data which it receives previously processed by the sense organs it goes on working structurally on what at the outset was already structural. And it can only do so in as much as the mind, the body to which the mind belongs and the things which body and mind perceive, are part and parcel of one and the same reality [p. 21].

That is to say ' "the understanding" takes over and developes intellectual processes already operating in the sensory organs themselves' [p. 22]. Unfortunately however, we are not told about the *mechanism* through which this 'taking over' becomes effective, so that the link Lévi-Strauss suggests between the physiological/natural level of perceptual processes and properly intellectual ones governed by the unconscious/'mind'/'understanding' remains somewhat speculative.

X   One overall result of all this which may be noted however, is the subjection of the mind/unconscious to a double determination – it must realise ideal elements and at the same time conform to natural determinations. This compound of two determinations only serves to blur even further the question of the supporting conditions of the unconscious in Lévi-Strauss's texts, for in the last analysis the nature of neither form of determination is fully explained by the author: the existence and reproduction of the entity itself is unaccounted for.

Beyond all the specifications I have mentioned above, the *exact* nature of the unconscious or of 'mind' in Lévi-Strauss's discourse remains something of a mystery – commentators have constantly referred to its vagueness. While the schematic outline I have given cannot exhaust all of Lévi-Strauss's comments on this constitutive entity, it must be accepted that nowhere is there an elaborated account of this entity specifying its all-important mechanisms of operation. We are given, rather, as we have seen, a series of notions of a little-elaborated nature. The question of the operative conditions of existence of the entity or faculty are, however, very important: granted its constitutive and determinant position within Lévi-Strauss's problematic the *failure* to provide a detailed account of its functions and make-up over and above the three types of broad specifications I have sketched above is highly significant.[16] Lévi-Strauss affirms the necessary *a priori* existence of a constitutive basis of the symbolic (and *ipso facto* of 'culture') but the real conditions of existence of this entity are *neither demonstrated nor elaborated*. The mechanisms of its causation are never clarified.

In this respect Lévi-Strauss resorts to appealing to work done in disciplines other than anthropology for 'evidence' of its operation – to philosophy and psychology in part, but in particular to *linguistics*. The recourse to existing philosophical and psychological positions is, however, substantively very limited. Lévi-Strauss's references to his project as quasi-Kantian and his varied references to Freud and to others in psychoanalysis and psychology (e.g. Isaacs, Piaget) tend to constitute in the main simply attempts by an author to sketch affinities and similarities between his ideas and those of others, rather than precise adoptions and assimilations of specific *forms of conceptualisation*.

The case with his recourse to linguistics is however quite different: here a particular position within linguistic theory is adopted and utilised as 'evidence' for the nature of the 'unconscious'/the 'symbolic function'. The particular position is of course that which is attributable to 'Prague Phonology' and in particular to that variant developed by N. S. Trubetzkoy and R. Jakobson in a number of texts. From a very early date Lévi-Strauss had always considered that 'phonemics' demonstrates the operation of an implicit system of mental constraints, whose mode of action is binary and oppositional, at the basis of language as an ordered system. On the one hand, certain aspects of the findings of the 'Prague school' on the phonological structure of language are 'affirmed', while, on the other, these findings are regarded as the most faithful manifestations of the true nature of the 'unconscious' – the latter being present most clearly in the structural order of language, where its 'traces' are most easily discernible.

To begin with, Lévi-Strauss accepts and assumes the validity of Jakobson's conception that it is a universal feature of all languages to be based, at the phonemic level of organisation, on binary oppositional choices between certain types of elements. For the latter[17] (and thus for the former also) *binarism is absolute* – the phonetic systems of *all* languages can in principle be described by means of a dozen 'distinctive features'[18] all of them binary, being present, absent or irrelevant as the case may be. Thus in a paper on 'linguistic universals' we are told by Jakobson that

> There is an inventory of simple relations common to all tongues of the world. Such relations pertain both to the early acquisitions of children's language and to the most stable properties in those types of aphasic regress which display a mirror picture of infants' development. This *repertory* may be exemplified in phonemics by such simple relations as compact/diffuse (universally displayed in vocalism and usually in consonantism) grave/acute and . . . nasal/non-nasal [R. Jakobson (1967), p. 581].

Lévi-Strauss's affirmation of Jakobsonian 'universalist' theses in both his substantive and methodological essays is well known – for him the 'discovery' of the universality and centrality of binarism in language constitutes the true promise of linguistics and the most valuable general fruit of its 'structural reorientation'.

Beyond this however, Lévi-Strauss goes one crucial step further by regarding this presumed universality of binarism as overwhelming testimonial evidence for the true nature of the 'unconscious' – the findings of phonology are assumed to show that at the very heart of culture (in language as the cultural *par excellence*) and of the 'symbolic function' an immutable system of mental constraints operates universally and constantly *according to binary mechanisms*. Significantly, Lévi-Strauss further does not avoid the temptation of linking the presumed universal phonological distinctions to a *natural* basis in the structure of *the brain* 'beneath' the symbolic function (we have already noted this tendency to try to relate the 'unconscious' to a natural foundation above). Thus for instance, we are told that the study of the phenomenon of the association of colour frequencies with phonemic interrelations may not only disclose

> much of importance to the psychological and theoretical aspects of linguistics, *but it leads us directly to the consideration of the 'natural bases' of the phonemic system – that is, the structure of the brain* [*Structural Anthropology*, p. 92; my emphasis].

Now, nothing is more tenuous than the two aspects of this appeal or recourse to 'linguistic evidence' by Lévi-Strauss. First and foremost the Jakobsonian tenets whose validity Lévi-Strauss assumes and whose substance he assimilates, are very far from having *universal acceptance* within linguistic theory, as Barthes, Malmberg and others[19] recognise, but as Lévi-Strauss flatly assumes and accepts. The controversial theoretical status of these ideas within linguistics must be fully recognised especially when one realises that they are being used by Lévi-Strauss as given *evidence* for a particular argument about universal structures of language[20] (the 'Mendelian table' ideal of the phonological traits). This is a fact which is *not* reflected in Lévi-Strauss's highly selective adoption of only specific linguistic theses (and a concomitant ignoring of others) in his work. While many linguists express agreement with the position of Jakobson numerous others express distinct reservations.[21] In particular, as Malmberg notes,

Andre Martinet accuses the Jakobson-Fant-Halle system of being *a prioristic*, a pre-established system for which the authors have postulated general validity. Martinet admits[22] the necessity of defining the (phonemic) oppositions in terms of sound substance. These terms as such are indifferent, but any attempt to make them descriptive (grave – diffuse, strident – mellow) will necessarily be arbitrary. What seems important to Martinet is the proportionality of the relations between units and this proportionality is revealed by the parallelism in the variations. And it can hardly be denied that at least some of the terms which Jakobson *et al.* have chosen to symbolise their fundamental entities – the 'distinctive features' – seem arbitrary, even directly misleading. *The idea of the universality of the basic features may seem fascinating but needs further evidence. Martinet cannot accept the general validity of the binary choice. In fact it seems as if several writers are inclined to look upon it as the simplest principle of interpretation although by no means the only possible one ...* [B. Malmberg (1963), p.123; my emphasis].

The mere citation by Lévi-Strauss of Jakobson's conceptions is *not* in itself sufficient to support the assertion of the existence of universal binary operators at the basis of all languages: the very real theoretical controversy over this question within linguistic theory has to be assessed in some detail and this position *substantiated* before it is used *arbitrarily* by another discourse to support a certain conception of the structural foundation of the cultural/symbolic *per se*. Nowhere in Lévi-Strauss's work do we find a fully adequate discussion of these issues: we are faced rather with a partisan adoption of certain specific linguistic perspectives which is without full justification.[23] So far it has nowhere been adequately proved conclusively that all languages have a universal and absolute structured binary foundation at the phonemic level and it must follow that such a proposition cannot be regarded as evidential of the nature of the structure of a universal cultural capacity ('mind', 'the unconscious', *'ésprit'*).

A *hypothetical* universalism such as this, as manifest in Lévi-Strauss's work, does not provide *proof* of the structure of this proposed mental apparatus and it is arguable that even if such a thesis were proven (that is, if it were proven that all languages have an identical universal binary substratum) it would *still* be illegitimate to assume that the organisation of an immutable human apparatus had been uncovered simultaneously. Establishing the universal nature of the order and constitution of a type of social phenomena (linguistic, economic, political, etc.) is a task at one theoretical level; providing an answer to the question of the 'origin' of this order (perhaps in 'external' determinations) is one at *another* level. The two are not coterminous and should not be conflated.

It is thus contended here that Lévi-Strauss cannot legitimately assume that phonology provides evidence for the nature of the structure of the 'unconscious' as he conceives it within his problematic. Despite his attempts to use certain types of non-anthropological arguments and positions as supportive of his own notion of this apparatus it cannot be said that its theoretical basis is thereby strengthened. It remains an ambiguous and paradoxical entity, as I have said above: it takes on the character of a *'constitutive essence'* within Lévi-Strauss's work in being propounded as highly conceptually necessary on the one hand (serving a definite *explanatory* role with respect to certain questions)[24] but, on the other, remaining somewhat theoretically indeterminate, almost as an entity without specified conditions of existence and operation.

This theoretical indeterminacy is moreover bound up directly with the conceptual function which the concept plays within Lévi-Strauss's problematic: as an *essential origin* or *source* of diverse activities the conception provides a *methodological* support for the structural theoretical project (and provides a distinctive element of a theory of symbolic action).

That which makes possible the whole undertaking of a structural comparative analysis of culture is the effective essentialist action of 'the unconscious' as its structuring origin: the diverse cultural regions are in principle all phenomena of this same original essence, *a priori*. It is linguistics which moreover is supposed to reveal the true mode of operation of this essence, and thus a 'quasi-linguistic' approach to other cultural domains might be expected to reveal *their* true nature (that is, 'explain' them) as comparable structural realisations of the action of the same capacity. In other words, if one can discern an entity such as an 'unconscious' at the very heart of the mode of signification or 'semiosis' peculiar to language 'the very paradigm of culture', then is it not likely that all symbolisms in their own particular 'semioses' bear its imprint in some way? Lévi-Strauss's 'unconscious' is the central feature of his general conception of symbolic action and at the heart of his conception of the object of anthropology. Through its role as a mechanism for the realisation of ideas or 'meanings' this entity is productive of the socio-cultural as a domain formed by the fusion of natural and ideal components. But because its action can only be conceived by Lévi-Strauss as 'expressively causal' there must be a reliance upon a dogmatic teleology in the understanding of its mechanisms,[25] which renders the way the social as a distinct domain is understood highly unsatisfactory. In the last analysis the substantive concept of the socio-cultural within structural anthropology is fraught with difficulties generated by this expressivism.

II The Epistemological Justification of Structural Method

We have just seen how Lévi-Strauss conceives of the realm of culture and how he tries to formulate, in accordance with this, a certain substantive conception of the object of anthropology in order to found a 'semiotic' type of analysis of it using certain structural principles. These principles are represented in his work as 'quasi-linguistic' and are supposed to produce a *scientific analysis* of the object under consideration (this or that cultural domain or region) by revealing the *structure* of the object (as its most fundamental and essential nature) beneath its mere given empirical 'appearances'. (This structured nature, as explained above, is conceived as the result of the essential operations of the 'unconscious'). If the essence of real culture is its structure, then for Lévi-Strauss scientific anthropology must deploy a conceptual apparatus which can isolate and abstract the structures of different sets of empirical socio-cultural phenomena. For Lévi-Strauss this is to be achieved (as we shall soon see) only by using certain specific conceptual means (chiefly a 'model' or theoretical construct) which can be established as *epistemologically* sound.

In this part of Section II I want to discuss these methodological principles and means, and how Lévi-Strauss provides epistemological justifications for the adoption of his methodological orientation to his objects by advocating a certain conception of the 'scientific method' and of the knowledge processes underlying it. We shall see that this part of Lévi-Strauss's methodology rests upon a wholly inadequate understanding of the nature of the process of the production of knowledge – his representation of science, his reflections on linguistics and other discourses and his particular epistemological statements can all be shown to be based upon important theoretical errors. The demonstration of these errors must have definite effects for Lévi-Strauss's 'structural methodology' (and also for that of similarly orientated authors such as L. Sebag,[26] R. Barthes, U. Eco) in that the whole *epistemological basis* for the advocacy of structural techniques of analysis of social phenomena in a methodological programme must collapse.

Linked with the removal of the substantive justifications for Lévi-Strauss's structural methodology (see Section I above) the overall conclusion here must be that the methodological claims for structural anthropology are without any adequate theoretical foundation.

THE STRUCTURAL PRINCIPLES AND MEANS OF INVESTIGATION OF THE OBJECT

The corpus of conceptual means to be used by structural anthropology with respect to its cultural 'objects' can be briefly characterised in this section. As such these are the principles and techniques which Lévi-Strauss advocates as apposite to the task of the formulation of the structures/essential mechanisms of cultural objects. How then is this structure/essence to be reached? Lévi-Strauss gives a number of theses on this question, but most of them centre upon a basic and fundamental point: the structured essences of real empirical (social) relations are attainable through the construction, by the investigator, of models or theoretical constructs (satisfying, as we shall see, a number of conditions) which represent the mechanisms underlying these relations. The *model* is to be the privileged conceptual means by which the order generated by 'the unconscious' in cultural reality is to be established and through which a methodological unity is affirmed between 'explicit' concepts of 'structure' and of 'model' and an 'implicit' concept of the essence of the real. Within the concept of structure (and this accounts for its analytical ambiguity in structuralism) substantive theses about the basically semiotic constitution of culture are fused and conflated with epistemological theses on the conceptual means of grasping the essence of that constitution. The trinity of 'structure/essence/model' traces the basis of the methodology:[27] the aim of the model is to reveal the structure as the essence of the phenomenon which is under consideration. Knowledge is the result of the fabrication of a model independently, and in abstraction from the real, which is prior to theory. I shall consider this general epistemological position shortly, but first, for Lévi-Strauss, what are the fundamental characteristics of models and of model construction?

In a number of publications Lévi-Strauss outlines the following basic features of the latter conceptual means. To begin with, models are conceptual constructs which, to be satisfactorily explicative (i.e. to establish the structure of a set of empirical social relations) must be 'systematic', 'transformational', 'predictive' and explanatorily 'exhaustive'. Thus Lévi-Strauss tells us that

we can say that a structure consists of a model which meets the following requirements. *First*, the structure exhibits the characteristics of a system. It is made up of several elements, none of which can undergo a change without effecting changes in all the other elements. *Second*, for any given model there should be a possibility of ordering a series of transformations resulting in a group of models of the same type. *Third*, it is possible to predict how the model will react if one or more of its elements are submitted to certain modifications. *Finally*, the model should be constituted so as to make immediately intelligible all the observed facts [*Structural Anthropology*, pp. 279–80].

These requirements are supplemented and qualified by two further characteristics of the model building process. First, it is suggested that a rigorous distinction must be made between the observational and the experimental levels of the process; and, second, it is suggested that models may be of four basic types: conscious or unconscious, mechanical or statistical (ibid. p. 280ff). Overall, there are two basic types of conception embedded in these theses which I wish to stress. These are:

(a) Lévi-Strauss's epistemological conception of the explanatory power of models *per se* – his understanding of how and why models do provide an adequate explication of the real phenomena (independent of them) to which they are 'applied';

(b) his conception of the nature, content, and different types of models (as theoretical constructs *per se*) needed for various methodological tasks (e.g. explaining different types of social phenomena at different levels of social organisation).

Particularly pertinent to (a) are the requirements of *prediction* and *exhaustive explanation* and the attempted demarcation between the *observational* and the *experimental* levels of model-building procedure. This latter demarcation is of particular importance because the manner in which Lévi-Strauss conceives of the relation between the observable and the theoretical, the pre-theoretical real/empirical and the conceptually constituted model, commits him to an epistemological position whose inadequacy is stark. Here theory and the knowledge of some object are implicitly regarded as the result of a process of manufacture by the subject – here the observer/scientist – of a 'model' which somehow fabricates and reveals the essential nature of the observed real empirical data which exist prior to theory. What is particularly crucial here is the exact kind of relation which is held to exist between models/theory and the pre-theoretical object, because it is this relation upon which depends the whole claim for the explanatory efficacy (i.e. the *predictiveness* and *exhaustiveness*) of theoretical models. While Lévi-Strauss asserts that the model must 'make intelligible all the observed facts' (idem.) this is only possible on condition that the nature of the relation between the model and the pre-theoretical observed facts is clarified so that criteria are available for the acceptability or non-acceptability of this or that model with respect to the specific domain of 'the real' which is investigated. Otherwise various models constitute no more than different versions or fabrications of the 'observed', whose validity we can know little about and whose relativity is beyond doubt. Their selection and retention is *essentially arbitrary for this epistemology*, given its failure to explain the relation between the model and its object, as the following quotation from Lévi-Strauss reveals. We are told that

> though many models may be used as convenient devices to describe and explain the phenomena it is obvious that the *best* model will always be that which is *true*, that is, the simplest possible model which, while being derived exclusively from the facts under consideration also makes it possible to account for all of them. Therefore the first task is to ascertain what those facts are [ibid., pp. 280–1; my emphasis].

But at what time are we certain that the richness of the real has been taken into account: that is, that *all* the facts (*whose selection must also be arbitrary because prior to theory and without consequent specification*) have been explicated? Lévi-Strauss's epistemological position is saturated with an arbitrariness which is the direct result of a fairly crude concept of the nature of scientific production as model construction which parallels that offered by authors such as Von Neumann and Morgenstern (themselves cited favourably very often by Lévi-Strauss) and many others within the social sciences. Both Badiou and after him Hindess[28] have demonstrated the weaknesses of the kind of epistemology of model construction which Lévi-Strauss *et al* hold and at the same time correctly differentiated this conception of theory from the far more rigorous formulation offered by 'neo-positivism' as embodied in the advanced work done by Carnap.[29] These demonstrations need not be repeated here but certain salient points about Lévi-Strauss's epistemology need to be emphasised and the methodological effects of its inadequacies need to be gauged.

I have just mentioned the essentials of this epistemology but it is worth stressing that what Lévi-Strauss presents is in essence *one variation of an 'invariant' epistemological position* whose primary terms are (1) an epistemological subject who in this case is the human individual; (2) an epistemological object or 'real object' which is assumed to be independent of, and prior to, theory; (3) the theoretical model which the subject constructs, which 'explains' the real object by a process of abstraction of its implicit and essential mechanisms. Having committed himself to this general epistemological framework (one shared by other authors), however, Lévi-Strauss's particular concepts mark out a particular 'variation' (demarcating him from other variants) on this theme. Accordingly Lévi-Strauss's own methodological problematic contains the concepts of different aspects of the process of model building and also of different types of models (reflecting the way Lévi-Strauss postulates the necessity for different types of theoretical constructs to be adequate for different types of real object investigated) despite the adherence to the general epistemological position outlined.

On page 23 we have already mentioned some of the concepts categorised in (b), but what is of the utmost importance to stress is that the inadequacies at the level of Lévi-Strauss's epistemology (the weaknesses of the conception of theory as the construction of models previously mentioned) *must* have definite effects for the theoretical adequacy of these same concepts because they are directly dependent on this general epistemology for their validity. That is, the stipulations that models be 'systematic, transformational, predictive and exhaustive' along with the distinction between 'conscious and unconscious', 'mechanical and statistical' types of models have a theoretical status which is determined to a large extent by the adequacy of the general epistemology underlying them. This is discussed in what follows.

(i) The requirement of '*systematicity*' for models is an effect of the overall need for the latter to contain precise 'quasi-syntactical' relations (of a coherent nature) between types of variables. As a theoretical construct *per se* the model must be subject to an *internal rigour* if an explanatory function with respect to a real object is to be fulfilled at all — this much is obvious. For Lévi-Strauss the ideal to be reached within ethnology is the achievement of models whose rigour approximates those constructions with which phonological linguistics has (according to Lévi-Strauss) demarcated the structured nature of the phonemic level of language (see above). The *substantive* thesis that sectors of culture are structured like languages (in accordance with the teleological action of the 'unconscious' discussed above) supports the contention that ethnological models of these sectors have to represent '*their syntax*' in a theoretical construct which interconnects, in a fairly precise manner, those variables which are dominant in the functioning of the sector.[30] In practice of course, however, ethnological models cannot achieve such a high level of rigour and their construction is often based on seemingly *ad hoc* procedures. This is exemplified in Lévi-Strauss's methodological comments on the analysis of the system of cultural representations traditionally called 'totemism'. Here we are told that in order to fabricate a model of its syntactical mechanisms of operation,

> The method we adopt in this case as in others, consists in the following operations:
> (1) define the phenomenon under study as a relation between two or more terms, real or supposed
> (2) construct a table of possible permutations between these terms
> (3) take this table as the general object of analysis, *which at this level only can yield necessary connexions*, the empirical phenomenon at the beginning being only one possible combination among others, the complete system of which must be reconstructed beforehand [*Totemism*, p. 84; my emphasis].

Levi-Strauss's accounts of the modes of procedures in structuralist anthropological model construction do not include reference to a theoretically founded technique which is capable of guiding the procedure of the division of the 'text' or 'semantic discourse' considered into the all-important significant units – unlike linguistics[31] – and thus accounts for the procedural arbitrariness present in the passage cited and also for the relatively *ad hoc* nature of the proposals for the definition of the constituent significant units of myths (their 'gross constituent units' or 'mythemes') in methodological statements on myth analysis. The all-important constituent units are almost treated as 'givens'.

But if ethnology falls short of the ideal,[32] its methodological ambition nevertheless remains the attainment of more sophisticated and rigorously formulated models: in this respect structuralism is held to constitute a first step in the correct direction towards scientificity in anthropology. The epistemology of models is preserved in the statement of the necessity of systematicity in the internal (conceptual) order of theoretical constructions.

(ii) The suggestion that models should be transformational along with the thesis of the necessity of experimentation with them leads us to a second specification of the nature of theoretical activity in the situation of the advocacy of the epistemology of models: it is the heart of the *comparative* nature of structural analysis. Thus

> No science today can consider the structures with which it has to deal as being no more than a haphazard arrangement. That arrangement alone is structured which meets with two conditions: that it be a system, ruled by an internal cohesion; and that this cohesion, inaccessible to observation in an isolated system, be revealed in the study of transformations through which the similar properties in apparently different systems are brought to light [*The Scope of Anthropology*, p. 31].

And

> By experimenting on models we mean the set of procedures aiming at ascertaining how a given model will react when subjected to change and at comparing models of the same or different types [*Structural Anthropology*, p. 280].

It follows that the study of transformations and the model experimentation appertain to the purely *deductive* as distinct from the *observational*. Because models are 'systems of symbols which preserve the characteristic properties of the experiment, but which we can manipulate', the introduction of different types of variable and the modification of the terms of the construct can result in the calculation of various ideal logical possibilities of syntactical organisation and a concomitant generation of different and *comparable* types of models. However, the epistemological constraints of Lévi-Strauss's position remain in force. For every logical construction generated (i.e. every model) it is conceived that a sector of the social is accordingly 'mapped', it being epistemologically necessary here that the model maintain a definite relation with the real which is external to theory (the semantic level of the procedure); but, as we have seen, Lévi-Strauss fails to give any adequate conception of this crucial relation which would eliminate the conclusion that models are only reasonable simulations or fabrications of pre-theoretical real situations. In the last analysis theory and the real are left in an arbitrary relation once more. The validity and usefulness of 'experimentation' on models and 'transformational' activities must as a consequence, remain doubtful, for at all times (to be methodologically consistent) it should be possible to specify the exact mode of the *relation* between the model and the real domain it is supposed to explicate.

(iii) This of course anticipates what must be said about the requirements of *predictiveness* and *exhaustiveness* of models and it also provides fuel for arguments that there are severe doubts about the theoretical distinction between *types* of models which Lévi-Strauss provides. For Lévi-Strauss, predictiveness and exhaustiveness must be two crucial theoretical requirements relating to the explanatory efficacy of models but, as we have mentioned above, no adequate *theoretically* based criteria are provided which specify when, why, and to what extent a particular model explains exhaustively the richness and complexity of the real object or situation to which it is applied: the selection of this or that model is not guided by adequately theorised principles and the possibilities of exhaustiveness and theoretically founded prediction recede before the stumbling block of the absence of any formulation of the necessary links between theory/deduction (the model) and the observable real.

With respect to the problem of the selection between different models as possible explanations of the same phenomenon it should also be noted that the invocation of 'the scientific principle of parsimony' does not offer a way out. In a reply to his critics Lévi-Strauss states that

It is a healthy attitude, at certain stages of scientific investigation, to believe that in the present state of knowledge, two interpretations of the same facts are equally valid. Until the twentieth century physics was in this position. The error consists not in recognising this state of affairs when it exists, but in being satisfied with it and in not seeking to transcend it. Structural analysis already offers a way out of this situation through the principle of parsimony which Jakobson among others had constantly utilised after borrowing it from the physicists: 'Frustra fit per plura quod fieri potest per pauciora'. This principle leads us in a direction opposite to that of pragmatism, formalism and neo-positivism, since the assertion that the most parsimonious explanation also comes closer to the truth rests, in the final analysis, upon the identity postulated between the laws of the universe and those of the human mind [ibid., p. 88–9].

Two points should be made here. First, the theoretical, and particularly epistemological, basis of this 'principle' (through which explanations are selected) is nowhere elaborated in Lévi-Strauss's texts. So that we have no way of instituting *theoretical* guidelines which govern the differentiation of explanations into those which are most parsimonious and those which are least. This it seems must be decided by an *arbitrary* decision of the investigator: in Lévi-Strauss's problematic it cannot be a question of theory and of *proof*. That which is parsimonious in explicative terms is almost reducible to that which is most plausible and logically economical. Second, we have stated here in a nutshell once more the conjunction of epistemological with substantive theses: the principle of parsimony has a substantive justification in a postulated homology between the laws of nature and of 'mind'. However, in view of the fact that, as we have shown above, this 'homology' rests upon highly unstable theoretical foundations, its invocation adds little help to the methodology of model construction. Confronted with such limitations at the level of prediction and exhaustiveness the task of the human sciences accordingly becomes the more humble one of 'bringing out necessary relationships between phenomena'[33] ['Criteria of Science', p. 543], or of replacing 'a less intelligible complexity by one that is more so' [*The Savage Mind*, p. 248].

Turning now to the distinction of different types, within the overall category of 'model', it is important to recognise the conceptual basis of the classification into those which are *mechanical* or *statistical* and those which are *conscious* or *unconscious*. The former distinction is methodologically the most important[34] and consists essentially in an attempt to differentiate types of models using as a criterion the '*relation between the scale of the model and that of the phenomena*'. It is stated that

According to the nature of these phenomena, it becomes possible or impossible to build a model, the elements of which are on the same scale as the phenomena themselves. A model the elements of which are on the same scale as the phenomena will be called a 'mechanical' model; when the elements of the model are on a different scale we shall be dealing with a 'statistical' model [*Structural Anthropology*, p. 283ff.].[35]

Now the vague and unelaborated nature of this distinction and the role of the notion of 'scale' within it has been recognised by many commentators[36] (in particular within the context of an analysis of its role within the methodological discussion of procedures for the analysis of kinship structures) and correctly emphasised. Without such elaboration there seems little point in conjecture and speculation over 'what Lévi-Strauss really means', but in the light of the critical comments made above we *can* say the following:

First and foremost, the schematic distinction between the mechanical and statistical models refers to the connection which may exist between models and the real phenomena they are supposed to explain. 'Scale' of the phenomena is supposed to dictate 'scale' and type of model but unfortunately exactly what is meant by the former crucial notion we are nowhere told. Because, in the epistemology of model construction, the phenomenon is defined as *prior* to theory (theory being the logical interrelation of variables implicit in the abstractive model) it is *impossible* for Lévi-Strauss to give an adequately theorised conception of 'scale' as an attribute of the real. It must follow that in Lévi-Strauss's problematic the 'scale' of this or that real phenomenon must be defined *arbitrarily* by relying on a more or less *ad hoc* understanding of the object of investigation. Furthermore, because of the unsatisfactory nature of the way Lévi-Strauss conceptualises the explanatory function of models (*viz*, the arbitrary relation between the real and theory/models) it is necessarily the case that a further distinction which relies upon this conceptualisation has very doubtful theoretical utility. In the last analysis the distinction of models as mechanical or statistical is of little methodological worth: it merely compounds errors which are necessarily implicit because of constraints within the methodology of an epistemological nature.

Now the above points have not been fully realised by previous commentators (some of whose positions we shall now consider) although certain implicit weaknesses and corresponding vaguenesses have been delineated, and this is mainly because of the failure to recognise the inherent inadequacies of the epistemology of model construction itself *in all its variations*, including the most rigorously formulated.

The bases of most authors' criticisms or endorsements of Lévi-Strauss's methodological position stem from their attempts to judge this position *in relation to their own conception of 'scientific method'*: thus Lévi-Strauss's position is either acceptable or non-acceptable depending on how far it deviates from this conception.

Those who are most in agreement with Lévi-Strauss[37] usually suggest that the latter's texts embody an attempted transposition of the true universal 'scientific method' into the ethnological domain – structuralism's problems derive not from the shortcomings of its epistemology, but on the contrary are problems generated by the difficult task of applying what is essentially a correct scientific method to an object with highly specific and problematic characteristics. Epistemologically structuralism is heading in the right direction – model building constitutes in principle the method of science *par excellence*.

On the other hand, those who are most critical of Lévi-Strauss's methodological formulations in the main postulate that what is inadequate about the latter is precisely its *deviation* from the essential features of scientific method.[38] Structuralism is castigated for failing to embody those means of proof and investigation which are (it is claimed) the distinctive features of any scientific analysis.

The common ground of these types of position is quite evident – in both cases what is at issue is the extent of the adherence to, or deviation from, what is considered to be the unified 'scientific methodology' of structuralism. Different authors have different conceptions, of course, of what are the essential features of 'the scientific method' – a plethora of different epistemological positions are held within the social sciences.

Now this is not the place to enter into a detailed consideration of different philosophies of science and their attendant epistemologies. What must be attended to, however, is the inadequate level of existing criticisms of Lévi-Strauss's methodological position. In many cases Lévi-Strauss's position is criticised *for the wrong reasons – his position cannot be attacked for failing to express the essentials of a 'scientific method' when the conception of the latter held by the critic (as the ideal to be achieved) is itself misconceived and erroneous.* (At the same time his methodology *as a whole* should not be subjected to a type of criticism which concentrates upon only one aspect of its constitution, as for example occurs when critics focus upon the *purely epistemological* side of the discussion of structure and of models without recognising that the

particular nature of 'structures' for Lévi-Strauss relies on 'substantive' theses (as we have shown above) relating to the 'semiotic' nature of sectors of culture).[39]
The position of H. G. Nutini is particularly interesting in this respect. For Nutini[40] Lévi-Strauss's conception of science and of a scientific anthropology is basically correct *in orientation* (this must be an enterprise of model-construction) but what is lacking is the provision of a fully adequate rigorous concept of the relation of models themselves, as analytical constructs, to the real phenomena to which they are applied. Structural anthropology thus heads in the direction of scientificity, but what is further required is a fuller development of the epistemology of model construction along *neo-positivist* lines. Our commentator never doubts the methodological importance of the content of structural anthropology. Thus he suggests that

> the fact will still remain that he was the first, and perhaps only, anthropologist who clearly recognised the correct logical and epistemological implications of the new scientific stance by addressing himself to the problem which I regard as central to anthropological theory: the nature and configuration of the concept of model and its relationship to a body of empirical social phenomena [H. G. Nutini (1970b), pp. 551–2].

Furthermore he suggests that

> it is a condition *sine qua non* in advancing anthropology on the road to a mature stage of conceptualisation that we come to grips with a variety of theoretical considerations related to this problem, such as the epistemological rules that must mediate between the supra-empirical nature of models and the empirical nature of social facts; the logical (deductive) and epistemological (inductive) basis of model building, which must never be confused if one wishes to construct a model which is the most efficient and explanatory in explaining a body of social phenomena . . . the quality and quantity of the data which must go into the construction of models; the synchronic and diachronic components of structural models and so on [ibid., p. 552].

What then is wrong with Lévi-Strauss's position? In a nutshell only the *absence* of one highly important set of theoretical parameters which, once provided, would lead anthropology to scientificity. These are supposed to constitute theoretical factors which 'co-ordinate and link analytical or formal systems' (i.e. models) 'to empirical reality': they are held to be vaguely equivalent to the 'co-ordinate definitions' of Reichenbach, Carnap's 'semantic rules', Nagel's 'correspondence rules' and Northrop's 'epistemic correlations', all of which (it is claimed) confront the problem of forging a rigorous connection between the analytic and the empirical. Thus Nutini postulates the necessity of a more rigorous and theoretical formulation of the relation between the model and the real within anthropology: Lévi-Strauss's anthropological methodology is judged against the standard of the nature of the scientific method formulated by Reichenbach, Carnap and Nagel – if the unitary method of *all science* consists in the formulation of rigorous analytical constructs which have a demonstrable rational connection with the real (demonstrable through the 'correspondence rules') then (for Nutini) the social sciences, like physical science, must develop such rules and connections.

Now while Nutini's plea for a more rigorous theorisation of the relation between models and the real is quite understandable from within his own epistemology, it must be noted that this epistemological position itself, and hence his comment on Lévi-Strauss, is quite misconceived and erroneous. If as I have said above, the basic point is that the 'epistemology of model construction' in all its variations is inadequate then Nutini's plea for a more rigorous model-building enterprise using 'correspondence rules' linking theory and the real is vacuous because he will remain *within* its confines, despite his criticisms of the cruder variations. That is to say, Nutini merely proposes a more rigorous theoretical formulation of the epistemology of the model: the rigorous neo-positivist variant (*viz.* Carnap *et al.*), is advocated instead of a more simple structuralist conception. However, neo-positivist epistemological positions are themselves confronted by insuperable theoretical difficulties deriving from general problems inherent in all attempts to formulate knowledge *per se* as a form of 'correspondence' or 'adequation' between thought and theory on the one hand, and given basic elements of experience/reality on the other. Althusser has suggested that any prescriptive theory of knowledge which attempts to legislate for and 'guarantee' its status by specifying certain requisite conditions governing the confrontation between an epistemological subject and given data of experience[41] is inescapably circular and must collapse precisely because it can never authorise *knowledge of these conditions* on its own terms.[42] Hindess has further demonstrated the effects of these difficulties within particular types of epistemological position which posit a correlation between thought and experience, knowledge and being, under a variety of guises.[43] This demonstration cannot be repeated here but we should note the principal theoretical problems of all neo-positivist theories of knowledge: first, reconciling the acceptance of certain *basic* theoretical conceptions about the character of knowledge production (whose analytical content is not reducible to experience) with its general thesis that all true knowledges *are*; second, avoiding a crucial arbitrariness in the account of knowledge generated by the ultimate primacy of judgements of experience.

We can see this for both rigorous neo-positivism and structuralist model fabrication. The problem of connecting theory to the empirical prior to theory takes the form of interrelating the model as an analytical construct governed by internal (syntactical) connections between abstract variables, and the real pre-theoretical domain which this construct (in a semantic relation) 'explains'. Despite the attempt by Carnap *et al.* to produce rigorous correspondence rules which link the theoretical to the observation (pre-theoretical) levels, for neo-positivism, and of course for structuralism, the primacy of subjective observational judgement (external to all rational principles in effect) must in the last analysis be maintained. Thus

the positivist domain of interpretation [for its models] is extra-theoretical, its structure is the (unknown) structure of the real itself. In this framework the observation language [for neo-positivist epistemology] plays a double role. On the one hand it belongs to science; its terms are in principle the terms of scientific observation. On the other it designates the elementary constituents of the real . . . the observation language represents the very frontiers of knowledge, the ultimate point beyond which theory cannot go. There can be no *demonstration* that an observation language does indeed designate the basic elements of the real. Any such demonstration would of necessity prove circular: it would require reference to a more 'basic' observation language with respect to which the same problem would arise. In the last resort for positivism observation represents the place where demonstration ceases. What remains is the confrontation between the observer and the brute fact, the real object in all its nakedness. The observer can only recognise the fact or fail to recognise it for what it is. For Carnap . . . knowledge rests in the last analysis on nothing more than an irrational or non-rational act of judgement [B. Hindess (1974), p. 245].

And if this is the case for neo-positivism then it is the case *a fortiori* for

Lévi-Strauss's epistemology: the rift between the pre-theoretical and the theoretical forged by this theory of knowledge cannot be bridged except in a wholly arbitrary fashion and this arbitrariness will find its fullest expression in the more simple epistemologies of model construction. As Badiou (1969) notes, they present us with a stark choice

Le cerle est évident: à la question qu'est-ce qu'un modèle? on repond: l'object artificiale qui rend raison de tous les faits empiriques considérés; mais à la question: quel est la critère du 'rendre raison', quel est le vrai modèle? On repond derechef: le vrai modèle est celui qui rend compte de tous les faits. On ajoutera pour faire bonne mesure, la classique condition d'élégance: le modèle doit être le plus simple . . . Pour l'espistemologie des modèles, la science n'est pas un procès de transformation du réel, mais la fabrication d'un image plausible [The circularity is plain: to the question 'What is a model?' one replies: 'The artificial object which explains all the empirical facts considered'; but to the question 'What is the criterion for "explaining", what is the true model?' one replies once again, 'The true model is the one which accounts for all the facts'. One can add for good measure the classical stipulation of elegance: 'the model must be the most simple . . . ' For the epistemology of models science is not a process of the transformation of the real, but the fabrication of a plausible image.] [*Le Concept de Modèle*, p. 20.]

We can see then that Nutini's position embodies an understandable plea for rigour but basically a misguided one. No matter what kind of rigour tried for the epistemology of models remains theoretically inadequate in its basic structure as an empiricism of the real. Accordingly the assessment of Lévi-Strauss's conceptions against the standard of neo-positivist concepts of theory must be regarded as without foundation with all its limitations.

The above comments enable us now to say a number of things about the celebrated debates over the methodological trinity '*empirical reality — structure — model*' which is central to structural social theory. In the past there has been constant confusion over basically two aspects of this trinity: on the one hand its reference to an *epistemological* process, and on the other the *substantive ontological* characteristics of constituent components. This has been stimulated no doubt by Lévi-Strauss's tendency to conflate these two aspects in his discussions of methodological issues: while usually these discussions stick to the characterisation of models as theoretical representations/abstractions of the real object which express the structured relations governing the real (and hence its 'structures') quite frequently the nature of the 'reality' of structures themselves is posed. Thus they are often represented as 'behind' or 'beneath the surface' of empirical reality: they constitute an unconscious and 'hidden reality' *in the manner of an essence*. Now the reason for this lies in the basic structure of Lévi-Strauss's methodology — while structures are the result of an epistemological empiricism (they consist in the models which are constructed 'out of' empirical reality which is prior to theory) they are at the same time *substantively* conceived of (as we established in Section I) as having an *ontological* status equivalent to that of an 'essence' of the real. This latter 'essentialism' accounts for the metaphorical representation of structures as 'beneath' reality, etc., and it is important to realise that only by grasping the nature of the operation of this 'essentialism' in Lévi-Strauss's problematic that certain of his formulations can be understood. The counterpart of his epistemological empiricism is an 'essentialism' of the real — both are *necessarily linked* in his discourse.

This conjunction and the distance which it establishes between a problematic such as that of Lévi-Strauss and that of Radcliffe-Brown has generated much confusion and hesitation among critics who fail to grasp the theoretical status of the concept 'structure' for the former and how it differs from the more crude conception of the latter.[44] However, the common ground of both critics and criticised *must* be acknowledged: the essential point concerns the empiricist confusions which are created by effecting a distinction between the 'conceptual' on the one hand, and the empirical, observational or 'real' on the other and then attempting to discuss the 'reality' of that which appertains to the conceptual and theoretical. *'Social structures' or 'economic structures' or 'political structures' of course have only a theoretical existence* because they are *concepts* — they are never reducible to a real or concrete status and it is futile to discuss the nature of their 'reality' as Lévi-Strauss (and also Godelier)[45] tries to do. This is the crux of the issue: it is only by being prey to an empiricism which separates the real and the theoretical into *separate* components that one can fall into confusions about the 'reality' or 'unreality' of that which is always formulated at a conceptual level. The basic fact remains however that this epistemology and this *de facto* separation of theory and the real is illegitimate on logical and theoretical grounds: theory does not have to 'map' the real which is prior to theory because the real is always 'interiorised' within theoretical formulations from the very beginning. There is in knowledge no raw domain of 'facts' independent of concepts for facts have concepts for their conditions of existence – all constituted fact requires classification and the operation of categories and concepts, and therefore all facts are embodiments of theory in various forms and varieties.

With Lévi-Strauss, as I have said, these confusions crystallise around the nature of his representation of structures as 'beneath' the real and as having some kind of *ontological* status of their own. This must be seen as a spurious formulation in view of what I have just said: all representations of structures are the *concepts* of structures and, for Lévi-Strauss's particular problematic to be consistent, the structures are mechanisms which are conceived as governing the real phenomena as their essence and which can only be delineated at the conceptual level via an epistemological process of model construction. The model must be the conceptual expression of the structure or essence of the real.

Yet of course, however, this is a consistency to a position within epistemology which is, as we have established, theoretically incoherent. Lévi-Strauss's epistemology of model construction represents an *impossible* project in that it requires an *extra-theoretical* comparison between the model and the real which is not theoretically achievable. No anthropology on earth as a consequence, could fulfil this project.

III Conclusion

We must briefly conclude this chapter by taking stock of the critical comments we have made on Lévi-Strauss's project for a scientific anthropology. First, we have seen that his 'structuralism' as a methodological project attempts to effect a substantive (preliminary) conception of the objects of anthropology as comparable in certain ways to what is regarded as the essential domain of 'culture', language; i.e. to demonstrate the object of anthropology as 'semiotic'. Above in Section I we have shown that Lévi-Strauss tries to do this by relying upon the postulates of the existence and effectivity of a mental apparatus (which he calls 'the unconscious') which is conceived as the common structuring origin of all domains of culture, but that this attempt is fraught with theoretical inadequacies. We concluded by suggesting that these inadequacies necessarily implied that Lévi-Strauss's methodological formulations on the nature of anthropology were without an adequate *substantive* basis.

In Section II, we turned to the epistemological component of the methodology and showed that at the heart of Lévi-Strauss's concept of the nature of the scientific means to be used by anthropology with respect to its substantive objects was an epistemology which is classifiable as a specific variant of classical empiricism. Quite simply it was demonstrated that Lévi-Strauss's notion of scientificity and of the process of production of knowledge embodies specific shortcomings hinging upon a fundamental arbitrariness in the theoretical model and the realities it is held to explain. The conclusion of Section II therefore is that the *epistemological* aspect of Lévi-Strauss's methodological protocols is also theoretically invalid.

The results of both Sections add up to an overall conclusion which by now will be evident: in both component areas of his methodology which we have discussed, theoretical errors exist which make Lévi-Strauss's formulations for a scientific anthropology both impossible and illegitimate.

In the form in which they are cast by Lévi-Strauss, methodological prescriptions for a social theory as a 'semiology' are both incoherent in themselves and incapable of realisation.

PART TWO
Structural Anthropology, Primitive Social Organisation and History

INTRODUCTION

Whatever the restrictions and limits upon structural anthropology claimed by its representatives it cannot avoid those requirements which are imposed upon *all* discourses which claim to provide the substance of any anthropology – to provide concepts adequate for the analysis of primitive or archaic societies as totalities and for the analysis of the forms which make up these societies as duly defined. In this section of the text it will be my concern to examine one aspect (a highly important one) of the contribution of Lévi-Strauss's 'reformulation' of anthropology to the provision of correct categories and forms of conceptualisation for this task. As such, the examination will concentrate upon his analysis of the *kinship formations* of 'primitive' societies, but at the same time a general concern here will be that of assessing the overall worth and validity of the whole mode of orientation which his anthropology advocates with respect to forms of social organisation generally called 'primitive'.

It will be a basic assumption here that no analysis of the regions, domains or sub-systems of societies can in the last analysis legitimately take place in abstraction from an *implicit* conception of the overall 'global' constitution of the these same societies which are the points of reference of the 'regional' analysis. It is from this particular perspective that I shall look at Lévi-Strauss's work on kinship and social organisation, so that, instead of repeatedly dwelling upon the minutiae of the complexity of the empirical concerns in the attempted resolution of orthodox anthropological bones of contention by the latter (as in the retrospective discussion of various interpretations of elements of particular systems such as the Murngin), I shall try to remain concentrated upon the overall conceptualisation of kinship relations in relation to particular types of social organisation.

Lévi-Strauss's work will thus be examined from a general theoretical level with reference to its status as *a theory of society* and in this respect an additional element of what follows will be the 'situating' of Lévi-Strauss's concepts with respect to those of other authors who have been recognised as the founders of the 'French' school of sociological theory: Durkheim and Mauss. We have already seen that there are implicit points of correspondence between the *concept of the social* of Lévi-Strauss and those of Durkheim and Mauss and now in this section we will be interested in establishing the significance of the more specific substantive formulations of structural anthropology by discussing in passing the divergent features of their differing concepts. In the last analysis the system of concepts which makes up the problematic of structural anthropology forms a unique set in its constitution – it is *not* the sum of a set of 'influences' which are combined in an arbitrary manner – but it will be noted that the different types of conceptualisation that these embody *do* fall into errors common to other positions in sociological and anthropological theory.

In terms of organisation and content, this part of the book is structured as follows. In the next two Sections, I and II, I attempt to provide an exhaustive sketch of the way Lévi-Strauss conceives of the nature of primitive societies, and of kinship relations within them, by stressing what I understand to be the major different levels of conceptualisation within his analysis. After separating out these different levels and examining their make-up in some detail, I suggest in Section III that each is predicated upon definite theoretical shortcomings which Lévi-Strauss is unable to solve with his concepts. The implications of the criticisms are examined so that the overall worth of Lévi-Strauss's achievements within anthropology may be assessed in some detail: this entails a more detailed examination of the positive value of the rupture created within social anthropological theory[1] by his concepts and the suggestion that structural analyses must be 'deconstructed' and reconstructed within the compass of a problematic which avoids the pitfalls of the one upon which the analyses were based and which is able to provide a true knowledge of social forms in history.

This Section is predicated upon the conviction that social theory can only advance on the basis of a full critique of the different 'levels' of conceptualisation in structuralism – a critique which has to be more

detailed and specific in certain important areas than those which have
hitherto appeared.

I proceed now to discuss Lévi-Strauss's understanding of society-in-
general and 'primitive society' and then go on to examine his morphological theory of kinship relations within the latter type of society.
My criticisms of each of these elements follow in Section III.

I Lévi-Strauss's Concept of 'Society' and of 'Primitive' Societies

Lévi-Strauss, along with many others in anthropology, effects a
distinction between types of society which is essentially a dichotomous
one: on the one hand we have the societies whose bases and institutions
are discussed by anthropologists – these are called 'primitive' or
'archaic'[2] – and on the other hand we have 'modern' societies whose
study is the concern of the sociologist. I am particularly concerned here
with Lévi-Strauss's conception of the former and not with the classification itself, but it is useful to point out initially its theoretical weakness
as an important typology.

Our author characteristically uses a variety of metaphors to express
the dichotomy (primitive and modern are respectively opposed as 'cold'
and 'hot'[3] or as having 'stationary' and 'cumulative histories')[4] or quite
simply makes a contrast between societies governed by 'blood ties' and
those dominated by economic relations;[5] but whatever means he uses it
cannot be said that it constitutes a detailed morphology of societal types
embodying established criteria for distinguishing different historical
forms. We are given no comparative theory of social forms – Lévi-
Strauss's concern is with societies he calls 'primitive' and others are
referred to for purposes of contrast. What then, in particular, is
distinctive about the former type itself?

For Lévi-Strauss, all societies (referring now to his general concept of
the social whole) must be regarded as organised unities of different but
interrelated structured levels. The complexity of societies derives from
this existence within them of different 'orders' or 'levels' which have
varied functions and which operate according to mechanisms which are
in principle specifiable. Thus he says that 'anthropology considers the
whole social fabric as a network of different types of orders' [*Structural
Anthropology*, p. 312] and that a society may be characterised as
possessing an 'order of orders' which is ' . . . the formal property of the
whole made up of sub-wholes, each of which corresponds to a *given
structured level*' [ibid, p. 323; my emphasis]. Now this idea of society as a

'network of orders' or as a composite of different 'levels' is very important within structural anthropology because it is constantly implicit in the discussions of different features of primitive social organisation, but we should note at the outset that it always remains at the 'notional' level (attention is not directed *in detail* to the theoretical connotations and specifications of the idea itself in Lévi-Strauss's work) and that *usually* attention is actually focused more explicitly upon the particular discrete 'orders' or 'levels' which this conception of a society engenders. The focus of structural anthropology is nearly always upon discrete and particular regions or domains of societies, while the theoretical problem of the situation of these domains within the whole of which they are a 'sub-whole' is displaced: *the domains (regions or levels) are defined more or less in abstraction from this issue.* The whole way in which Lévi-Strauss conceives of the project of structural analysis attests to this abstraction/displacement. Of the 'dual' character of structural studies a key element is

> *isolating strategic levels*, and this can only be achieved by *'carving out' a certain constellation of phenomena.* From that point of view each type of structural study appears autonomous, entirely independent of all the others and even of different methodological approaches to the same field [ibid., p. 285; my emphasis].

This 'isolation' or 'carving-out' process (a theoretical one) is of course crucial and it should be noted that it necessarily refers us back to some concept of the totality at hand (i.e. the social whole) – the process cannot be *arbitrary* for the demarcation or carving out of orders and levels is dependent upon such a concept at all times.

Now, in practice Lévi-Strauss gives the discussion of these 'levels' or 'orders' and the attempt to demarcate their internal mechanisms *priority* over the question of the overall position of these levels within the society (this being dependent upon a further elaboration of his idea of a 'society') being considered and it is *within this context* that the analyses of structural anthropology of primitive social organisation must be considered. For, to return to the question posed above, what is precisely distinctive for Lévi-Strauss about those societies called 'primitive' is the nature of the complexity of organisation and uniqueness of societal function of one particular 'level' or order (as an isolatable sub-whole) – this level being of course, *the network of kinship relations.* Accordingly his work on these relations (which I shall discuss presently) is predicated upon two standpoints which must continually be borne in mind:

(1) the notion of kinship relations as constituting an isolatable 'level' of primitive societies having a particular *function* within the overall society considered as a compound of such different 'levels';

(2) the attempted specification of the mechanisms governing the order of this level in different primitive formations and of the social effects of this type of determination.

Having stated this, we are now in a position to approach Lévi-Strauss's discussion of the mechanisms which he does indeed posit as operative within kinship phenomena.

Central to this discussion is an emphasis upon the great importance of the ubiquity of institutions of transaction and exchange within primitive societies, which Lévi-Strauss shares with earlier anthropologists (Thurnwald, Malinowski, Frazer, Mauss, etc.). This emphasis itself has strong affinities with that of Marcel Mauss, who not only conceives of primitive exchange phenomena as multi-faceted ('total social facts', being at the same time legal, economic, religious, etc., in varying degrees) but also regards them as absolutely fundamental for normative order (demarcating a form of archaic social contract).[6]

Lévi-Strauss is in agreement with Mauss on the last point – if it is ethnographically recorded that relationships of transaction permeate the primitive social order, then this can only be because of the generalised integrating function which they serve in satisfying functional pre-requisites. Some form of order necessarily structures the mode of distribution of the product and of marriage alliances, regulates relationships through informal and legalistic practices, and so on, and Lévi-Strauss adopts such a position despite no proper statement of the elements of a functionalist theory (specifying pre-requisites and their mechanisms, etc.).

He diverges from Mauss (and Malinowski), however, on the question of what it is which lies at the foundation of primitive exchanges. For both the latter, different transactional behaviours and institutions retain a discrete quality which is given to observation. Lévi-Strauss on the contrary, characteristically posits the necessary operation of unobservable 'essential mechanisms' which structure the multiplicity of exchange relations. It is the overall domination in Lévi-Strauss's work on social organisation of the idea of the necessary intervention in the real of 'hidden' constitutive mechanisms that it is important to emphasise. The notion of a 'principle of reciprocity' is the conception of such a mechanism in the analysis of kinship formations, but it is also determinant in the few places where Lévi-Strauss discusses primitive 'political' relations.[7] Reciprocity as an organisational principle, and somewhat in the manner of a metaphysical 'essence', can be realised and crystallised under quite distinct and varied forms.

Lévi-Strauss's celebrated 'structures' which are supposed to 'lie beneath empirical reality' are in fact logically governed by these forms, principles or mechanisms which generate them and are operative within different levels of societies. This will now be seen in Lévi-Strauss's specifications of the internal mode of operation and external societal effects of these mechanisms within the domain of kinship.

II The Structures, Mechanisms and Functions of the Kinship 'Level'

For structural anthropology, primitive societies are social forms largely dominated by complex networks of kinship which perform crucial functions for the maintenance of the whole social order. These networks are conceived as an analytically isolatable domain of facts which make up one 'level' of the whole social form, and in this Lévi-Strauss shares a common perspective with other 'schools' of social anthropology as a whole. In particular for the latter, however, this domain may be represented as a 'communication structure' whatever the society considered. Thus his position is that

the complete set of marriage regulations operating in human societies and classified usually under different headings, such as prohibitions on incest, preferential forms of marriage and the like, can be interpreted as being so many different ways of insuring the circulation of women within the social group or of substituting the mechanism of a sociologically determined affinity for that of a biologically determined consanguinity [*Structural Anthropology*, p. 60].

For all forms of society it will, in principle at least, be possible to demonstrate the internal mechanisms articulating these structures of communication and under certain conditions these mechanisms will consist in different variant forms of '*the principle of reciprocity*' or, more generally, of *exchange*. As is well known, it is mainly in *The Elementary Structures of Kinship* (hereafter *ESK* for brevity) that this claim is qualified and the concepts of the variant mechanisms and types of structure so generated are established. The whole work is predicated upon the ambition of demonstrating the possibility of a reduction of the number of factors involved in empirical ways of regulating alliances in primitive[8] societies to a small and well defined number, specifying the logically possible alternatives of prescription and prohibition in the functioning systems. It is the *novum organum* of what Buchler and Selby and Fox call 'Alliance theory' within social anthropology.[9]

Before an exposition, however, a word of caution. Inevitably, it will only be possible here to give a schematic outline and resumé of the major concepts established in the texts and, as always, this will reflect a particular type of pre-occupation or focus of concern. Like Rossi[10] I shall be concerned less with Lévi-Strauss's marshalling and treatment of detailed ethnographic evidence (although this cannot be ignored)[11] and more with *the categories* constructed within his problematic which dominate any utilisation of 'facts'. Accordingly concern will be directed principally at the 'architecture' of a body of concepts and not at derivative forms of argument deployed in the treatment of detailed empirical cases.

Above, we have already stressed the key role in structural anthropology of an abstract principle called 'exchange' or 'reciprocity' which may operate as an essential 'trans-empirical' mechanism within various levels of primitive societies as Lévi-Strauss conceives them (chiefly kinship and the political as we have seen, but also the economic).[12] For kinship networks, variant forms of this principle fit into the following logical schema of major concepts.

In brief, those societies which practise the ascriptive classification of individuals into classes of possible or prohibited spouses are conceived as having levels of kinship governed by three possible 'elementary structures'. These in turn are articulated by two basic variants of exchange or reciprocity; either exchange which is 'restricted' or 'direct' or that which is 'generalised' or 'indirect'. The operation of these mechanisms of regulation is furthermore dependent upon what is called the nature of the 'regime' obtaining in the society considered. A regime expresses the mode of articulation between the rule of residence practised (the determination of the place of habitation of the children of a marriage: matrilocal or patrilocal) with that of the rule of transmission of descent (matrilineal or patrilineal if unilineal). A regime is 'harmonic' if locality and descent follow the same principle (matrilocal/matrilineal or patrilocal/patrilineal) and 'dysharmonic' if they follow opposite principles (matrilocal/patrilineal or patrilocal/matrilineal). The claim made for these mechanisms and principles should not be under-estimated. At the conclusion of *ESK* Lévi-Strauss states:

There are only three possible elementary kinship structures; these three structures are constructed by means of two forms of exchange;

and these two forms of exchange themselves depend upon a single differential characteristic, namely the harmonic or disharmonic character of the regime considered . . . Ultimately the whole imposing apparatus of prescriptions and prohibitions could be reconstructed 'a priori' from one question and one alone: in the society considered, what is the relationship between rule of residence and rule of descent? Every disharmonic regime leads to restricted exchange just as every harmonic regime announces generalised exchange [p. 493].

For Lévi-Strauss once a minimum of 'institutional material' is historically provided (a number of local groups or bands, variable rules of residence, for example) the combination of a number of simple principles is able to provide the *logical possibility* of the formation within a society of structured networks binding these groups according to specific mechanisms. The above concepts form part of a logical schema with definite interconnections whose resultant *different conceptual levels* must be emphasised. As a result it may be diagramatically represented in full as in Figure 1.

As can be seen, the substantive analytical lynch pins of the set-up are the variant forms of exchange and regimes, because these are the concepts which are most directly implicated in explaining the empirical features of various primitive kinship formations; but, remembering what was said about the concept of the *unconscious* (in Lévi-Strauss's concept of the social *per se*) in Part One, we should note that in this context it again occupies the role of a 'constitutive agency' – this time at the root of the explanatory principle of reciprocity or exchange – in accordance with its function for Lévi-Strauss as the general mechanism of the condition of realisation of any domain of cultural facts (the 'culturalisation of nature'). Before the principle is subject to variation in form in whatever domain, it is 'always already' the result of the effectivity of the unconscious (particularly in *ESK*).[13] This is made quite explicit in the discussions of the relationship between 'nature' and 'culture', of the 'prohibition of incest' and 'exogamy' in general: while the latter two are all realisations of the principle of reciprocity – its variant forms – this is only possible in the last analysis because of the power of the unconscious (mind or *ésprit*) in transforming ostensibly natural phenomena (consanguinity and undetermined alliance) into cultural forms (modes of societal regulation of alliance endowed with a meaning) through the utilisation of a mediating principle of organisation. The 'unconscious' and the ubiquitous 'principle of reciprocity' are

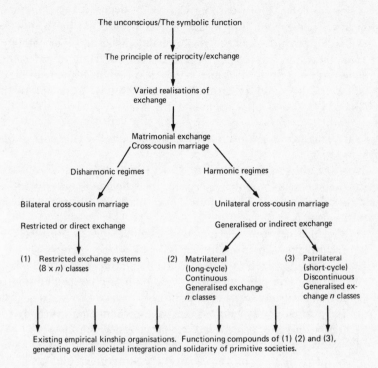

FIGURE 1

directly conceptually linked at a specific level: (i) the former makes possible the latter, and (ii) the latter inaugurates the domain of kinship as a sphere of 'symbolic exchange' as a consequence. We are told that 'the emergence of symbolic thought must have required that women, like words, should be things that were exchanged', and that exchange in general (in contradistinction to Marcel Mauss as we saw above)

n'est pas un édifice complex, construit à partir des obligations de donner, de recevoir et de rendre, à l'aide d'un ciment affectif et mystique. C'est un synthèse immédiatement donné à et par la pensée symbolique qui, dans l'échange comme dans toutes autres formes de communication, surmonte la contradiction qui lui est inhérente de percevoir les choses comme les éléments du dialogue, simultanément sous le rapport de soi et d'autrui et destinés par nature à passer de l'un à l'autre. [is not a complex building constructed from obligations of giving, receiving and returning with the help of an emotional and mystical cement. It is a synthesis given immediately to and by symbolic thought which, in this exchange as in all other forms of communication, overcomes its inherent contradiction of perceiving things as elements of dialogue, simultaneously under the relation of self and others and as naturally destined to pass from one to the other.] ['Introduction à l'oeuvre de M. Mauss', p. xlvi.]

Culture, language and kinship are commonly conceived as 'born at one fell swoop'.

Now the above refers to the first two ((1) and (2) below) of three distinct and equally essential aspects of the schema of concepts I have just sketched above. They must be emphasised (they govern my exposition) and are:

(1) the link between the unconscious/mind and the principle of reciprocity accounting for the basis of symbolic exchange;

(2) the variation in the *manifestation* or *realisation* of the principle of reciprocity in different forms within kinship: the prohibition of incest, exogamy, dual organisations, cross-cousin marriage, the fully developed systems of marriage exchange governed by the 'restricted' and 'generalised' reciprocity mechanisms;

(3) the action and social effects of the developed variants of exchange proper – that is, of the elementary structures – and their explanatory force with respect to existing empirical kinship organisations.

Together these account for the most important different but interconnected features of the way Lévi-Strauss conceptualises kinship, and it is important to consider *each in turn* in detail – no one of these on its own exhausts what the latter has to say on the subject and criticism of *one alone* is insufficient in Lévi-Strauss's overall theory of kinship: this may well lead to a reductionist interpretation.

(1) THE BASIS OF THE PRINCIPLE OF RECIPROCITY AND SYMBOLIC EXCHANGE

Taking the first, however, and referring back to what has just been said about the unconscious 'making possible' the principle of reciprocity and symbolic exchange, we must note the considerable difficulty which Lévi-Strauss has in actually theorising their interrelation. It is not enough to say as Rossi does that reciprocity simply is a 'corollary of the primacy of mind and of its dialectical mode of operation'[14] because, as Wilden notes, 'it is never *entirely* clear what he means either by 'unconscious' or by 'mind'.[15]

Despite this, however, it is possible to discern features of the type of interrelation Lévi-Strauss is trying to establish. To enable him to use the conception of a principle of reciprocity as a unifying explanatory principle accounting for the diversity of all the modalities of kinship in social organisation, its ubiquity has to have some basic causal foundation, and this is secured by reference, once again, to the faculties of 'mind'. Continually throughout the first chapters of *ESK* various kinship institutions are conceived as phenomenal realisations of reciprocity: the prohibition of incest, exogamy, dual organisations, cross-cousin marriage, all are based on this principle and at the same time conceived as having their locus in certain structures of the mind. For example, it is asserted that

> if dual organisation rarely reaches the institutional stage it nevertheless has to do with the same psychological and logical roots as all those sketchy and partial forms which are formulations of the principle of reciprocity for the same reason as dual organisation is just such a formulation . . . In all forms there is a difference of degree, not of kind; of generality and not of type. To understand their common basis, inquiry must be directed to certain fundamental structures of the human mind, rather than to some privileged region of the world or to a certain period in the history of civilisation [ibid., p. 75].

The ubiquity of the principle of reciprocity (and its explanatory efficacy) is rooted in the constant effectivity of these structures in organising the material at their disposal within different spheres of social organisation. The structures mark the response of all cultures to the functional necessity of imposing collective control where natural exigencies threaten the precarious conditions of the whole social group.

The origin of this response, and with it the basis of any socio-cultural existence, Lévi-Strauss sees manifest in the phenomenon of the prohibition of incest which reveals both the most primitive crystallisation of the mechanism of reciprocity and, as a consequence, the clearest representation of the manner in which the symbolic function marks its minimal imprint upon the socially necessary regulation of alliances: by constituting its *precondition*. For higher forms of the realisation of reciprocity to be effective within the domain of kinship the *initial* steps embodied in the prohibition must be taken: for complex systems of exchange of women to be possible at all there must first of all exist an elementary differentiation imposed through culture upon the chance and contingency of natural biological relationships, which decrees at the least a minimum stipulation of what is possible matrimonially and what is not. Lévi-Strauss conceives this differentiation (which says what must be, positively, as well as what must not be, negatively) as two things:

(a) it is the initiator and pre-condition of *exchange within kinship*: its logical end is to *make possible positive* forms of organisation (*ESK*, pp. 44–5).

(b) it is, considered as a phenomenon itself independently of its field of effectivity, the *pre-condition* for a set of significations or symbolisms. For any communication there must exist at the very minimum a cutting up of two domains into contiguous and discrete differentiated components so that they can be metaphori-cally matched (e.g. for language, the domain of sound images and the domain of ideas) and thus so that a refraction of *signifieds through signifiers* might take place. For Lévi-Strauss, of course, this work of differentiation is achieved by 'the unconscious': it represents the most basic *symbolising* capacity of that entity.

The differentiating action of the 'unconscious' is thus the *pre-condition* of the establishment of kinship as a sphere of symbolic exchanges. But what establishes that this will always necessarily be so? In other words why should kinship always reveal itself as a reciprocity/symbolic exchange – clearly the mere operation of the *differentiation* of the unconscious/the symbolic function is not enough to establish necessary and sufficient causal conditions for the *ubiquity* of reciprocity within kinship, since it merely affirms its possibility. There has to be *another causal element* which will establish this. Lévi-Strauss clearly recognises this in reference to the interpretation of dual organisations as realisations of the principle of reciprocity. He writes that

To assert, as we did . . . that a historical or geographical study could not exhaust the problem of the origin of dual organisations and that for a better understanding of these organisations we must take into consideration certain fundamental structures of the human mind would be a meaningless proposition if we were unable to perceive exactly how these structures were made up and what was the method by which we might apprehend and analyse them [*ESK*, p. 84].

The mere differentiating faculty of the symbolic capacity of the unconscious (upon which commentators like Wilden concentrate) is insufficient for explanatory purposes – it merely makes possible symbolic exchange, it does not define its modalities – and Lévi-Strauss attempts to establish constraints at the level of the structure of the mind/unconscious, over and above the differentiating faculty, *which would be able to account for the ubiquity of the principle of reciprocity* within kinship relations once formed. He goes on:

> What are the mental structures to which we have referred and the universality of which we believe can be established? It seems there are three: the exigency of the rule as rule: the notion of reciprocity regarded as the most immediate form of integrating the self with others: and finally, the synthetic nature of the gift, i.e. that the agreed transfer of a valuable from one individual to another makes these individuals into partners and adds a new quality to the valuable transferred [idem.].

In *ESK*[16] it is the concept of the constant operation of these structures within the mind which causally accounts for the constancy of reciprocity within primitive social life and for the 'totalness' of the social phenomena of exchange. Lévi-Strauss acknowledges that for the principle of reciprocity to have any explanatory force its conditions of existence and its origin have to be established and in the latter text these are rooted not in social but in psychic exigencies. Does he adequately establish these conditions and exigencies?

Chapter 7 of *ESK* attempts to marshall certain evidence from developmental psychology (Isaacs, Piaget, etc.) for this purpose, but this must be seen within the context of Lévi-Strauss's other writings on the mind/intellect/unconscious. What we have in that chapter, in fact, is the suggestion that infant thought must be closely considered because it . . . provides a common basis of mental structures and schemes of sociability for *all cultures*, each of which draws upon certain elements for its own particular mode' [ibid., p. 85], and that

> observations made on infant psychology reveal, in a concrete and striking form, mechanisms which, corresponding as they do to needs and very basic forms of activity and which for this reason are buried in the deepest recesses of the mind, are somewhat difficult to arrive at through theoretical analysis. These are apparent in the child not because his mind represents an alleged 'stage' of intellectual develop-

ment but because his experience has been less influenced than an adult's by the particular culture to which he belongs [idem.].

The mechanisms which these 'observations' (chiefly those of Isaacs) uncover are moreover the ones which were quoted above (the quotation from *ESK*, p. 84). *Lévi-Strauss contends that because these appear to be operative within the thought of infants this necessarily implies their contancy in thought-in-general* (and *ipso facto* in *primitive* thought). His concern is the relation between primitive thought, infant thought and thought in general and the following passage exemplifies his basic postulate that 'infantile thought represents a sort of common denominator for all thoughts and all cultures':

> Adult thinking is built around a number of structures which it specifies, organises and develops from the single fact of this specialis-ation and which are only a fruition of the initial summary and undifferentiated structures in the child's thought. In other words the mental schemata of the adult diverge in accordance with the culture and period to which he belongs. However they are all derived from a universal resource which is infinitely richer than that of each particular culture . . . Every new born child comes equipped, in the form of adumbrated mental structures, with all the means ever available to mankind to define its relations to the world in general and its relations to others. But these structures are exclusive. Each of them can integrate only certain elements out of all those that are offered. *Consequently each type of social organisation represents a choice, which the group imposes and perpetuates.* In comparison with adult thought, which has chosen and rejected as the group has required, *the child's thought is a sort of universal substratum the crystallisations of which have not yet occurred and in which communication is still possible between incompletely solidified forms* [ibid., p. 93; my emphasis].

Now what is crucial here is whether or not the recourse to child psychology in this chapter of Lévi-Strauss's book does indeed provide the *universality* of the three 'mental structures' mentioned. My opinion is, however, that the answer to this question must be *negative*. Later on in my criticisms I shall suggest that the kind of arguments proffered in *ESK* and elsewhere fail to satisfactorily establish the psychological conditions of existence of the principle of reciprocity, for reasons which are linked to the whole way in which Lévi-Strauss conceptualises the 'mind' itself as a strategically causal agency at the basis of the practices of different social groups.

(2) THE REALISATION OF THE PRINCIPLE OF RECIPROCITY

However, if the principle of reciprocity has its conditions of existence within psychic structures, its effectivity within the social domain is more crucial for the way Lévi-Strauss explains kinship organisation, for we have seen that it is regarded as the unifying and essential mechanism governing all forms of kinship, from those which he refers to as least 'crystallised' or institutionalised (e.g. the prohibition of incest) to those which are most (at the extreme the fully constituted 'symmetrical' and 'asymmetrical' exchange systems and even 'complex' systems). Now these different 'degrees of crystallisation' of the principle of reciprocity can be simply exemplified if we bear in mind the distinction Lévi-Strauss makes between the 'prohibition of incest' and 'exogamy'. Basically the former, in its prime function as a rule of differentiation, serves the simple function of providing a logically sufficient condition for the establishment of the reciprocal exchange of women[17] while the latter is established as the simplest concrete form of marital exchange. 'Reciprocity' is indeed at work in both phenomena, but in the case of the prohibition we are told that its presence is 'only inorganic' and not appreciably organised; while for exogamy reciprocity is expressed in a conscious, organised social differentiation of pre-existing classes between which individuals will be exchanged; for the prohibition 'exchange may be neither explicit nor immediate' (although the fact that ego may obtain a wife is only a consequence of the fact that a brother or father has 'released' her) – the rule itself not specifying the person or class of persons to whom another shall be offered in exchange. The difference between the two is thus purely formal to Lévi-Strauss: one merely establishes the logically necessary primitive basis for a system of reciprocal relationships while the other, at one remove from this level, gives reciprocity a more distinct *organisational form*: that is to say, 'crystallises' it more fully.

Above and beyond exogamy Lévi-Strauss conceives this process of 'crystallisation' to continue – logically and *not* historically – by degrees of complexity from exogamy through 'dual organisations' and into the fully formed 'elementary structures' themselves, and shortly I shall discuss this logical schema of the higher forms of exchange in kinship in more detail. For the moment however, I want to say something about the mode of *causality* which is implicitly attributed to exchange/the principle of reciprocity in Lévi-Strauss's problematic.

The *action* of the principle can most effectively be designated as the realisation, manifestation or 'expression' of an 'essence' in diverse phenomenal forms. The relationship between these empirical forms and totalities and the essential principle which 'explains' them is one which, following Althusser and Balibar, we may call 'expressive causality' and its effectivity is, as they point out, implicitly *teleological*.[18] Thus, the principle has to be accounted for in part by the varied nature of the contingent social/institutional material existing *prior* to the principle but which the principle succeeds in *moulding to its purpose*. The principle is 'always at work and always oriented in the same direction', continually using 'brittle and almost always incomplete institutional structures to realise the same ends', revealing a contrast: 'between the functional *permanence* of systems of reciprocity, and the contingency of the institutional matter placed at their disposal by history and moreover ceaselessly reshaped by it' [ibid., p. 76]. Cross-cousin marriage, the prohibition of incest, exogamy and endogamy, dual organisations and systems of more elaborated 'restricted' and 'generalised' form (we shall come to these shortly) all constitute 'realisations' of the principle in different guises. All are transformations or variations on an invariant structure and all mark the place of an intervention of a structural necessity into historical contingency; as we shall see later, however, it is the question of the nature of this 'intervention' which is important and which presents problems for Lévi-Strauss's modes of explanation of what really lies at the basis of Maussian 'total social facts'.

(3) EXCHANGE AND THE THEORY OF KINSHIP SYSTEMS

(a) Exchange, Dual Organisations and Cross-Cousin Marriage

However, having made those brief critical points (to which I shall return later), it is now time to turn to Lévi-Strauss's concepts of the more 'crystallised' forms of exchange to see in detail how they govern his discussions of empirical kinship organisations.

We have already seen that the principle of reciprocity is conceived as being empirically realised in its most primitive form within the prohibition of incest and exogamy, which constitute the minimal *preconditions* for the setting up of a system of matrimonial exchange. At this stage the modalities of this exchange are ill-defined: while exogamy necessarily requires that exchange between social groupings take place, the exact number of these groups and the nature of the pattern of alliances is left indeterminate because all that is required is that marriage should be with an individual outside a particular social unit.

However, a higher degree of crystallisation of reciprocity consists in what anthropologists have called 'dual organisations'. The latter are quite simply types of social organisation in primitive societies in which *all* individuals of the community are divided into two groups or 'moieties' (nearly always exogamous) which maintain varied types of interrelationship (in kinship, in religion and ritual, in politics, in economic organisation). The basis of the definition of the relationship of one individual to another is in moiety membership, however this may be transmitted (patrilineally or matrilineally), and the distinction between father's and mother's collaterals forms one axis of the system so formed (*ESK*, p. 72). When kinship relations are organised dualistically in this fashion (as in a system of exogamous moieties), one of its effects is the generation of certain concomitant rules of marriage. Irrespective of descent, children of the father's brother and mother's sister are placed in the same moiety as ego (*parallel* cousins being thus formed whereas those of the father's sister and mother's brother are placed in the *opposite* moiety (*ESK*, p. 98). Thus, in such an exogamous system 'the latter are the first collaterals who are possible spouses of ego'. Furthermore

this remarkable feature is expressed in a number of ways. Firstly, the cousins descended from the father's brother or from the mother's sister cannot marry for the same reason as brothers and sisters (they belong to the same moiety) and are designated by the same term. Secondly the cousins descended from the mother's brother or the father's sister belong to the opposite moiety and are called by a special term, or by the term for husband or wife since the spouse must be chosen from their division. Finally, the father's brother and the mother's sister whose children are called brothers and sisters are themselves called father and mother while the mother's brother and the father's sister, whose children are potential spouses are called by special terms by a term for 'father in law' or 'mother in law'. This terminology . . . satisfies all the requirements of a dual organisation with exogamous moieties. It might be an expression, in terms of kinship, of the social organisation based on moieties [ibid., p. 98].

At the same time, however, this terminology is coincidental with the widespread primitive form of alliance — 'preferential marriage between cross cousins' — so that ' . . . it might as just easily be said that dual organisation is the expression, on an institutional plane, of a system of kinship which itself derives from certain rules of alliance' [ibid., p. 99]. Which then derives from which, the rules of alliance from the institutionalisation of exogamous moieties or the latter from the former? Lévi-Strauss avoids all temptation (unlike Tylor, Rivers, *et al.*) to see one as *derivative* from the other:[19] on the contrary he conceives them as mutually implicative and as having a *common foundation* so that neither is secondary. Thus they are related in that

> Both are *systems of reciprocity* and both result in a dichotomous terminology . . . But while dual organisation with exogamous moieties defines the actual spouse vaguely, it determines the number and identity of possible spouses most closely. *In other words it is the highly specialised formula for a system which has its beginnings, still poorly differentiated, in cross cousin marriage.* Cross cousin marriage defines a relationship, and establishes a perfect or approximate model of the relationship in each case. Dual organisation delimits two classes by applying a uniform rule guaranteeing that individuals born or distributed into these classes will always stand in this relationship in its widest sense. What is lost in precision is gained in automation and simplicity. *The two institutions are in contrast, one being crystallised, the other being flexible* [ibid., p. 103; my emphasis].

Both have the same functional value — to establish reciprocity — but 'dual organisation' *represents its institutionalisation* (and therefore a more crystallised level of its realisation) while 'preferential cross cousin marriage' is more precise in its actual definition of possible spouses.[20] Each realises reciprocity in a different logical and structural way. Of the two, however, Lévi-Strauss accords logical priority to the latter: it is conceived as 'the veritable "experimentum crucis" in the study of marriage prohibitions'.

Here it is necessary for us to understand why this is the case and also to grasp how the discussion of this institution (along with that of dual organisations) fits into the framework of concepts which I schematically outlined above.

The kind of demarcation procedure which cross-cousin marriage sets up is one which differentiates within a category of relatives (cousins) 'who from the view-point of biological proximity are strictly interchangeable'. For Lévi-Strauss the significance of this cannot be underestimated because of the link between this institution and the incest taboo. Thus he states that

> if we can understand why degrees of kinship which are equivalent from a biological point of view are nevertheless considered *completely dissimilar* from a social point of view, we can claim to have discovered the principle, not only of cross-cousin marriage, but of the incest prohibition itself [ibid., p. 122].

What then is the *basis* of cross-cousin marriage? All of its varying modalities are characteristically conceived as variations or transformations of a single central invariant process of exchange whose skeletal features Lévi-Strauss represents diagrammatically (Figures 6 and 7 on p. 131 and 145 of *ESK*). The basic features of this process are directly associated with *a principle of opposition*, found *independently* of dual organisation and thus irreducible to it, which is 'the distinction between collaterals of the same degree according as kinship is established through a relative of the same or of different sex'. This is

> the idea that the *brother-sister* relationship is identical with the *sister-brother* relationship, but that these both differ from the *brother-brother* and *sister-sister* relationships, which are identical . . . it is the principle whereby there are considerable differences of status attached to whether the structure of collateral relationships (viz the arrangement of the sexes) is symmetrical or asymmetrical [ibid., p. 128].

Prior logically to the variant forms of cross-cousin marriage (and as a condition of their existence) there is the unconscious or conscious recognition[21] of an opposition between two types of relationship (cross and parallel) resulting in both positive (e.g. prescription, affinity) and negative (prohibition and antipathy) social consequences each of equal 'value', in that (*contra* Frazer) 'cross cousins are recommended for the same reason that parallel cousins are excluded'. The overall reason unifying the latter and providing the purpose of the oppositions referred to lies in the representation of cross-cousin marriage as the 'most elementary formula for concrete marriage by exchange'. This formula of exchange by 'crossing' Lévi-Strauss represents diagramatically (*ESK*, p. 131). A structure of exchange is thus built so that a group which receives must give, and vice versa. Whatever the group, parallel cousins are always from families in one formal position and cross-cousins from those in opposed positions, the mode of exchange relationship between these elements *itself* being important, independent of the things exchanged. It is the logical characteristics of this type of exchange which are important, placing it as they do at a crossroads leading to two different manifestations of reciprocity as extreme types: on the one hand dual organisation in societies cleaved into exogamous moieties, and on the other the more or less universal prohibition on incestuous unions.

(b) Restricted and Generalised Exchange and Types of Regime

At this point however, it is essential to connect the above discussion to the concepts of the 'restricted' and 'generalised' variants of exchange which Lévi-Strauss constructs, within the context of the examination of the 'classical' kinship organisations of Aboriginal Australian tribes Cross-cousin alliance is central to the operation of marriage systems which are governed by *each* of these mechanisms. To understand how the latter are conceived it is necessary to consider how as concepts they 'emerge' from the treatment of certain Australian systems as exemplars or 'types'. The latter serve as exemplary material for a study of the nature of the implicit 'logic' governing the regulations of alliance in a variety of kinship formations. How is this logic related to regular divisions of the tribes into marriage classes and to the various forms of cross-cousin marriage which are empirically encountered? Some tribes not only differentiate (in alliance) between cross- and parallel cousins, but also between the 'matrilineal' and the 'patrilineal' cross-cousins while others present symmetrical groupings of marriage classes (two moieties, four sub-sections and eight sections, for example)[22] which are linked to the different marriage regulations in ways not previously fully understood (according to Lévi-Strauss) by other theorists – chiefly Lawrence and Radcliffe-Brown.

Lévi-Strauss's own position is that progress can only be made analytically through the retention of a notion of exchange but as split into two variants with different formal characteristics ('restricted' or 'generalised', 'direct' or 'indirect') and through the concentration on the detailed inter-play of factors of residence and descent in effecting dichotomous classifications of the kinship statuses of groups and the individuals belonging to them. Here we cannot give an *exhaustive* account of the whole analyses of different systems and of the 'anomalies' which they present (which results in Lévi-Strauss's 'classification of the principal types of kinships systems'), but the following exposition attempts to reproduce the two major points: firstly the demonstration of how possible alliances in two- , four- and eight-class systems can be explained as effects of the operation of restricted and generalised exchange as structural mechanisms, and, secondly of how rules of residence and descent are central to the issue of which mechanism can become operative in a particular system.

Lévi-Strauss proposes the concept of *restricted exchange* to tackle systems divided into two, four or eight marriage classes in an attempt to interpret all initially on the basis of (a) a simple *reciprocity* process entailing organisational symmetry, connected to (b) a *dichotomising* process. Thus

> The term 'restricted exchange' includes any system which effectively or functionally divides the group into a certain number of pairs of exchange units, so that for any one pair X − Y there is a reciprocal exchange relationship. In other words, where an X man marries a Y woman, a Y man must always be able to marry an X woman. The simplest form of restricted exchange is found in the division of the group into patrilineal or matrilineal exogamous moieties. If we *suppose* that a dichotomy based upon one of the two modes of descent is superimposed upon the other the result will be a four section system. If the same process were repeated the group would comprise eight sections instead of four. *This is a regular progression* and embodies nothing faintly resembling a change in principle or a sudden upheaval [ibid., p. 146; my emphasis].

The first stage of this scheme takes in the relation between a system of two classes/moieties (dual organisation) and cross-cousin marriage. It has been seen that the system of two moieties places into opposite classes groups of individuals[23] which include cross- and parallel cousins (so that this form of social organisation is equivalent to a terminology of preferential marriage with the cross-cousin) to produce a vague specification of individuals as possible spouses. Many systems however, 'prefer' the cross-cousin *before all others*, so advocating, from those possible, a more rigorous specification of the spouse than a simple dual organisation of marriage classes allows. Lévi-Strauss interconnects the two not only by supposing them to be varying levels of crystallisation of reciprocity, as we have seen above, but by postulating that the increased specificity in the prescription is the result of the imposition of a second dichotomy of the social group adding to the first (due to moieties) to produce four (not two) variables in the definition of marital status. This does not modify the marriage rule because the four-class marriage system produced merely manifests a more rigid definition of the preferred spouse than that in the two-class system, while there is no dichotomy of possible spouses:

> In both, the class system considered as such prohibits the same types of collateral relatives (brothers, sisters, parallel cousins) and leaves the same types in the category of spouses sanctioned by the system (cross-cousins and those identified with them) [ibid., p. 147].

The postulated dichotomising or splitting process which is proposed specifies the *preferred* spouse more sharply but does *not* split into two the whole group of *possible* spouses, as the example of the Kariera shows. Lévi-Strauss finds this quite surprising:

> one would normally expect something entirely different. Since the first division of the group into two moieties results immediately in the division of the women into two groups, one including possible wives and the other prohibited wives, i.e. in dividing the number of spouses by two, it would be natural that a second division should repeat the process . . . that it should divide the number of spouses regarded as possible in the first dichotomy again into two [ibid., p. 159].

Why then is this not the case? Lévi-Strauss's analysis of the four-class (Kariera type) system suggests that this is because of the *nature* of the action of the second (matrilineal) splitting process, which acts upon the initially given (patrilineal) moieties. The two dichotomies do not operate in the same way in the determination of status: for the four-section system the matrilineal rule is followed in connection with descent, while the patrilineal one determines residence or local origin. Children take their family name from their mother and the name of their place of origin from their father. See Figures 2–4.

If a man	marries a woman	the children are
Durand of Paris	Dupont of Bordeaux	Dupont of Paris
Durand of Bordeaux	Dupont of Paris	Dupont of Bordeaux
Dupont of Paris	Durand of Bordeaux	Durand of Paris
Dupont of Bordeaux	Durand of Paris	Durand of Bordeaux

FIGURE 2
SOURCE: *ESK*, p. 161.

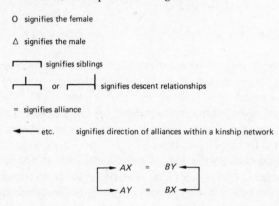

Durands of Paris *(A) = (B)* Duponts of Bordeaux

Durands of Bordeaux *(C) = (D)* Duponts of Paris

FIGURE 3
SOURCE: *ESK*, p. 161.
Key to Symbols used in kinship network diagrams.

O signifies the female

△ signifies the male

⌐—⌐ signifies siblings

⌐—⊥ or ⌐—⌐ signifies descent relationships

= signifies alliance

◄——— etc. signifies direction of alliances within a kinship network

$$AX = BY$$
$$AY = BX$$

FIGURE 4
SOURCE: Ibid., p. 162.

Each of the four classes in Figure 3 is the result of the combination of a couple of nominal terms and a couple of place terms, given that the former are transmitted matrilineally and the latter patrilineally. If A and B are moieties, X and Y names of hordes of origin, then alternatively we have the representation set out in Figure 4, where marriage is with the cross-cousin, as in the moiety system, but where a second link is added to the first moiety link (i.e. between Durands and Duponts) which 'continues to unite them as in the past' but also unites those of the two places Paris and Bordeaux, so that 'a dialectic of residence, *both reducing and reaffirming the social ties*, will be added to the dialectic of descent'.

A similar demonstration is repeated for the eight-class (Aranda type) system by showing that it can be conceived as the result of a connection between *four* local groups and (again) two moieties. Diagrammatically this situation is more complex than the Kariera type (although it is equivalent in principle of operation). See Figure 5. There, however, the consequences for *alliances* are fundamental. Unlike the case of the transition from a two-to a *four*-class system (which 'does not in *itself* bring about any innovation with regard to the degree of kinship

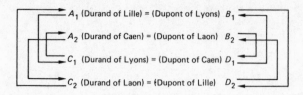

Figure 5
Source: Ibid., p. 164.

sanctioned or prohibited by marriage') the eight sub-section system has the logical effect of making the preferred spouse belong to the class of cousins descended from cross-cousins. *Both* the latter produce the distinction of cousins into cross-(prescribed) and parallel (prohibited) cousins, whereas the former distinguishes 'cousins descended from cross-cousins' from other cousins.

Lévi-Strauss stresses the logical qualities of each of the systems as parts of a series (2 class $\longrightarrow$ 4 class $\longrightarrow$ 8 class) and from a logical point of view, the four-class system presents two anomalies. The first is that it does not divide the number of possible spouses by two as do the others, and we have just referred to the way Lévi-Strauss accounts for this. The second, however, concerns the dichotomies of spouses in the series. If we consider these, it is apparent that the process (conceding a logical relation 2 class $\longrightarrow$ 4 class $\longrightarrow$ 8 class) *misses out* one dichotomy of cousins which would be intermediate between the first and last stages. That is, stage (2) in the series of systems of restricted exchange. See Figure 6.

No. of classes		Rules of alliance
(1)	Moiety	Dichotomy of cross-/ parallel cousins — the latter excluded.
(2)	Sections	Dichotomy of matrilateral / patrilateral cross-cousins — *one* excluded.
(3)	Sub-sections	Dichotomy distinguishing all cousins as (a) cross-cousins and (b) as cousins descended from cross-cousins — former excluded.

Figure 6

It is apparent there that the dichotomy (1) corresponds to both the moiety and section stages so that dichotomy (2) *is absent*: the theoretical stage which is logically required (if one accepts a direct relationship between class and alliance) does *not* obtain. Can this second anomaly of the four-class system be explained?

This is attempted within the context of the involved discussion of the empirical kinship systems of the Murngin tribe and through the construction of the concept of *generalised exchange*. Now a detailed consideration of the former discussion cannot be given here: we must concentrate upon Lévi-Strauss's more general concern with the *logical qualities* of the classical systems as 'types'.

We have seen that the two-, four- and eight-class systems are conceived by Lévi-Strauss as variations on a general structure of reciprocity, which he calls 'restricted exchange', establishing interconnections between two partners or between partners in multiples of two. For a two-class or moiety system, as we have seen, 'restricted exchange' is the *only* matrimonial exchange possibility; but this is not the case, we are told, for the four-class (or section) system. There *two* modes of exchange may be constituted. First, as in the Kariera, the restricted variant may be set up: the classes are split into two pairs between which a direct reciprocity is effective. Second, however, a 'directional' exchange between the marriage classes may be instituted 'satisfying at the same time the exigencies of class exogamy and of the division into moieties'. Thus

The possibility may be expressed by the formula: if an A man marries a B woman, a B man marries a C woman. Here the link between the classes is expressed simultaneously by marriage and descent. We propose to call the systems using this formula *systems of generalised exchange* indicating thereby that they can establish reciprocal relationships between *any* number of partners. These relationships moreover are *directional relationships*. For example, if a B man depends for his marriage upon class C placed after his own, a B woman depends upon class A, placed before [ibid., p. 178].

Lévi-Strauss gives a formal analysis of this type of four-class system and compares its features with that of the Kariera (for restricted enchange) by considering (1) the relations between the classes of the spouses and their children [24] and (2) the type of regulation of marriage practised. (1) Analysis of the three aspects (pair, couple and cycle) of the interrelationships of classes (see note 24) of the system of generalised exchange reveals that pairs are univocal/directional (as here $A = B$ is not equivalent to $B = A$) that cycles also are, but that couples are 'oscillatory'. This means effectively that we have two cyclical or rotatory structures (pairs and cycles) and one 'oscillatory' structure placing it in an intermediate position between the Kariera type (where all class relations are oscillatory, there being no cyclical/rotatory structures) and the Aranda type (where we have two oscillatory structures (in both cycles) and two rotary structures – pairs and couples). (2) On the other hand, examination of the marriage regulation of the four-class generalised exchange system reveals the operation of preferential marriage with only one cross-cousin within a continuous chain of matrimonial exchange, as Figure 7 shows (here the *matrilateral* cousin is chosen, the four-class generalised system corresponding to preferential marriage with the mother's brothers daughter).

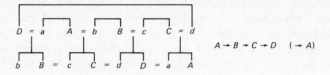

FIGURE 7   Generalised exchange among four classes
SOURCE: Based on *ESK*, Figure 28, p. 180.

For Lévi-Strauss the result of this formal analysis is that it is the four-section system of generalised exchange (and *not* the Kariera restricted type) which is the correct occupier of the intermediate position in the classical series between the moiety and the eight sub-section systems, explaining the transition from the prohibition of parallel cousins to the prohibition of all first cousins. The anomalous gap in the classical series, into which the Kariera type system was wrongly inserted, is filled through the provision of the concept of a different (generalised or 'directional' or 'indirect') exchange mechanism. It is with this concept that Lévi-Strauss aspires to abstract the logic of those Australian systems which had always been anomalous in the classical series, and, as we have mentioned, the discussion of the Murngin is dominant here.[25] Lévi-Strauss asserts that

If our analysis is correct, the problem of peripheral systems which are without classes or have an aberrant number needs to be seen in a new light. A typology based *exclusively* on the Kariera and Aranda systems would prove inadequate in the north and south of Australia where there are systems with not two, four or eight lines, but an odd number . . . these systems practise the dichotomy of cross cousins into patrilateral and matrilateral, though this seemed impossible in the previous systems [ibid., p. 197].

These 'peripheral' systems are indeed discussed in general terms in Chapter 12 and 13 of *ESK* and throughout the whole of the text, using the concept of generalised exchange, but here we must mention one more concept deemed by Lévi-Strauss to be necessary for an adequate full typology of systems: namely the concept of *regime*.

'*Regime*' expresses the mode of articulation, in any system, of the rules of residence and of descent, and Lévi-Strauss conceives of two types, *harmonic* and *disharmonic*. For the former the rules will be equivalent or symmetrical (either matrilineal/matrilocal or patrilineal/patrilocal) and for the latter they will be asymmetrical or inverted (matrilocal/ patrilineal or patrilocal/matrilineal).

It follows that the nature of the regime of a system is important for the way in which the social status of individuals can be defined (in terms of descent and residence) . The simplest system of exogamous moieties can function whatever the rule of residence or descent and whatever their relationship, but for more complex systems with greater than two classes both variables are in play (their mode of interrelation producing either 'harmony' or 'disharmony' of regime). If we consider a system composed of four classes it can be seen that when the regime is disharmonic (as in the Kariera type) we have the co-operation of two dichotomies each acting in a different direction to produce restricted exchange and preferential cross-cousin marriage. When the harmonic possibility is considered, however, the system has two alternatives:

(a) The production of a compound of two dual systems through the splitting of the two local groups each into two parts correspond- ing to the moieties.[26] Here (and in the eight sub-section harmonic system which also will split into dual systems) the variable of residence/locality does not significantly raise complexity above multiple forms of dualism.

(b) The institution of *generalised* or 'directional' exchange between classes $(A = B = C = D (= A))$ which can theoretically handle a high level of complexity by the incorporation of an unlimited number of groups.

The outcome of this is the suggestion that it is possible to construct a general typology of the classical kinship systems with two principal axes: one associated with the variants of restricted exchange (discussed above in some detail) under the heading of disharmonic regimes, and a second of the forms of generalised exchange under the heading harmonic regimes. At the termination of a lengthy process of analysis Lévi-Strauss is able to put forward a schema logically interrelating different types of system using the basic concepts of types of exchange and regime defined as above. See Figure 8.

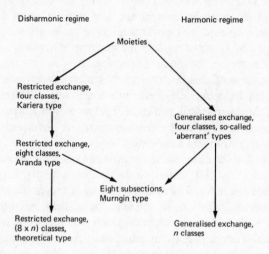

FIGURE 8
SOURCE: *ESK*, p. 216.

(c) Structures of Kinship and Forms of Social Solidarity

Now, of the many important features which Figure 8 expresses, relating the different types of systems its most important feature is the overall *contrast* between harmonic (generalised) and disharmonic (restricted exchange) types. *Both their developmental possibilities and their integrationist capacities are distinct*; they are contrasted in the following important passage:

The development of restricted exchange goes hand in hand with the admission of an even greater number of local groups participating in the exchange, e.g. two in a Kariera system and four in an Aranda system. Organic development (i.e. development in the degree of integration) goes hand in hand with a mechanical development (i.e. numerical increase in the number of participants). Conversely, generalised exchange, while relatively unproductive in the matter of system (since it can engender only one pure system) is very fruitful as a regulating principle: the group remaining unchanged in extent and composition, generalised exchange allows the realisation of a more supple and effective solidarity within this mechanically stable group [ibid., p. 441].

The bilateralism of the restricted exchange systems favours stable organisations into discrete marriage classes precisely because its formula of direct reciprocity can use these in an efficient way to realise a highly satisfactory overall *societal* integration.

What then are the more specific organisational possibilities of systems with harmonic regimes and generalised exchange? We have already noted that, in contrast to the bilateral nature of marriage under restricted exchange, for the generalised variant a dichotomy of cross-cousins is effected so that marriage (being with only one class of the two, either matrilateral cross-cousins or patrilateral cross-cousins) is necessarily unilateral, and have illustrated the simple generalised system which corresponds to the adoption of the matrilateral alternative. So far little has been said about the second possibility (patrilateral marriage) and the first has been mentioned solely to exemplify the general principle of generalised marriage. In order to be more specific about the modalities of this form of exchange in relation to the two different forms of unilateral cross-cousin marriage and to get a more precise understanding of the *contrasts in logical operation and social function* which Lévi-Strauss constructs between these and the restricted or bilateral forms, it is important to bear in mind the structure of Part Two of *ESK*. There the discussion of the characteristics of generalised exchange unfolds in conjunction with a reassessment of a wide variety of kinship systems distributed throughout Asia, beginning first with 'concrete systems based clearly and simply on a structure of generalised exchange' (the Kachin of Burma, the Gilyak of Siberia) and then going on to less straightforward manifestations in China and in India.

In the former systems, preferential marriage, with the mother's brother's daughter is held to be able to provide a simple and continuous directional exchange so that, for three units *A*, *B*, *C*, *A* surrenders a daughter or sister to *B*, who surrenders one to *C*, who in turn will surrender one to *A* to complete the cycle, as illustrated in Figure 9.

It is suggested that the system entails 'credit' and, according to Lévi-Strauss, 'trust', in that each group, having given women to one group, must be prepared to wait to receive from *another* different one when the cycle is completed. As Lévi-Strauss puts it, the individual groups *A, B*

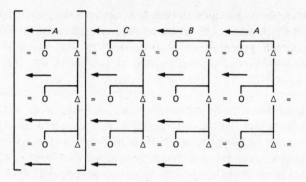

FIGURE 9

and *C* must take part in a 'collective speculation' entailing certain risks
in return for the high level of overall collective cohesion which the
cyclical structure allows.[27] The system '. . . by the multiplicity of the
combinations which it sanctions and the *desire* of the safeguards that it
arouses, invites the particular and private speculations of the partners'
[ibid., p. 265]. It seems furthermore that there are two ways that these
collective desires for safeguards may be satisfied: first, by multiplying the
number of cycles of exchange participated in ('widening the circle of
affines'), and second by 'cornering as many women as possible from the
wife-giving lineage' (i.e. polygamy). For Lévi-Strauss this tendency
within the system towards polygamous privilege (of a whole lineage)
implies a quasi-feudal orientation, but.more particularly raises the fact
that it has egalitarian conditions of existence leading (paradoxically) to
aristocratic consequences. Thus

> For the system to function harmoniously, an 'a' woman must be
> equivalent to a 'b' woman, a 'b' woman to a 'c' woman and a 'c'
> woman to an 'a' woman, i.e. that the lineages A, B, C shall be of equal
> status and prestige. By contrast, the speculative character of the
> system the widening of the cycle, the establishment of secondary
> cycles between certain enterprising lineages for their own advantage
> and finally the inevitable preference for certain alliances resulting in
> the accumulation of women at some stage of the cycle, are all factors
> of inequality which may at any moment force a rupture . . . One
> comes to the conclusion that generalised exchange leads almost
> unavoidably to 'anisogamy', i.e. to marriage between spouses of

different status; that this must appear all the more clearly when the cycles of exchange are multiplied or widened; but that at the same time it is at variance with the system and must therefore lead to its downfall [ibid., p. 266].

Both the egalitarian and inegalitarian tendencies manifest themselves, it follows, in different ways. While the preferential unilateral marriage rule codifies an egalitarian slant, inegalitarianism may well be expressed through complex customs of *bride-purchase* which become super-imposed upon the debtor—creditor cycle which the marriage rule expresses. Bride wealth becomes a tribute paid by an inferior to a superior group within the egalitarian context of the operation of the system of generalised exchange, as Lévi-Strauss attempts to show in simple terms for the Kachin and Gilyak systems.

Let us turn now, however, to the more detailed look at the *structural* qualities of this matrilateral exchange which Lévi-Strauss provides. If cross-cousin marriage *in general* is considered, bearing in mind what we have already said above, it can be understood to be based upon a 'fundamental quartet' between brother and sister, son and daughter, establishing a structure of reciprocity between one man creditor and one man debtor, one woman received and one given. We have two structural possibilities: either matrilateral or patrilateral forms. See Figure 10. According to Lévi-Strauss matrilateral generalised exchange, Quartet I in the Figure, has a 'better structure'[28] than Quartet II, in being the most satisfactory realisation of 'crossing' (see above) upon which cross-cousin marriage is based. Moreover

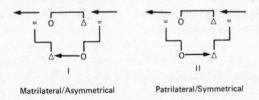

Matrilateral/Asymmetrical   Patrilateral/Symmetrical

FIGURE 10
SOURCE: After *ESK*, p. 443.

however the structure is analysed, men and women appear in regular alternation as must do those from whom cross cousins . . . are descended. The quartet of marriage with the matrilateral cousin is the sytematic application to all degrees of kinship, of the formal alternation of sex upon which the existence of cross cousins depends [ibid., p. 444].

The consequence for the functioning of the *whole* matrilateral system is that the three constituent marriages of this 'cell' are *all in the same direction* (as illustrated below and in the Figure 9), generating an 'open structure' so that the 'various cessions and acquisitions of wives' by which the quartet is constituted, presuppose *a whole chain* on which a wider but self-sufficient-system of the same type can be built. As Figure 11 shows, all marriages are linked in the same way into a total continuous chain of relationships so that integration of the whole social group proceeds from 'the participation of every individual and biological family in a collective harmony.' That is to say,

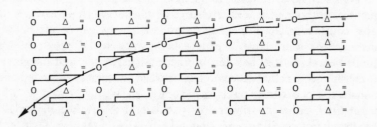

FIGURE 11
SOURCE: Ibid., p. 452.

a human group need only proclaim the law of marriage with the mother's brother's daughter for a vast cycle of reciprocity between all generations and lineages to be organised, as harmonious and ineluctable as any physical or biological law . . . the overall cycle of reciprocity is coextensive with the group itself both in time and space, subsisting and developing with it [ibid., p. 450].

Despite his concern with the *integrationist efficacy* of matrilateral cross-cousin marriage, however, Lévi-Strauss is quick to remind us of the dangers, already glimpsed, which this marriage form entails for the society which adopts it. The longer the cycle of reciprocity becomes, the more complete the societal integration but at the same time the more it becomes 'a long term speculation which continually verges on bankruptcy, if the unanimity of the collaborations and the collective observance of the rules should ever come into default' (ibid., p. 451).

Matrilateral marriage thus becomes 'a great sociological venture', 'so richly promising and productive of results but also so full of hazards'.

There does remain however another alternative: marriage with the father's-sister's daughter, the second possibility allowed (as we saw above) by the structure of cross-cousin marriage. It is enough to return to Quartet II above to realise that in this case the structural cell of the system is quite different. Here the unit is composed of only two asymmetrical pairs (brother-sister, husband-wife) along with two which are symmetrical (father-son, mother-daughter), in contrast to the *four* asymmetrical pairs (brother-sister, husband-wife, father-daughter, mother-son) of the matrilateral quartet. This has the overall effect of producing *a change in the 'direction' of marriage* when we turn from the older to the younger generation, so that unlike Quartet I, we have a closed structure so that 'a woman is ceded in the ascending generation, a woman is acquired in the descending generation, and the system returns to the point of inertia'. So, for a *network* of such interconnecting relations,

Instead of constituting an overall system as bilateral marriage and marriage with the matrilateral cousin do in their own respective spheres, marriage with the father's-sister's daughter is incapable of attaining a form other than that of a *multitude of small closed systems juxtaposed to one another*, without ever being able to realise an overall structure [ibid., p. 445; my emphasis].

We have, as Figure 12 reveals, a discontinuous exchange system of short cycles. Reciprocity in this instance, cannot attain a total structure

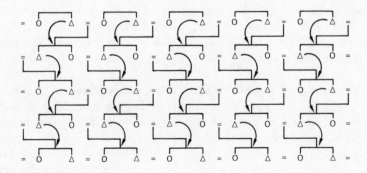

FIGURE 12
SOURCE: Idem.

integrating the whole social group: solidarity is 'mechanical and precarious', so that

> instead of the real unity of a single thread underlying the whole social fabric, there is an artificial unity of bits and pieces, proceeding from the fact that two interconnected elements are each coupled with a third element [ibid., p. 446].

This 'bits and pieces' discontinuity at the heart of systems of patrilateral marriage accounts for its relative empirical infrequency in contrast to the matrilateral form. While the latter can provide an assured integration, the former 'builds a precarious edifice' not expressible in a systemic law because of the directness and small-scale nature of the elementary exchanges forged by its constituent atoms. But if its solidary consequences are not highly satisfactory, its mechanism is 'safer' than the matrilateral form precisely because it avoids the 'risks' which the latter, according to Lévi-Strauss, must engender because of the length of its cycle. The short cycles of the patrilateral system offer *immediate* exchange returns, avoiding the speculative dangers which have been associated with the matrilateral alternative.

For Lévi-Strauss, this accounts also for the empirical presences of vestiges of patrilateralism where simple forms of matrilateral marriage in generalised exchange are encountered: social groups practising the efficient but risky latter form 'have remained obsessed by the patrilateral formula which offers none of these advantages but does not entail the same dangers' [ibid., p. 452]. Their 'collective anxiety' expresses itself in the attachment to 'a certain coefficient, or even a symbol of patrilaterality', however this may be realised, and as a consequence *societies always 'think of' the two forms together*. For this reason no temporal priority can be attributed to either matrilaterality or patrilaterality; both are always, consciously or unconsciously, *conceived* simultaneously together, so that

> *the two formulas are eternally coexistent*. All the historical hypotheses imaginable will never succeed in providing anything more than the incomplete and approximate transfiguration of a dialectical process [ibid., p. 454; my emphasis].

But if there is constant association there is also opposition in the sense that the patrilateral form engenders the shortest cycle of generalised exchange whereas the matrilateral form reproduces the longest in principle. The former is the limit of generalised exchange representing the 'negation' of the long cycle present in the latter.

We are nearing the conclusion of this exposition, corresponding to Lévi-Strauss's attempt to provide a simple *logical unification* of the principles of the three elementary forms of marriage constituted by bilateralism as restricted exchange, and two polar types of generalised exchange, patrilateralism and matrilateralism. Neither type, we are told, is ever manifest in a totally 'pure' form: each nearly always operates in the presence of an admixture of the others manifest alongside it. While the 'contamination' of generalised exchange is 'intrinsic', as we have just seen, for restricted exchange 'each system is simple and coherent, but is continually besieged by other systems based upon principles which are foreign to it' [ibid., p. 464]. None of these 'contaminations', according to Lévi-Strauss, can be seen as the product of evolution or diffusion but as the result of a *synchronic law of association*. He interrelates the three marriage forms in the following way:

> Matrilateral and patrilateral marriage represent the two poles of generalised exchange, but they are opposed to each other as the shortest and the longest cycles of exchange, and both are opposed to bilateral marriage as the general to the particular – since mathematics confirms that, in all combinations with several partners, the game for two should be treated as a particular case of the game for three. At the same time, bilateral marriage has the characteristic of alternation in common with patrilateral marriage whereas it resembles matrilateral marriage in that both allow a general solution, and not a collection of partial solutions, as is the case with patrilateral marriage. The three forms of exchange thus constitute four pairs of oppositions [ibid., p. 464;].

But if this system of oppositions (see Figure 13) is the logical interrelation of the forms, in what does *necessity* for 'contamination' and our 'synchronic law' consist? At this point our account turns full circle, for we return to the teleological efficacy of the mind for Lévi-Strauss's answer. The logical triad is conceived to be potentially always accessible to the mind, or at least the unconscious, so that 'it cannot evoke one [form] without thinking of this structure in opposition to – and also in correlation to – the two others.' Finally then, behind the diversity in the expression and realisation of the forms, in combinations and in degrees, we have the exigencies of the *recognition of*, and *choice between* discrete types of reciprocity each engendering quite specific

FIGURE 13   The system of oppositions between the elementary forms of
            marriage

= Bilateral marriage: no cycle $A \longleftrightarrow B$

− Patrilateral marriage: short cycle $\begin{cases} A \longrightarrow B \\ A \longleftarrow B \end{cases}$

+ Matrilateral marriage: long cycle $A \longrightarrow B \longrightarrow C$

SOURCE: Ibid, p. 465.

social effects. *Before* a particular primitive social group is able to adopt
one or a number of these forms to resolve its specific problems, the
triadic structure uniting *all three* has to be present to the unconscious so
that, in the last analysis, the actual *praxis* of primitive marriage, in
whatever form and for whatever social ends, ultimately rests upon its
apperception. According to the conclusion of the *ESK* at least, the
reasons for the adoption of one form or another cannot reside in *social*
exigencies: here, and elsewhere, as we have seen, it is the 'praxis' of the
unconscious which has the final word.

III An Integrated Critique

Now, after a long account of the third and final element entailed in Lévi-
Strauss's theory of kinship, it is necessary to set forth a synthesis of
critical comments which takes into account the specific conceptual levels
in it which I have sought to emphasise. Before doing this however, some
comment must be made about the character of the different critiques
already in existence.

   As one would expect, these are far from homogeneous, but they are, in
principle, classifiable into quite distinct types on the basis of the varied
nature of the theoretical problematics underlying and governing the
different modes of criticism. As a consequence of a particular understanding of the nature and role of theory in the social sciences in general,

and of Lévi-Strauss's theory in particular, each type usually concentrates its attentions on selected features of the latter's work on
kinship. This variation can be illustrated by contrasting two very
different types of assessment: on the one hand that produced by the
Anglo-Saxon anthropologists Leach, Needham and Korn,[29] and on the
other that advanced by the American theorists Rossi, Scholte and
Wilden,[30] among others.

Let us take the latter first. For these authors Lévi-Strauss's theory of
kinship is significant within anthropology less because of the force of its
substantive analyses and more because of the fact that it represents one
aspect of a novel theoretical approach to the social-in-general. *ESK*,
accordingly, is of interest really because it embodies a new 'paradigmatic' mode of explanation within anthropological theory which
differentiates it from pre-existing ones. It is part of a unique structuralist
'epistemic paradigm' (Scholte) or the product of a unique set of
epistemological assumptions (Rossi, Boudon, Wilden) and as such it is
these theoretical conditions of existence of the work on kinship which
these writers consider to be most important.

The situation is quite different for Leach, Needham and Korn, who,
while far from unconcerned with the type of issues stressed by the writers
we have just discussed, usually direct the greater part of their attention
to the empirical *adequacy* of the analyses of the particular systems of
kinship which Lévi-Strauss provides (the Kachin, Murngin, Dieri, Mara
'cases', for example). The abiding concern here is whether Lévi-Strauss's
forms of conceptualisation themselves adequately represent the bases of
specific cases of kinship organisation (the sheer scope and generality of
ESK is regarded as one of its main weaknesses: the book 'attempts too
much'). At the same time, however, despite this objection, some of these
authors do support certain aspects of the overall basic orientation to
primitive kinship which Lévi-Strauss advances. This can be clearly seen
in Needham's *Structure and Sentiment* (and also Leach's *Rethinking
Anthropology*): in spite of several objections to the content of *ESK*, its
basic formulations on the 'synthetic' and symbolic character of
exchange in primitive society, and on the modalities of matrimonial
exchange and the varied integrationist functions of the these modalities,
are upheld. Needham's text (dedicated to Mauss) does not doubt 'the
quality of Lévi-Strauss's insights' (that is, his concepts), but states at the
same time that regrettably, in spite of this, ' . . . it cannot be said that he
has employed them to *their proper effect* in the analysis of *any single
system*' [p. 3; my emphasis]. For Korn, Needham and Leach, what is
more important is the correct application of these valuable 'insights' to

the facts so that the real scientific contribution of Lévi-Strauss's work to a traditional anthropological line of interpretation of kinship systems — namely, the study of 'prescriptive alliance' — might be gauged. Once this part of structural anthropology has been decanted (its only really potentially scientific aspect for these writers) the rest, a typically Continental metaphysical dross (regarded with suspicion especially by Leach)[31] may be left on one side.

All these criticisms have a distinct place and effectivity in relation to Lévi-Strauss's theory of kinship, as we shall see. Here however, it is contended that the latter's problematic must be scrutinised in the following key areas:

(1) his mode of theorisation of what is at the basis of the rules governing alliances in all primitive societies (the nature and origins of the mechanisms governing their 'kinship levels') and thus of his kinship morphology;

(2) his more general understanding of the conditions of existence (the social determination) of kinship relations and of their social effectivity (their societal effects) within these societies.

(1) THE ROOTS OF EXCHANGE AND THE MORPHOLOGY OF KINSHIP SYSTEMS

(i) An Inadequate Theorisation of the Foundation of Primitive 'Exchanges'

Earlier (in Section I and II) I tried to suggest that there are certain shortcomings involved in the way Lévi-Strauss tries to theorise the basis of the generality of exchange phenomena — which he conceives, like Mauss, as 'total social facts'. This foundation, we have seen, (a) he attributes to the operation of an abstract principle (called the principle of reciprocity) within diverse areas of cultural life, and (b) he relates the *ubiquity* and *constancy* of this principle to the constant effectivity of certain mental structures (and behind them, of course, the mind or the unconscious).[32]

Now it is time to amplify the brief comments which I made above and to go on to suggest that because of *two* types of theoretical failure it cannot be said that Lévi-Strauss gives a correct explanation for what lies causally at the basis of primitive exchange phenomena. The first conceptual flaw — (b) — concerns the way Lévi-Strauss tries to show that the ubiquitous principle of reciprocity has psychic conditions of existence by relating it to certain 'structures of the mind'. Quite simply, the kind of arguments presented for this purpose fail to reach their objective primarily because of their reliance upon a set of hypotheses (about the unconscious and its immutable operation) of an eclectic and speculative character which are in themselves insufficient to provide a well-founded casual bridge between the domain of the psychic and the exchange principle.

As we have seen, the basic argument on the foundation of exchanges in *ESK* hinges upon the utilisation of certain findings of developmental psychology on the character of infant thought. These appear to suggest the constancy of a number of mental dispositions which in conjunction correspond to the basic need, desire and expression of reciprocity. Lévi-Strauss argues that this constitutes evidence for the *universality* of psychological exigencies which require in all forms of thought – primitive or modern, adult or infant – the apperception of reciprocal and oppositional relations. What it is important to note is that the latter is only able to do this on condition (i) that he conceives of all forms of thought (and all thought systems) as having a common substratum, and (ii) that he regards infant thought as a privileged case. This is quite clear from the quotation evidence cited in my exposition (see pp. 51–2). Infant thought is indeed conceived as privileged precisely because its operation is supposed to show most clearly – in a form relatively free from the cultural influences impinging upon adult thought – the form which certain universal parameters of all types of thought must take. *Before* the utilisation of developmental psychology Lévi-Strauss already pre-supposes the existence of constant psychic mechanisms which are the locus of all developed thought systems: Isaacs's work on infant psychology is simply regarded as showing further that the operation of these mechanisms must include the unconscious recognition of reciprocity.

Now whether developmental psychologists themselves would regard the work in question as having universalistic implications is open to doubt. And it is certainly the case (as Gardner notes)[33] that in his later work Lévi-Strauss drops this type of recourse to psychological 'evidence'. What is clear is that his assertion of the existence of a common foundation for infant and all adult (primitive and modern) thought processes is without satisfactory support, so that the condition which makes possible universalistic claims for the psychological evidence used is removed; this 'evidence' simply cannot have the significance which Lévi-Strauss attributes to it.

This has already been demonstrated in part in the first part of this book, when Lévi-Strauss's conception of the unconscious/mind and of 'constant psychic operations' were discussed (see pp. 12–21). Essentially, the point concerns the fact that Lévi-Strauss is unable to fully substantiate the claim that a common substratum of all thought (the unconscious/mind) does in fact exist and does operate in the determinate way he suggests. In effect this entity is characterised in such an essentialist and speculative manner that the structuralist reliance upon it as a causal agency engenders a direct theoretical paradox: on the one hand it is regarded as directly determinant of certain phenomena (so that an adequate account of these phenomena must refer back to it); but, on the other, the entity itself seems to be essentially mysterious and without specified supporting conditions. The result of this paradox is that it is often called upon to play the role of essence in a teleological and 'expressivist' causal manner,[34] and to 'explain' quite varied phenomena in a manner which effectively eliminates the possibility of understanding their complexity and the conditions governing their variation. It engenders, that is to say, an implicit reductionism.

In the last analysis the specifications which Lévi-Strauss provides do not establish that all thought has its origin in the formal structures of what he calls the unconscious and it must be accepted that, if this is the case, then his attempts (in the *ESK*) to establish a universal necessity for the ubiquity of the principle of reciprocity are far from successful.

This brings us to the second flaw—(a)—in the arguments on the foundation of 'total' social exchange phenomena: this time one concerning the actual *social effectivity* of the abstract principle of reciprocity itself. Once again (as we noted above on p. 54) we are confronted with an explanatory device whose mode of action reproduces 'expressivism' and all its attendant difficulties, and this is inevitable since, for Lévi-Strauss, the manner of the social *realisation* of the principle of reciprocity is only the obverse of its mode of foundation in the teleology of the unconscious. We are told that there can be a plethora of different types of realisation or crystallisation of this principle (not only within kinship but within other 'sectors' of primitive societies, as we have seen) which are duly catalogued as variations on an invariant principle, but if we demand to know the conditions which govern this variation in realisation what Lévi-Strauss offers is quite disappointing. What governs whether one particular variant is realised must be the product of two factors: on the one hand the nature of the 'contingent institutional material' empirically existing prior to the principle of reciprocity, and on the other the action of the unconscious in effectively *choosing* the particular form of the principle to be realised within these given social conditions.

This is a quite unsatisfactory form of explanation because, first, it entails a lapse into a reliance upon chance and contingency as a causal mechanism which is quite without justification and which denegates the possibility of understanding the phenomenon concerned in terms of its material, social conditions. Second, it relies upon the conception of an ephemeral mental capacity which must be assumed, again without adequate rational justification, to possess a 'recognition structure' capable of registering discrepancies, effecting certain choices and rejecting others, etc., in order that the principle of reciprocity may be manifested in one variant form or another.

Resultant exchange phenomena in the social domain – be they in the sphere of alliance, of the economic or of the political – are in the last analysis products of a process of the culturalisation of the natural. This process operates through the capacity of an unconscious mechanism to realise an ideal principle within natural conditions, but we must affirm that Lévi-Strauss's analysis of this procedure is not at all adequate. Ultimately it is subject not only to the specific shortcomings I have just mentioned, but, in addition, to the more general ones discussed earlier which stem from the fact that what we have here is one facet of his 'rationalist theory of action', with all its attendant difficulties.[35] It is precisely because of the analytical errors which such a position must engender that we must say that, in the final analysis, those primitive exchange phenomena which Lévi-Strauss considers cannot have the substratum and foundation which he postulates.

(ii) The Basis of the Kinship Morphology Undermined

If there are really basic flaws in the way Lévi-Strauss explains the foundation of primitive exchange phenomena in general, then there must also be serious doubts about his general thesis that it is possible to say that all forms of kinship and marriage are based on some type of principle of exchange, which can be established on theoretical grounds independently of Lévi-Strauss's empirical analyses. There are two aspects of this thesis, which I have mentioned above. First, there is the common anthropological assertion that some collective control of alliances is necessary for the integration and maintenance of any social whole; and, second, there is the supplementary assertion that this mode of control must always be a policy of exchange, itself in turn a transformation of the principle of reciprocity. Lévi-Strauss supports the latter assertion by (i) the general arguments on the character of primitive exchange which I have already discussed, and (ii) empirical analysis in the bulk of *ESK* which attempts to show that a whole diversity of alliance systems is governed by the mechanisms of restricted and generalised exchange.

Now in effect I have already undermined the basis of the general notions supporting the second assertion. The idea that the societal regulation of alliances must always be structured according to a principle of reciprocity depends wholly upon the notion of its ubiquitous purposive action within a number of domains. As I have just shown, however, the notion of this 'expressive' action cannot be supported. It must follow that the assertion by Lévi-Strauss that kinship relations always express an exchange falls into an unsupportable dogmatism. More importantly, it must mean that the prohibitions of incest, cross-cousin marriage and the variant mechanisms of exchange do *not* have the universal foundation which Lévi-Strauss suggests they do in an abstract principle related to the structures of the mind. If Lévi-Strauss's conceptualisation of primitive 'total' exchanges in general is undermined, then this has definite effects on the concepts used to delineate mechanisms of exchange within specific domains. Thus, although Lévi-Strauss provides a typology of basic alliance rule mechanisms, his attempt to *found* this typology on the omnipresence of a 'principle of reciprocity' behind exchange must fail.

What, however, about the adequacy of the typology itself? It is a putative morphology of kinship 'invariants', and alongside this question of Lévi-Strauss's failure in trying to establish the conditions of existence of these invariants we have to consider whether they have any explanatory efficacy. They are defined as we have seen above, in an exceedingly formal and abstract way and it is this formalism in the major constituent concepts of the typology which is the root of many problems. This has been interpreted by many commentators (Leach, Needham, Barnes, for example)[36] as a consequence of the fact that these are 'models' of the empirical constituted by Lévi-Strauss in accordance with his methodological protocols. However, this is not the case. They are in fact simply substantive concepts, never fully commensurable with the empirical, constructed by Lévi-Strauss relatively *independently* of his methodology and epistemology,[37] and in some cases it is possible to give them diagrammatic representation.

The morphology is built around the concepts of restricted and generalised exchange (as invariant features of elementary kinship structures) whose specification interrelates three internal features of kinship: a genealogically specified rule of marriage; a reference to the number of kinship groups exchanging in the system; and the character- istics of symmetry or asymmetry in the form of the movement of exchanges (reciprocal or directional). That which has logical priority, however, is the rule of marriage: the attempt is made to show that restricted and generalised exchange correspond to three types of marriage rule (bilateral, matrilateral and patrilateral cross-cousin marriage) in the sense that they are possible products of the logical facilities for exchange which Lévi-Strauss conceives the latter to possess in the sphere of kinship. His formal discussion of the marriage of cousins shows that under certain conditions it may logically permit a structure of reciprocal relationships to emerge, providing that the procedure of crossing is followed, differentiating between cross- and parallel cousins. Given this procedure, Lévi-Strauss understands the organisation of reciprocity to be capable of transformation into different forms corresponding to bilaterality (R. E.) matrilaterality (continuous G. E.) and patrilaterality (discontinuous G. E.). In order to explain *how* this can come about he has recourse to two important features: (a) the number of groups in the system, and (b) the articulation of residence and descent rules in it, making up its 'regime'. (We have shown this above in detail for bilaterality.) The latter is particularly important: if a regime is harmonic reciprocity can be either patrilateral or matrilateral (giving generalised exchange), whereas if it is disharmonic the only result can be bilaterality (and restricted exchange). This demonstration utilises the factors of residence and descent as purely formal modes of classification which synchronically combine and together provide a classification of marriageable individuals in the systems considered. This is perhaps most clear in the morphological classification Lévi-Strauss tries to construct for the Aboriginal 'classical series' of systems. Starting with the simple moiety system, two types of logical – not historical or temporal – transformation are possible. On the one hand reciprocity may become a symmetrical or direct exchange between an even number of classes, and on the other it may be asymmetrical or directional between any number. In the first case it is the joint combination of locality or residence (in the existence in Australia of different systems with varying numbers of patrilocal groupings) with a dichotomy of descent (postulated as matrilineal) acting in the definition of kinship status which is used to give the systems a common foundation. In the second case no such cross- cutting of residence and descent principles is present and any number of groups may be accommodated.

Now it is undoubtedly true that, using the notion of *residence* as a 'structural principle', Lévi-Strauss is able to present (particularly for the disharmonic progression of systems) a logically interconnected schema of possible kinship systems on a transformational basis. However, it is precisely this feature of the kinship typology which constitutes its basic point of inadequacy. If we question exactly *why* the element of residence is introduced and why it plays such an important role for particular kinship organisations, what we are given is quite unsatisfactory — residence is selected it seems purely because to effect transformation within discharmonic types two contrasting rules of filiation are ideally required (descent being the other). Its importance can in fact be justified only *formally* by Lévi-Strauss and this is reflected in the rather limp assertion in *Totemism* that the legitimacy of using the rule of residence as a structural principle really derives from the fact that ' . . . every ordered society whatever its organisation and degree of complexity has to be defined in one way or another in terms of residence . . . ' [p. 105]. Now this assertion cannot be doubted but it is undoubtedly a flimsy basis for the recourse to residence as such an important analytical element within a morphology. It reflects the essential arbitrariness entailed in the connotations of the concept of regime (which rely on the simple contingent presence or absence of two kinship characteristics), an arbitrariness which can only undermine the theoretical and practical efficacy of the overall typology.

Its ethnographic adequacy has of course already been put under heavy attack by kinship specialists. It is impossible to consider in detail the various types of criticism which have been advanced, but those of Korn and of Barnes, which have direct bearing on those particular systems which Lévi-Strauss conceives as ideal examplars of particular stages in the transformations of particular types of exchange, are typical. While Korn analyses the paradigm eight-class disharmonic system of the Aranda and finds it in fact to be harmonic in Lévi-Strauss's terms (Korn, F., 1973, Chapter 2), Barnes (1971, p. 161) raises doubts about the position of the Kariera as an exemplar of four-class disharmony. Now, without taking a position on particular analyses and joining the disputes over particular systems, we can situate the empirical inadequacies of the typology within its overall theoretical status.

From what we have said about the 'expression' of exchange and the arbitrariness which is central to its mode of classification we can say that *the comparative ambition of the morphology has been undermined*: Lévi-Strauss quite simply is unable to provide a set of adequate theoretical reasons for why this typology should have the scope which he attributes to it. If this is the case then the vast analytical contents of the *ESK* have to be conceived as resulting not in a *general* morphology, but in a set of particular analyses of particular kinship systems in specific forms of social organisation *which must be judged individually*. The utility of its analyses is then the extent to which particular forms are analysed in an adequate manner for the type of social formation being considered, and not their contribution to a putative general classification of known kinship systems.

This point is important to bear in mind because recent Marxist anthropologists, though critical of Lévi-Strauss's general conceptions of the nature of primitive social organisation, appear to accept without argument the morphology of kinship systems which Lévi-Strauss provides. Both Godelier and after him Friedman[38] attempt to integrate Lévi-Strauss's classification of kinship forms into a Marxism which would be able to provide a correct analysis of the true social *function* of these forms. Structuralism, it is argued, can indeed 'explain the logic of forms but ignores the logic of functions' – its attempt to provide the basis of a vast number of systems of kinship in transformations of two exchange principles is correct but it fails to theorise the social functions which the variant forms fulfil. Two points must be made here. First, as I have just stated, the morphology itself cannot be accepted at face-value, as Godelier clearly thinks;[39] and, second, Lévi-Strauss does (and *must* in fact precisely because of the nature of the issues being tackled) provide us with a number of reflections on the societal effects of different forms which make up the morphology, which must be examined.

(2) THE SOCIETAL PLACE OF THE KINSHIP FORMS

At this point we return to the general issue of the whole way in which Lévi-Strauss conceives of kinship relations in primitive societies considered as totalities. We have already seen that structural anthropology usually regards its objects as isolatable systems for methodological reasons, but Lévi-Strauss does state that what he calls relations of kinship have to be thought of as one 'level' of primitive societies entertaining definite relations with other levels. There is an explicit recognition in some parts of his work that (a) kinship relations have definite societal effects – that is, they are *determinate*; and (b) kinship relations are *themselves* subject to social constraint – they are *determined*.

The Determinations of Kinship: Its Social Consequences and Conditions of Existence

It was seen how for Lévi-Strauss kinship in general has a crucial permanent functional integrationist value for primitive societies and how specific forms of kinship result in different degrees of integration (see pp. 66–72). The three central structural realisations of exchange in kinship – bilateral cross-cousin marriage and matrilateral and patri-lateral cross-cousin marriage – are each regarded as having *specific solidary effects* for the society which adopts one in particular (though a combination may be operative). Restricted exchange (bilateral cross-cousin marriage) can generate a number of transformable systems (by segmentation from $2 \to 4 \to 8$ classes) but these are always limited in their integrationist capacities to linking pairs of symmetrically placed groups. Generalised exchange, on the other hand, 'can engender only one pure system' of n groups, but its integration can encompass two forms (the 'continuous' and the 'discontinuous') each with better prospects for the integration of the social whole than restricted systems. The second generates a 'multitude of closed systems' while the first produces an overall cycle of great cohesive power.

Now, what are the theoretical statuses of these reflections of Lévi-Strauss on the kinship forms and primitive social solidarity? A number of authors, and in particular those who see Lévi-Strauss's kinship morphology as a contribution to the generalised 'theory of social exchange',[40] seem to suggest that they are front-rank developments and refinements of Durkheim's 'mechanical' and 'organic' solidarity. This claim however, cannot be seriously upheld. It is true that Lévi-Strauss does use the terms 'mechanical' and 'organic' in a *metaphorical* sense to express the effects of different systems (see *ESK* pp. xxxiv and 484), but this in no way commits him to detailed reflection on the specification of the original Durkheimian concepts,[41] which have a very particular content moulded by the nature of the latter's social morphology. Lévi-Strauss's reflections are quite different in the sense that they are concerned with the purely *formal possibilities* for interconnection between social groups pre-given in the system, and are advanced with no specific connection to a theory of social types: the constitution of the different primitive societies as wholes is not rigorously examined and kinship relations are seen as having cohesive effects relatively inde-pendently of other forms of social determination (e.g. political or economic). There are two important issues here: first, the status of what Lévi-Strauss says about the particular social consequences of the adoption by a society of one or another of his kinship mechanisms; second, the status of his reflections on social solidarity in general.

If we take the second issue first, we can note that there is indeed an implicit Durkheimianism in Lévi-Strauss's position in the sense that he also, like the former, is only able to conceptualise the generation of social solidarity by first assuming the prior existence of social forms which must be understood as already integrated. Where Durkheim takes the band or horde as the primary datum for a social morphology, Lévi-Strauss in his kinship morphology also presupposes the 'givenness' of primitive bands, local groups and descent groups:[42] for both authors the problem of social solidarity is begged precisely because the solution offered presupposes a group solidarity to be already present in society.

Turning now to the first issue, we must problematise also Lévi-Strauss's thesis that from a formal consideration of the operation of each alliance mechanism (bilateral, patrilateral, matrilateral) it is possible to deduce consequences for the whole social order. If we presuppose for the moment that the concepts of the mechanisms are unquestionably well-founded it seems to be quite clear that the extent to which Lévi-Strauss will be able to specify these 'consequences' will be directly dependent upon his understanding of the organisation of the particular society as a whole within which a mechanism is considered to be operative (in the domain of kinship relations). He appears to accept this theoretical necessity when he suggests that if no 'external factors' were affecting a kinship mechanism

> it would work indefinitely and the social structure would remain static. This is not the case however, hence the need to introduce into the theoretical model new elements to account for diachronic changes of the structure on the one hand, and on the other for the fact that kinship structure does not exhaust social structure [*Structural Anthropology*, p. 309].

Despite this acceptance however, no 'new elements' are introduced and, in practice, in the analysis of particular social forms alliance mechanisms are considered in relative isolation from other levels of social organisation such as the economic and the political, and to be capable of generating specific societal consequences independent of their influence. Why does this happen?

It must be seen as a direct effect of the quite unique *comparative* approach to kinship in societies which Lévi-Strauss takes. His very project for the construction of the invariants (and transformations of these invariants) governing the kinship 'communication structures' of quite different forms of primitive social organisation through the breadth of its comparative ambition itself tends to militate against an adequate understanding of the specific place of kinship in particular societies. This leads to the dilemma we have just mentioned: precisely because of the comparative scope of the concepts of restricted and generalised exchange Lévi-Strauss is forced into positing 'general' social consequences which are theoretically achievable by each mechanism *independently* of factors external to kinship, whose influence, it is asserted elsewhere, it is expedient to take into account. We can accept Lévi-Strauss's theses on the social consequences of the mechanisms only if we concede them to operate independently of external social determination. This concession the latter is quite willing to make in analysis, although it forces him into theoretical contradiction, but we should be clear about what it entails: ultimately the proposal to analyse sectors of specific types of social organisation in *abstraction* from the wider social whole of which they are a part.

Similar remarks are apposite for another set of issues relating to another aspect of this 'abstractionism': Lévi-Strauss's failure to account for the social conditions of existence of particular types of kinship organisation. Accepting again that Lévi-Strauss's representations of particular systems are adequate, the kind of crucial questions which are raised at this level concern the *reasons for* the dominance of kinship relations in primitive societies in general and the conditions which govern the adoption by a particular society of a certain kinship form (or the evolution to a new form). Here the neo-Marxist criticisms of Godelier and Friedman have great efficacy despite the shortcomings I have already mentioned above. The former makes a crucial point when he observes that

> The majority of anthropologists, when faced by a multifunctional institution . . . infer that it is because of its multifunctional character that the institution dominates the structure of the whole society and the logic of its reproduction. The analysis however, stops there in the blind alley of a tautological empirical 'explanation'. If one should then ask 'why is it kinship . . . that is multifunctional in this society?' the answer is 'because it is dominant'. *An institution is dominant because it is multifunctional and multifunctional because it is dominant.* This type of explanation can take us no further but continues in an abstract vein creating phantom explanations, pseudo analyses, which do nothing but reproduce the empirical appearances of the

facts . . . [Godelier in M. Bloch (ed.) (1975), p. 13; my emphasis].

It is certainly true that Lévi-Strauss *is* one such anthropologist forced into this kind of circularity: kinship may be held by him to be 'the very warp and weft' of primitive society but if we ask why, references back to its integrationist efficacy lead into the blind alley Godelier castigates.

The observation that Lévi-Strauss cannot explain 'the logic of functions' also has a modicum of truth in connection with the issue of what it is that determines why one particular mechanism of exchange rather than another becomes operative in a particular society. Even if we accept that Lévi-Strauss does isolate the invariants of different kinship systems in an adequate manner, accounting for the occurrence of a particular variant in a particular society constitutes an insuperable problem for him, as we noted above in connection with the teleology associated with the 'realisation' of reciprocity. We find him in fact giving two different and quite inconsistent attempts to resolve it: on the one hand (the most frequent), by appealing to the exigencies of group thought; and, on the other (far less frequently), by appealing to the determination of material social conditions.

The first we have already more or less disposed of as theoretically inadequate. Here we usually find the combination of a 'voluntarism' attributed to societies as 'human subjects writ large' (consistent with Durkheim), with reflections on the internal constraints of the thought of this group subject, based ultimately on the unconscious. This is quite clear in the discussions of why some societies adopt a matrilateral form of exchange (with its concomitant 'risks') while others opt for the 'safer' patrilateral one. Societies holding to the first type are said to be 'obsessed' by the safeness offered by the second and as unable to rid themselves of the 'disquiet' engendered by the collective risks which they perceive in the system they have adopted. The constant co-presence of the two formulae is then explained on the basis that the 'society–subject', in adopting one, always 'has in mind' the other as an alternative possibility offering different potentialities. 'Always', because the thought of the 'society–subject' is subject to unconscious constraints present to all minds. The adoption of a particular variant may be based on voluntaristic recognition and choice by the group as a whole, but it is a choice between only three possibilities governed by a triadic set of oppositions (see above p. 74).

These ideas however fail to resolve the problem, as we have noted. Lévi-Strauss fails quite demonstrably to give both the thesis of the 'group voluntarism' (the group necessarily being understood as having will, consciousness, perception, a 'recognition structure') and that of the unconscious constraints of its thought an adequate theoretical foundation.

Lévi-Strauss's second type of reflection on the problem is in contrast to the first, purely notional and only indirectly involved with the major concepts of the alliance mechanisms in his theory of kinship. In a number of places we find him acknowledging that forms of kinship answer to the exigencies of *social* conditions, but it is undoubtedly true that the level of reflection here is limited to the recognition that for many primitive societies production of the necessities for subsistence and the reproduction of the social group could not be secured without some collective control over the regulation and distribution of alliances. Lévi-Strauss may link the general necessity for control to exigencies of an economic nature but in no sense does he offer an explanation of the occurrence of particular types of control in terms of economic causes and determinations as Friedman seems to suggest.[43] Lévi-Strauss has no theory of the structure of the primitive economy and its subsidiary non-economic conditions of existence. We are given a general reflection on the general importance of the control of alliance, but for explanation of the existence of specific modalities of control in Lévi-Strauss's work we have to settle for the spurious and speculative expediencies of collective thought (just discussed) in order to add to the support of the teleology of exchange.

IV Conclusion: Society and History

All the previous comments bring us to a suitable place at which to take stock of the criticisms established, and to make a few somewhat more general points about their general implications.

We can say that we have established three basic levels of inadequacy in Lévi-Strauss's discussions of kinship and primitive social organisation. First, we have shown that his attempt to theorise the basis and foundation of primitive exchanges (and of matrimonial exchanges in particular) is fraught with unsatisfactory theoretical features deriving from failures implicit within his conception of the teleological social action of the unconscious and its putative predilections for reciprocity. Second, we have tried to reveal shortcomings in the morphological classification of kinship forms (as realisations of exchange) which stem from utilising for its construction principles whose selection is arbitrary and without adequate overall justification. Third, we have suggested that the construction of this comparative morphology is accompanied by an overall understanding of the social place of kinship in primitive societies which must fail to provide an adequate account both of the social determination exercised by kinship and of the social determinations experienced by kinship relations through other social conditions (accounting for the conditions of existence of kinship forms). The combined result of these criticisms must be that crucial aspects of Lévi-Strauss's theory of kinship are undermined – in particular its whole ambition of being an exhaustive comparative morphology of possible types in primitive societies.

Now, this is not to say that we can negate all of Lévi-Strauss's analytical conclusions, for the possibility still remains that in the analysis of particular kinship formations the latter's concepts of restricted and generalised exchange do indeed provide the keys to the analysis of the formal mechanisms operative behind empirical regulations of alliance *in specific types of society*. While the comparative morphology as a whole cannot be regarded as well-founded, the structural analysis of particular systems entailed in its construction could well be used (to an extent which cannot be specified easily in advance) and placed within a theoretical framework which is able to think out, more adequately than hitherto, the exact social effects and conditions of existence of kinship for the particular type of society concerned.

What would this theoretical framework be? One thing is certain: Lévi-Strauss's own problematic cannot provide the necessary constituent concepts. Throughout this section we have seen that it fails to elaborate a proper morphology of primitive societal types, within which kinship relations could be situated, and that the latter are almost always discussed (despite objections to the contrary) in relative *abstraction* from an elaborated overall theory of the articulation and interdependence of the different regions of the social whole. This crucial lacuna in structuralism means that, despite its comparative sophistication at some levels, in the last analysis it is inadequate as a theory of society and of history.

Even in the light of Lévi-Strauss's series of laborious reflections on the problems of history and social change this conclusion must be upheld. In nearly all his texts we find him consistently arguing against explanations of social institutions which rely on an implicit 'evolutionism' or 'diffusionism' or more generally which bear the mark of certain 'philosophies of history'. We see a constant polemic against positions which conceive of different cultural forms as the bearers of distinct positions within 'stages' of a general plan of development or which conceive of historical progression as a linear and cumulative succession of discrete temporal units. For Lévi-Strauss these, as Gaboriau[44] notes correctly, are positions where

> The only diversity between past and present societies is that of the stages of a genesis, where all aspects of social life . . . are simultaneously developed by 'approximations' and progressive complication: as we find in Hegel, each society illuminating a 'degree' of history is animated by the same 'idea' [p. 158].

Lévi-Strauss's attack (in *Race and History*, in the Introduction to *Structural Anthropology*, and in *The Savage Mind*, Chapter IX, in particular) charges such notions with an implicit 'reductionism' in the treatment of the richness of cultures: difficulties are generated either by attempting to assimilate different cultures to a single process or plan or by the possible availability of an infinite number of causal evolutionary sequences, between which no priority can be adequately established, produced by the attempt to overcome gross simplification. In the 'debate with Sartre' (Chapter IX of *The Savage Mind*) – and by extension Hegel – the thesis of history as non-problematically linear and cumulative is attacked on more theoretical grounds. It is regarded as 'an illusion sustained by the demands of social life, rather than the object of an apodictic experience', a philosophical thesis reproducing an ideological reliance upon the 'evidence' of experience in a situation where such experience can provide no evidence at all: it is a misrecognition of history shackled to humanist ideology. The counterpart of historicism is humanism.[45]

Lévi-Strauss's own alternative position on history tries to avoid both reductionism and an ideological assumption of the superiority of 'the diachronic' by, first, postulating the theoretical necessity of a multitude of histories (and not one single *general* process) and, second, by postulating the primacy of what he calls the 'synchronic' order of a set of facts over its diachronic order. Thus, (a), historical knowledge becomes always the knowledge of different types of temporal sequence, each of which is a specific dimension of time (from the millenial history of geological concerns to the hourly history of 'biography and anecdote') – 'history' is a complexity of 'histories' each referring to different orders of temporality;[46] and, (b), knowledge of a social and cultural domain must appeal to its diachronic or historical dimension only secondarily and *after* recourse to another order of the facts which reveals their essence (preserving the richness of their diversity) prior to the changes which take place in them. This latter dimension is of course what Lévi-Strauss calls the 'synchronic' order of the social, and it is in the manner by which synchrony is thought in relation to diachrony that Lévi-Strauss hopes to provide a 'structural history'. Now this notion of 'synchrony' is central to Lévi-Strauss's whole conception of the nature of the objects of social theory (discussed in detail on pp. 9–21 above) because it is directly connected to the thesis of the primacy of the knowledge of the essential internal structural determinants of social phenomena conceived as semiotic systems. Such knowledge abstracts the essential structural mechanisms governing a particular putative semantic field at a particular temporal conjuncture or, more exactly, at a particular conjuncture in their development, their diachrony. This conjuncture is the 'synchrony' of the phenomena and their history – a 'structural' one – is a diachronic succession of synchronies.[47]

We must point out, however, that this conception of a 'structural history' is far from satisfactory. It has to tackle two types of question: first, there is the problem of the analysis of diachronic changes within distinct and finite individual systems (kinship, myth, language) of which structural anthropology conceives the social whole to be composed; second, there is the wider problem of the diachronic dimension of entire social wholes or totalities themselves, of which the above systems form parts in combination with others.

On the first problem Lévi-Strauss explicitly recognises that, for both linguistics and anthropology, the history of the discrete systems which are its objects of investigation entails taking into account internal structural reorganisations which take place within them as they progress from one synchronic state to another. Thus it is acknowledged in *The Scope of Anthropology* that ' . . . the history of symbolic systems includes logical evolutions which relate to different levels of the structural process and which it is necessary first to isolate' [p. 29]. Unfortunately however, we are provided with no detailed reflection on the theoretical problem of how to account for these crucial structural reorganisations. At times these are explained on the basis of *contingency* and *accident*, while at others it is acknowledged that material social factors have to be those which are causally responsible for change. We have already seen that this acknowledgment is evident in Lévi-Strauss's discussion of the necessity of specifying the social factors external to kinship structures which cause the operative mechanisms to be modified in operation, but that, despite Gaboriau's hopes for a structural history,[48] this acknowledgment is a token and nothing is offered as a theoretical approach to the problem. In practice a causality of contingency and accident is the dominant means which Lévi-Strauss profers for the explanation of transitional change in social sub-systems: historical change is the product of extrasystemic accident, synchrony and diachrony being opposed as 'structure and event'. And this, of course, is no explanation at all, because through a recourse to chance (by definition an unknown force) it acknowledges theoretical impotence. Recourse to chance, as Godelier has emphasised in his discussions of Lévi-Strauss, is the symptom of a theoretical lack.

This is no less the case when we turn to the second and most crucial problem of the diachrony of *whole societies* as complex articulations of structures. Precisely because, as we have seen above, Lévi-Strauss can only acknowledge this complexity (in his conception of an 'order of orders' and of the necessary articulation of kinship with other social features) but not explore it conceptually, he is bereft of the means to transcend mere speculation. In an interesting discussion[49] Gaboriau asks

> why is it that a given society transforms itself over time? In certain parts of your work . . . you insist on the fact that the factors behind transformation should not be looked for in the social sub-systems in isolation, but in the way they are superimposed on one another and articulated together. You claim that the latter constitutes a series of factors which must be studied before considering external influences. I should like you to throw more light on this series of factors ['Confrontation over Myths', p. 64].

The reply which Lévi-Strauss gives is particularly illuminating. Of the 'general question', as he calls it, he says:

> I must admit that I am unable to answer it. I think that ethnology, sociology and the human sciences in general are unable to answer it *because societies develop very largely through the action of external factors which fall within the scope of history not that of structural analysis.* So the construction of a theory of social development demands the observation of a large number of societies which have been immune from any external influence . . . which is obviously impossible . . . there would have been no Darwin had there not previously been a Linnaeus; the problem of the evolution of species could not have been posed *without initially defining what is meant by a*

species and defining them. Now we are far from possessing . . . even a
taxonomy of societies comparable to pre-Linnaean taxonomies, such as
Tourneffort's. So I see this as a question which – yes we can *speculate*
about, such speculation is not futile – but which we can never say
anything serious about [ibid., p. 65; my emphasis].

A number of comments need to be made on this statement:
(1) The old dichotomy 'history versus structure' is reintroduced,
    history being the domain of influences external to and impinging
    upon structures in a more or less chance way.
(2) The task of the construction of an ideal classificatory typology of
    societies (an absolutely necessary one, as we have already
    suggested) is formulated in positivist terms, and because of the
    difficulty of achieving the required conditions, rejected as
    unachievable.
(3) Because of this failure *speculation* is admitted to be the only
    course of action.

If we turn to the second point for the moment, we can see that it is
quite understandable why Lévi-Strauss does not try to develop a
morphology of societies if he sees the construction of concepts of types to
be necessarily dependent upon the observation of 'pure' social instances.
This places upon theory construction impossible empiricist restrictions
which ought not to exist – theory is regarded as the product of
correlations of discrete observations prior to theory, but in fact no such
raw data independent of concepts exists.[50] If the appropriate observations cannot be made, then, for Lévi-Strauss, the fully adequate
typological concepts will not be produced. This effectively denegates a
comparative sociology (by restricting its concept formation to the
narrowest empiricism) and, as Point 3 indicates, raises in its place the
crude alternative of speculation.

The impotence of structural anthropology in the face of the really
important analytical questions posed to a comparative understanding of
types of social organisation could not be more clearly revealed. At the
level of an understanding of societies in history its forms of conceptualisation are necessarily inadequate.

PART THREE
Ideology and 'Mythic Thought': The Structural Interpretation of Symbolic Representations

The remaining part of the substantive work of Lévi-Strauss that we have yet to consider constitutes the great bulk of his analytical work since the 1950s and may be taken in its unity as furnishing the zenith of his effort (whose outlines we have already discussed) to formulate the conceptual foundation stones and first practical results of a scientific semiotics of systems of 'collective representations'. The 'objects' which occupy Lévi-Strauss's reflection here are forms of thought within societies, and modes of action held to be governed by this thought – systems of social knowledge and of ideological representation – and it is his aim to demonstrate and interpret the internal structural articulations operative within these systems. In considering the modes of representation usually dominant in primitive social forms (magic, totemism, myth, and ritual in particular) this work falls firmly within the traditional contribution of 'symbolic anthropology' to the examinations usually broadly referred to as the 'sociology of knowledge and ideology': following Durkheim, Mauss, Malinowski, et al.[1]

In this section of the book I hope to critically evaluate certain aspects of Lévi-Strauss's contributions in this area. Testifying to its scope and diversity we find him providing important reinterpretations of a number of primitive ideological forms: totemic classifications and practices, ritual, sacrifice, magic, sorcery, and of course mythology. Now while, on the one hand, each of these reinterpretations is in a sense a self-contained piece of analytical work referring closely to specific ethnographic data, on the other we are able to discern a concept being constructed so as to form the foundation of all these practices. We find, that is to say, a

94

concept of 'mythic thought'; i.e. a characteristic discursive form upon which all those systems of ideological representation dominant in 'primitive' societies, can be based.

It is particularly important to stress the existence of this general concept of 'primitive ideology'. From the very earliest of Lévi-Strauss's writings it has been possible to glimpse the unfolding of a unitary project – in which different studies constitute 'moments' and landmarks – whose ultimate ambition was to formulate theses on the character and foundation of 'primitive thought in general'; of that which is peculiar to those forms of knowledge and representation which are particularly dominant in primitive (but not *only* primitive) societies.[2] Particular empirical studies – of the practices mentioned above and of aspects of kinship also – whose aim it is to bring to light specific forms of order or rationality in ethnography which was hitherto seen as chaotic or as unintelligible, are in Lévi-Strauss's work predicated upon the thesis that it is possible to specify an integrated substratum of what is specific to primitive ideology, which is itself responsible for the orders revealed.[3] This thesis and its qualifications (set out most fully in *The Savage Mind*) are logically prior to the corpus of particular studies within Lévi-Strauss's texts: the former gives the results of the latter a basic analytic foundation by inserting them into a theoretical framework of concepts. The empirical excavation of structural order relies on theory for its capacity to be at all meaningful.

Characteristically, however, Lévi-Strauss wishes to extend the implications of this thesis itself. His strictures on the nature of a unitary 'mythic thought' or 'science of the concrete', as it is called, contain implicit conceptions of its origin and basis which attempt to relate its organisation and action to two parameters which are regarded as constant. On the one hand, to· analogical thinking processes and dimensions; and, on the other, to what are supposed to be ahistorical (or transhistorical) immutable structures of all thought, which not only form the basis of mythic representation, but also all those other modes which are elaborated and which different societies (and not merely 'primitive' ones) come to adopt, either alongside it or in its stead – such as philosophy, science, political ideology, etc. In the final analysis Lévi-Strauss refers us to what we are to understand as the preconditions of all societal thought in its diversity of manifestation: to a limited number of invariant features upon which social representation in all its guises is built.

The above suggests that, once more, as with the work on kinship and social organisation dealt with in the previous section, we shall be examining a corpus of analysis and interpretation which must be regarded as composed of distinct but logically interconnected levels, each containing a particular set of theses irreducible to those at other levels. In this section an attempt will be made to consider each of these in turn, so to facilitate a detailed evaluation and criticism of their constituent elements. Accordingly what follows is split up into distinct areas:

(1) a consideration of the way in which Lévi-Strauss interprets distinct spheres of primitive ideology and presents details of their mechanisms of operation; and

(2) a consideration (a) of his concept of 'mythic thought' or the 'science of the concrete', the suggested logical foundation of the spheres of ideology he reinterprets; and (b) of his understanding of the general process of the production of ideology embedded in the conception of 'mythic thought'.

While Section I will deal with the coherence and value of particular efforts of analysis of spheres of primitive symbolism, Section II will turn to a set of notions of higher generality concerning symbolism and ideology-in-general, which the former analyses rely on implicitly. In both Sections of this final part of my book an attempt is made to do full justice to the detail and complexity of Lévi-Strauss's thought in the above areas and to analyse it in such a way as to provide not merely an appraisal of its originality and fecundity, but a critical assessment of it which facilitates a demarcation of what is analytically valid and invalid in the structural interpretation of ideological systems and what, accordingly, can and cannot form a basis for theoretical development in the study of ideologies.

I The Structural Interpretation of Ideological Systems: Totemism and Mythology

Lévi-Strauss offers a number of important reinterpretations of the kinds of ideological thought and practice with which 'symbolic anthropology', as it has been called, has always been concerned. He discusses a number of such practices within a wide collection of books and articles, but it may be said that dominant in his work is a concern with, first, *totemic phenomena*, and, second, and above all others of course, *mythology*. Although he offers discussions of magic, shamanism and ritual in general, it is his concern with totemism and myth that will be regarded here as the principal areas of importance, and it will be convenient to begin with his discussions of totemism and to end with the protracted myth analyses. The reason for this order of treatment stems quite simply from their strategic position within Lévi-Strauss's work as a whole: while the reinterpretation of totemism exemplifies with great clarity the bare outlines of his putatively quasi-semiotic analyses of symbolism, the myth studies show perhaps their complete fulfilment and the absolute stretching of principles and concepts to their highest limits in specific discussions of ethnographic data. Between *Totemism* and *L'Homme nu* we have the opportunity to witness the levels and stages of the unfolding of the unitary project of the comprehension of primitive thought which we have referred to above as being the distinctive mark of this aspect of Lévi-Strauss's anthropology. We must consider what these various stages of analysis really do achieve, bracketing at certain stages what Lévi-Strauss himself tells us they achieve.

TOTEMISM

Lévi-Strauss's interpretation of totemism is justifiably famous precisely because of the way it effects a distinct break with most of the orthodox modes of interpretation of constituent totemic practices. His critique of previous 'solutions' to the problem of totemism displaces existing theories of the symbolic in favour of a quite new conception. In this critique Lévi-Strauss:

(1) rejects the thesis of the American school (Lowie, Kroeber, Boas) that totemic phenomena are not a reality *sui generis*, on the grounds that they cannot be fully explained (as suggested) as the simple manifestation of a general primitive disposition to identify individuals and social groups with the animal and vegetable worlds;

(2) rejects 'functionalist' contentions (Malinowski, Durkheim, Radcliffe-Brown [in his first theory],[4] Firth and Freud)[5] that totemism has its unitary origin in the satisfaction of *universal* naturalistic, utilitarian or affective *needs*, on the grounds that (a) they have no means of comprehending the empirical detail of totemic phenomena in a way avoiding arbitrariness, and (b) they posit as *causal* of totemism a set of factors (subjective dispositions and affective states) whose mechanisms cannot be established and whose social foundation itself is not taken into account;

(3) presents the work of Firth, Fortes, Evans-Pritchard and Radcliffe-Brown (in his second theory)[6] as containing the germs

of a correct interpretation of totemic phenomena making possible a fully adequate explanation of both their content *and* their form. The advance of the first two authors consists in recognising that the choice of specific natural species which are then totemically associated with social classifications is neither arbitrary nor the simple effect of a putative affinity or identification consciously recognised between species and group, but somehow connected to their objective association. They fail, however, in their understanding of the nature and logos of this discursive association: positing it as an objective and consciously perceived resemblance they face a mass of contradictory data, amply attested to by Evans-Pritchard,[7] which cannot be understood. Now in fact it is precisely the latter who, along with Radcliffe-Brown (B), for Lévi-Strauss effects a decisive and innovatory step in interpreting totemism – implicitly even if not explicitly.

This step is taken primarily because between them these two authors recognise *two* principles of interpretation which Lévi-Strauss deems fundamental. First, Evans-Pritchard understands (in his analyses of Nuer religion) that the basis of totemic phenomena lies in the interrelation of natural species with social groupings according to logically conceived processes of *metaphor* and *analogy*. Second, Radcliffe-Brown (B) realises the necessity of an explanation which illuminates the principle governing the selection and association of specific pairs of species and types used in classifications and respects the detailed ethnographic context in which these are operative. Together these two simple structures for Lévi-Strauss make possible ' . . . a reintegration of content with form . . . a genuine structural analysis equally far removed from formalism and from functionalism' [*Totemism* p. 158]. It is important to understand why this is asserted. The basic issue concerns what Lévi-Strauss conceives as analytically necessary for the comprehension of totemic classifications as empirical discursive systems, so that none of the ethnographic detail (reference to specific species, etc.) is left unaccounted for or simply regarded as contingent. Here we depart from preoccupation with previous partial accounts of totemism and begin to focus on what is positive about Lévi-Strauss's own theory.

This is predicated on a number of fundamental postulates which must be carefully outlined. To begin with, we have the very basic thesis that totemic classifications constitute 'semantic spaces' governed in principle always by a metaphorical association of two separate series or orders of phenomena. Different forms of totemism realise different modes of association of those series, and the series themselves: on the one hand that which is conceived as *natural*, and on the other that which is conceived as *cultural*, are understood as systems of differences. These differences are held to depend upon two types of logical parameter for each series: for the natural series distinctions of 'categories' and 'particulars', and for the cultural series those between groups and persons. Thus

> There are four ways of associating the terms, two by two, belonging to the different series; that is, of satisfying with the fewest conditions the initial hypothesis that there exists a relation between the two series:
>
> | NATURE | Category | Category | Particular | Particular |
> |---|---|---|---|---|
> | CULTURE | Group | Person | Person | Group |
> | | 1 | 2 | 3 | 4 |
>
> To each of these four combinations there correspond observable phenomena among one or more peoples [ibid., p. 85].

Once these invariants have been delineated, it can be postulated that various empirical totemic classifications follow such patterns: Australian totemism may be seen as positing a relation between natural categories (animal or vegetable species) and cultural groups (the moiety, marriage class, etc.), for example (Type 1 above), and Polynesian and African forms as positing relations of Type 4. Such a postulate implies a syncretic invariant foundation (of a logical nature) to all forms of totemism and at the same time proposes the inclusion of ritual classifications not usually termed 'totemic' at all as being also emanations of this basis. Lévi-Strauss condemns as illusory the attempt to arbitrarily carve up certain phenomena as totemic or non-totemic when for him they are the products of a general association of discrete and differentiated units of the natural and cultural orders.

But what of Lévi-Strauss's conception of this 'association' itself? Why does it take place, giving birth in varying societies to a series of novel identifications between natural and social life, and what are its conditions of operation? The notion is absolutely central to his understanding of primitive classifications, for while he points out that ' . . . *the principle underlying a classification can never be postulated in advance*. It can only be discovered a posteriori by ethnographic investigation, that is, by experience' [*The Savage Mind*, p. 58], it is also quite clear that this investigation will be to a large extent governed by a conception of the associational principle organising the classificatory domain under examination. Although a totemic classification presents 'extrinsic' interpretative difficulties because of its dependency on a particular detailed knowledge of natural and social facts to which the anthropologist may have only partial access (e.g. the associations which a particular animal may engender for a particular tribe), 'intrinsic' ones of a logical kind can for Lévi-Strauss be examined once it is understood that the logic of classifications may operate on several 'axes' simultaneously and according to mechanisms of contiguity and association (or metonymy and metaphor).[8] Elements within classifications have a 'positional' meaning which is the result of their being placed in relation to others, on the one hand by these metonymical and metaphorical connections, and on the other, we are told, by *ad hoc* coincidences or contrasts on varying axes or levels. It seems that while the former have a formal character of differentiation and substitution which is posited as necessary to *all* systems, the latter are independent cultural variables (elements may be contrasted at the level of sensible/intelligible, synchronic/diachronic, close/distant, static/dynamic according to Lévi-Strauss's examples) so that

It is possible that the number, nature and quality of [these] logical axes is not the same in every culture, and that cultures could be classified into richer or poorer on the basis of the formal properties of the systems of reference to which they appeal in the construction of their classifications. However, even those which are least well endowed in this respect employ logics of several dimensions [ibid., p. 63].

Endemic to the overall internal organisation of classifications is the *oppositional* arrangement of elements. Some *pairing* of elements, is, for Lévi-Strauss, the key practical expression of the metaphorical and metonymical classificatory processes. Opposition presupposes, first, differentiation and therefore contiguity within the domains from which the related elements are drawn; and, second, the possible substitution of resembling alternatives at each pole of the opposition. Thus it is suggested that ' . . . the practico-theoretical logics governing the life and thought of so called primitive societies are shaped by the insistence on differentiation . . .' [ibid., p. 75], which makes possible a classificatory 'grid' introducing ' . . . divisions and contrasts, in other words the formal conditions necessary for a significant message to be conveyed' [ibid]. What is necessary is the presence of the logical *possibility* of opposing terms which can be regarded as discursively distinct. For Lévi-Strauss what is socially valuable about totemic classifications stems from this formal organisation: their persistence and pervasiveness in primitive societies is a consequence of the fact that 'they are codes suitable for conveying messages which can be transposed into other codes, and for expressing messages received by means of different codes in terms of their own system' [ibid.]. Irreducible to a unique set of arbitrarily designated institutions, totemic phenomena form one aspect of a 'general classificatory ideology' which at base always operates using mechanisms of differentiation, opposition and substitution, 'metonymy' and 'metaphor'. *Totemism becomes analytically 'dissolved' and forms one expression of a general ideological mode of classification.*

Lévi-Strauss is always concerned with the *logical* facilities of the mechanisms he calls 'metonymy' and 'metaphor' to realise varying forms of classification and to modify the nature and extension of systems already in existence. In this respect it is particularly important to consider his conception that totemic systems have inbuilt capacities for 'equilibration' and 'transformation', and, second, his notion of an elementary regulatory mechanism or principle at the heart of these systems, known as the 'totemic operator'. Together these ideas form the heart of what is theoretically specific in Lévi-Strauss's reinterpretation of totemic phenomena and they have to be considered very closely. While there can be no possibility of doing justice here to the wealth of reassessment of empirical material connected with the exemplification of the ideas, we can address ourselves to the principles underlying the comparativist stance in their treatment.

Both the capacities for 'equilibration' and 'transformation' which Lévi-Strauss conceives to be endemic to totemic classifications are understood by him to be the products of a common internal logical dynamism which in the last analysis derives from the putative dominance within the organisation of primitive classificatory systems of a formal conceptual scheme termed the 'totemic operator', which has at its centre the concept of *species*. Not only does this scheme provide for Lévi-Strauss the logical wherewithal for given systems of classifications to adapt their internal organisation to modifications forced upon them by historical circumstances, so as to adjust their synchronic structure in the face of the contingencies of diachronic developments, but it also furnishes the principle demonstrating the way in which quite heterogeneous areas of primitive social life can be thought of and represented in terms of its parameters, so giving rise to systems of representation of varying 'scale' but of the same logical type.

The Savage Mind affords ample documentation of how totemic equilibrium is considered to assert itself in systems exposed to diachronic uncertainty. The classificatory equivalence which totemic systems posit between the world of natural species and the world of social groups can be upset, we are told, by factors which are analogous to those which induce strains in the synchronic structures of language: for example, extreme demographic variation. However, the quantities and qualities of disturbances which totemism and language can each tolerate are understood as discrepant precisely because they possess quite different *functions* which their respective equilibria have at all costs (and on pain of extinction) to preserve. While language is understood as being 'directed' synchronically to maintain a function which is communicational, for Lévi-Strauss totemisms have only to retain an equilibrium satisfying a function which is mainly *cognitive* or *intellectual*.[9] Totemic classifications are regarded as 'means of thinking' governed by less rigid conditions than means of communication such as languages and as inherently capable of satisfying these conditions fairly easily, even despite adverse impinging events. Now, in spite of the absence of a clear statement about the nature of these conditions (without which totemism would not function adequately as a cognitive instrument), from Lévi-Strauss's hypothetical examples it is quite easy to see *how* he supposes totemic systems to have various means for the re-establishment of a type of system affected by change. The example of the imaginary society composed of three clans totemically associated with bear (land) eagle (sky) and turtle (water) species respectively is particularly salient. Change affecting demographic composition of the clans and leading to the extinction of one (say the bear clan, symbolically associated with land) and the enlargement of another (the turtle clan), which subsequently splits into two parts, might be faced in two ways. First, the *same* totemic associations might be preserved in a damaged form so that the only classificatory/symbolic correlation is now between sky (eagle) and water (turtle) or, second, a new correlation may be generated by using defining characteristics of the species turtle to distinguish between two clans still identified with it and as the basis for the formation of a new symbolic opposition. If, for example, colour is used, yellow and grey turtles may become totemic associations and yellow and grey regarded as expressive of the basic distinction between day and night perhaps. A second system of the same formal type as the first is easily formed through the simple process of differentiation and opposition as Figure 14 shows. The opposition between sky and water is split and a new oppositional basis for symbolic association can be made possible by the contrast yellow/grey so that a structural resolution of the imbalances caused by demographic variation can be achieved, and the cognitive function of the system perpetuated.

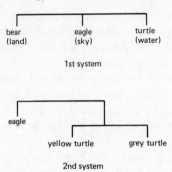

FIGURE 14
SOURCE: *The Savage Mind*, p. 67.

But if for Lévi-Strauss such classificatory systems of knowledge have as their core a formal framework which an elementary differentiation and opposition of terms can stretch out and modify, it is also the case that this framework can be utilised and modified *qualitatively* to produce 'the convertibility of ideas between different levels of social reality'. Totemic conceptions become even more important then because

for the societies which have constructed or adopted them, they constitute codes making it possible to ensure, in the form of conceptual systems, *the convertibility of messages* appertaining to each level, even of those which are so remote from each other that they apparently relate solely to culture or solely to society, that is to men's relations with each other, on the one hand, or, on the other, to phenomena of a technical or economic order which might rather seem to concern man's relations with nature [ibid., pp. 90–1; my emphasis].

In a nutshell, Lévi-Strauss is saying that the kinds of analytic conceptual operation endemic to totemic classifications provide primitive social groups with unconsciously or consciously held concepts which may be used by them to guide their social praxis *in any particular sphere* whatsoever. Ritual eating prohibitions, economic exchanges and kinship relations can, for instance, be conceptualised, rationalised and organised using schemata comparable to the totemic homology between natural species and social characteristics. Lévi-Strauss provides many examples with which to supposedly substantiate this thesis, most of which attempt to demonstrate the reliance of, first, a system of totemic classifications, and, second, a set of other primitive institutions (kinship, food prohibitions) upon a common logical foundation, the organisation of the terms of which is different in each case.[10] The most famous and detailed discussion is that which attempts to interrelate the logical foundations of classical totemism on the one hand, and caste regime organisation on the other. It has a number of details which if examined illuminate the principles behind the concept of 'transformation' and bring us to the great importance of the notion of a totemic conceptual 'operator'.

Beginning by suggesting superficial analogies between societies practising totemic exogamy (such as the classical Australian Aboriginal tribes) and those operating with caste endogamy, Lévi-Strauss goes on to suggest, first, that one aspect of their true relation is as differing institutional expressions of varying modes of effecting the thought homology between the natural and cultural domains. We have seen that totemic phenomena constitute a homologous relationship between the *differences between* natural species on the one hand and the *differences between* social groups on the other (that is between two systems of *relations*) and it is understood that exogamy very often operates alongside such a classification, so that while ' . . . social groups are distinguished from one another but they retain their solidarity as parts of the same whole', importantly, ' . . . the role of exogamy furnishes the means of resolving this opposition between diversity and unity' [ibid., p. 116]. Systems tending toward caste endogamy are also conceived as based upon a homology between what is thought as natural and what is thought as cultural, but in this case *the form* of homologous relation is quite different. Instead of being set up between two systems of difference it is – in a pure form at least – understood as transposed towards a set of direct homologous relationships between *specific* natural species and *specific* social groups, which identify in various ways with the species concerned.[11] Endogamy is represented as one natural result of a tendency to operate with a series of 'closed' social representations of specific social groups by specific natural entities. Lévi-Strauss understands societies which operate with such classifications (e.g. the American Chickasaw) as intermediate types between those practising totemism and those with caste organisation, 'recalling' castes as conventionally understood, despite the fact that here the 'castes' are coded in terms of natural species, totemically.[12]

Caste organisations such as those manifested in India are understood as based ideologically on a similarly 'displaced' totemic homology to that just mentioned, but it is now thought of as being an identification not between social groups and natural species, but between social groups and socio-cultural phenomena. Thus in India,

a high proportion of totemic names are names of manufactured objects, that is, of products or symbols of functional activities which — because they are clearly differentiated in a caste system — can serve to express distinctions between social groups within the tribe or caste itself' [ibid., p. 121].

This, however, is not the only level at which Lévi-Strauss contrasts totemic and caste institutions. Turning to social organisation he suggests that they are both comparable in terms of specialised *social function*, in the sense that while, on the one hand, totemic exogamy of the Australian type centres upon an exchange of essential women, on the other endogamous caste organisations centre upon an exchange of essential produced commodities. Both are formally 'exo-practising', as he puts it, but each with a different set of elements, and it is this difference of content (between goods and women) which provides central contrasts between them. For Lévi-Strauss the fact that caste organisations are *culturally* defined, both in respect of the conceptual model embedded in their operation (*vis à vis* the differentiation of commodities and identification with them) and in respect of the nature of the exchanges they practise (an exchange of these manufactured goods), necessitates that their *natural* products ('women whom they both produce, and are produced by') be conceptualised in *natural* terms. Endogamy (as we have seen above) is the result because: ' . . . women are made diverse on the model of natural species and cannot be exchanged any more than species can cross with one another' [ibid., p. 124]. Totemism on the other hand, in utilising a *natural* model and exchanging *natural* phenomena (women), requires a cultural homogen-isation of natural species established in the assertion that all members are subject to the same type of social beliefs and practices (totemic identification, prohibition, exogamy). This abstruse formulation is recast using a dichotomous classification of structure and function. Thus the 'common properties of which occupational castes and totemic groups provide contrary illustrations'[13] are expressed as follows:

Castes are heterogeneous in function and can therefore be hom-ogeneous in structure: since the diversity of functions is real, complementarity is already established at the level of reality and the operation of marriage exchanges — between the same social units —

would be a case of accumulation of functions . . . of no practical value. Conversely, totemic groups are homogeneous as far as their function is concerned, for it makes no real yield and amounts to no more than a repetition of the same illusion for all the groups. They therefore have to be heterogeneous in structure, each being destined for the production of women of a different social species [ibid., p. 125].

While the former projects a social heterogeneity in a natural (the human) species – *vis à vis* women – the latter projects an already existent heterogeneity (that of animal and plant species) on to social homogeneity: each institution, according to Lévi-Strauss, uses a specific type of 'mediating set' with which to conceptualise the hiatus between, and distinctiveness of, natural and social relations.

The conclusion of the overall comparative analysis of the two institutions is that the kinds of distinctive contrasts excavated have demonstrated a *logical* affinity between them which expresses itself as an inversion of the content of their common properties (see Note 13). This is understood as delineating a *transformational* relation between totemic and caste institutions. This claim will be assessed shortly, but for the moment let us note that the essential feature of the putative 'proof' of transformation lies in the preliminary selection of and concentration upon certain levels (and concomitantly the ignoring of others) at which the two sets of phenomena will be compared. If this selection and concentration can be faulted analytically, then the logical affinities upon which transformation relations rely can legitimately be called into question. We shall see later that this is in fact the case, and that accordingly there are definite difficulties with Lévi-Strauss's placing of diverse cultural institutions upon a common foundation.

We are now, however, at a suitable point at which to return to the final key concept entailed in the analysis of totemic classifications, the concept which provides their true discursive 'logos'. We have seen that for Lévi-Strauss totemism is predicated upon a conceptual homology between natural and social differences, that the form of this homology permits logical extension into diverse areas and that the whole classificatory impulse or purpose conceived to be behind it is thought of as fluid and transformable. In the last analysis much of this is possible only because of the availability of a particular notion which is always at the heart of the human perception[14] of natural heterogeneity: the notion of *species*. Why is this the case?

Fundamentally this is because – as (Lévi-Strauss suggests) both

Rousseau and Comte had glimpsed[15] – the concept possesses properties
of a logical kind which can furnish social representation with a potential
means of focusing on all planes of existence: with a tool of conceptualisation. These properties concern

> a balance between the point of view of extension and
> comprehension . . . considered in isolation, a species is a collection of
> individuals; in relation to other species however, it is a system of
> definitions. Moreover, each of these individuals, the theoretically
> unlimited collection of which makes up the species, is indefinable in
> extension since it forms an organism which is a system of functions
> [ibid., p. 136].

In a nutshell,

> The notion of species . . . possesses an internal dynamic: being a
> collection poised between two systems, the species is the operator
> which allows (and even makes obligatory) the passage from the unity
> of a multiplicity to the diversity of a unity [idem.].

Its midway position between the categorical and the singular levels of
classification endows it with the privileged status of mediator between
these extremes. This can be understood more clearly if one considers
how Lévi-Strauss interprets the totemic utilisation of a particular
animal. What is at issue is the *position* of this animal within a system
structured by the levels the notion of species provides: on the one hand
we have the differentiation of this animal from others external to its
species and on the other hand we have the similarity and association
existing between its specific features (perhaps anatomical, perhaps
ecological) and those corresponding ones of animals in other species.
Together these two levels are supposed to provide 'a double movement
of detotalisation and re-totalisation' whereby

> The analytic procedure which makes it possible to pass from
> categories to elements and from elements to species is . . . extended
> by a sort of imaginary dismembering of each species, which pro-
> gressively re-establishes the totality on another plane [ibid., p. 148].

This analytic process provides a 'matrix', a 'system by means of a
creature', one axis formed by species differentiation and the other by
anatomical or perhaps ecological differentiation, as is shown in Figure

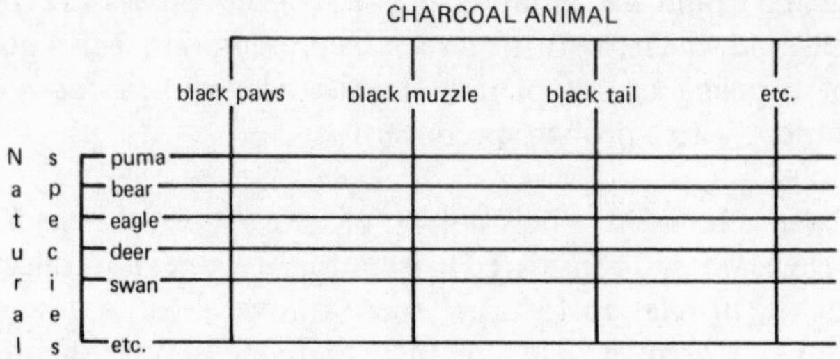

CHARCOAL ANIMAL

		black paws	black muzzle	black tail	etc.
N s	puma				
a p	bear				
t e	eagle				
u c	deer				
r i	swan				
a e					
l s	etc.				

FIGURE 15
SOURCE: Based on ibid., p. 147.

15. The constituted 'matrix' according to Lévi-Strauss then provides intellection with a rich store of progressive associations perfect for symbolic use. Species and anatomical or ecological differentiation together furnish a treasure of 'signifiers' which can be used to 'encode' relations which obtrude at any level of reality.

However, the potential scope of this richness can only be grasped when we consider the complex unitary cell — Lévi-Strauss's 'totemic operator' — which can be built up from just a threefold species and anatomical specification. This cell — whose diagrammatic representation is reproduced as Figure 16 — shows the potential three-dimensional nature of the matrix we mentioned above. From an initial differentiation into species, it reveals a 'detotalisation' of each into individuals and of these individuals into anatomical parts (heads, necks, feet). 'Re-totalisation' can be achieved in three ways: the regrouping of parts of animals within each species (all seals' heads, all seals' necks, etc.), the regrouping of classes of parts (all heads, necks, etc.), and finally the regrouping of parts to restore an individual as a whole. The fruit of the *conjunction* of a knowledge of two types of diversity within unity (between species, between parts of organisms), the totemic operator is considered to provide the basis for almost an infinity of classification[16] which can begin at a number of points and achieve varying degrees of specification.

There is one more point, this time concerning the *qualitative* potentialities Lévi-Strauss considers the operator to possess. We have already seen — when we discussed the 'equilibration' of totemic logic — how quantitative growth is understood to be possible provided that 'local logics' develop binary oppositions along their specific axes. In

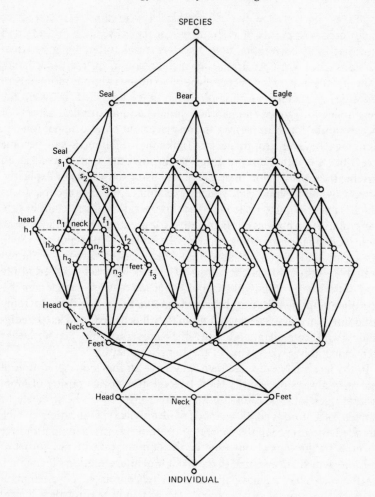

FIGURE 16   The totemic operator
SOURCE: Ibid., p. 152.

addition Lévi-Strauss posits two qualitative expansionist capabilities: universalisation and particularisation. Universalisation denotes a protraction and broadening of classification (using the species 'grid') beyond social segments to encode other domains: for instance the pathological (by developing, as do some North American Indian tribes, a morphology of diseases and their remedies using species and their organs as 'markers'),[17] the geographical (by organising social space using totems as points of reference as in the Australian Aranda and Aluridja) and, correspondingly, the territorial (often by inter-tribal divisions as in West Australia). Particularisation, on the other hand, embodies the narrowing of classification to its lower limits, ultimately to denoting or naming. A homology is simply effected between the constituents of groups (human individuals) and anatomical aspects of species (limbs for example) via the displacement of an original totemic homology beyond groups *per se*. Individual differences can become accessible to symbolic representation through the species grid: at an extreme the construction of *proper names* using, implicitly or explicitly, aspects of the totemic clan species exemplifies the microscopic-focus which is understood to be achieved by this operation. Thus, clans or sub-clans quite often possess quota of names for use solely by their members, each individual name being 'part of the collective appellation'. Such cases, for Lévi-Strauss, show that the particularising orientation available to thought via the notion of species has been realised at the level of the names of individuals. Individuation may use proper names – 'the quanta of signification below which one no longer does anything but point' – in classification, but ultimately it is understood as 'paradigmatic' with totemism and with the 'universalising' classifications mentioned above, partaking of the same foundation.

In the last analysis we see then how Lévi-Strauss's interpretation of totemism always necessarily leads beyond itself to the posing of more general questions. The dissolution of totemism into one instance or moment of a more generalised mode of ideological classification –which he called 'the science of the concrete' – putatively dominant in primitive societies, is the logical outcome of the combination of *two* forms of causality which are essential to the structural interpretation of ideology. On the one hand we have the series of reflections which attempt to establish the internal structures of totemism and the equivalent logical constitution of certain other systems which at first sight appear discontinuous with the former. As Figure 17 shows, the aim is to demarcate 'horizontal' relations of equivalence, of transformation[18] (*viz.* isomorphism, inversion). On the other hand, at another closely

| Myth, ritual, magic, totemism, food prohibitions | Caste, 'universal classifications' | Systems of naming, etc. |

FIGURE 17   TRANSFORMATION: HORIZONTAL RELATIONS OF LOGICAL AFFINITY

related level we have theses attempting to establish the common 'vertical' determination of all these phenomena as variant manifestations of the ideological substratum known as 'the science of the concrete' or 'mythic thought', a general discursive form, as illustrated diagrammatically in Figure 18.

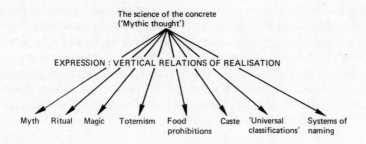

FIGURE 18

Now although these two 'determinisms' in Lévi-Strauss's conceptualisation of ideological practices cannot be considered separately without doing violence to the full character of the mode of interpretation entailed, what we must do at the moment is concentrate upon the *first* one and assess critically the quality of his arguments on the logical basis of totemic classifications. The second determinism will be discussed more fully later, after a discussion of Lévi-Strauss's principles of myth analysis, when the notion of the 'science of the concrete' is considered in the context of his general concept of ideology.

The Totemic Operator and the Concept of 'Species'

There are a number of levels of difficulty with Lévi-Strauss's discussion of totemism, but they may be said to begin with certain ones surrounding the idea that these representations are always based upon a central discursive mechanism whose driving force is intellectual or cognitive. An important issue concerns not whether the positing of the 'totemic operator' as an objective mechanism in classifications is sufficient for the interpretation of the empirical data Lévi-Strauss considers, but whether the mechanism as he portrays it is *necessary* and sufficient for the interpretation of totemic ideologies. It is quite clear that with the aid of the central notions of oppositional and metaphoric and metonymic association we are shown a coherence within totemic phenomena which previous theories had been unable to grasp. But in seeking to complete the revolution in interpretation initiated by Evans-Pritchard and Radcliffe-Brown (B), as we have seen, a lot more than a simple heuristic device for grasping elements in opposed and associated pairs is put forward. Once the primacy of metaphor and metonymy as objective 'laws' of totemism (compounded within the totemic operator) is posited, Lévi-Strauss has to provide for them a foundation and an origin – something, that is to say, to make them objectively *necessary* to primitive representations of the totemic type. It is at this point that the presence of the idea of *species* becomes crucial, for if, for Lévi-Strauss, a striking logicality within totemism can be shown to exist once classifications are considered from the standpoint of contiguity and association of elements, then this is only because

> the diversity of species furnishes man with the most intuitive picture at his disposal and constitutes the most direct manifestation he can perceive of the ultimate discontinuity of reality. It is the sensible expression of an objective coding [ibid., p. 137].

Or, in other words, because a primordial recognition by primitive man of 'a combination objectively given in nature' leads to the creation (by the mind) of varied taxonomies.

However, it is precisely this notion of a 'primordial recognition' which must be called into question. Essentially, for Lévi-Strauss, it forms one aspect of a knowledge process which is posited as being at the heart of primitive classifications[19] – the epistemological subject (the mind/intellect) confronts given natural and cultural reality, and perceives there basic patterns (e.g. the discontinuity of species); out of these basic patterns the intellect, in accordance with its peculiar constraints, builds the 'operators' which are the discursive mechanisms operative in systems of representation. What we must note at the moment, however, is that this epistemology is quite erroneous: neither science nor ideology as processes of knowledge production can be seen as predicated upon an original perception/recognition by a subject of a reality independent of categories of thought. We have only to refer to Althusser's critique of epistemological empiricism – whose basic elements we have outlined above in Part One and which need not be repeated here – to realise that Lévi-Strauss's 'primordial recognition' is apocryphal. Whether we are discussing the classifications of primitive tribesmen or modern botanists, and whether the former are regarded as 'true' or 'false', there is never a justification for grounding the morphologies they envisage in an original act of perception by a subject of an objectively given pattern.[20]

The implication of this criticism is that, first and foremost, Lévi-Strauss's 'totemic operator' cannot have the foundation he suggests it has. He may regard all totemic classifications as expressive of varied interrelations between two systems of discontinuous features (the world of natural species and the social world) but there is no necessity to posit an original 'raw' apperception of each domain by primitive man: *all* we are entitled to say is that totemic morphologies result from an association of *two sets of ideological categories* – one of predominantly 'natural' and another of predominantly 'cultural' orientation (using these terms very loosely) – each of which may employ particular points of reference (e.g. for Lévi-Strauss the cultural categories deploy a classification into 'groups' and 'persons', the natural ones a classification into 'categories', 'species' and 'particulars'). Neither set has its origin in the experiences of a subject (so that Lévi-Strauss's appeal for support from the philosophies of Bergson and Rousseau[21] must be regarded as futile) *and* neither has points of reference which can be guaranteed to have a particular value in *all* primitive cultures. This last point is worth stressing in view of the logical importance Lévi-Strauss attributes to the presence of a notion of species in the 'natural' set of ideological categories. Can it be assumed that this classificatory notion will have the same meaning and logical implication in all cultures practising totemism? This is an assumption which Lévi-Strauss appears to make, but we should note that it implies the *cultural invariance* of the type of notion of species he describes, with its specific logical parameters, and that this itself is not established. It cannot simply be assumed that all primitive ideological terms demarcating one animal or plant genus from another have the quality of providing a conceptual matrix with unlimited capabilities for classificatory extension and contraction. From Lévi-Strauss's account we can see how this would be possible, but we cannot find adequate substantiation for its necessity.

Totemic Systems and their Ideological Environments

This brings us to the question of the posited capabilities of totemic classifications *as systems* which we have sketched; 'equilibration' and 'transformation'. Equilibration, we have seen, is regarded by Lévi-Strauss as an essential teleological or purposive quality of totemisms concerning inbuilt tendencies towards the preservation of their major function – intellection – and we have also seen (by considering one of his examples) how this preservation is understood to take place in terms of their formal organisation. Unfortunately, however, and in spite of illustrations, there are large analytical gaps in the account, which stem from a considerable lack of specification of the precise role of the intellectual function itself: while on the one hand we are told little about the relation between this function and the affective one, except that the former is always dominant, on the other we are told little about the ideological conditions – for totemic classifications always exist alongside other systems of representation – which will govern the level of achievement of its goal. If, borrowing for a moment functionalist terms, we can say that totemic systems are considered to have an 'adaptive capacity' (in relation to an ideological environment) and a 'goal-attainment capacity' (directed to the achievement of a certain cognitive efficiency), then the problem concerns the fact that in general terms Lévi-Strauss cannot tell us anything about what the degree of efficiency for a particular system within particular ideological environments will be, and by what mechanism this degree will be achieved. We are told simply that totemic systems will adapt synchronically to diachronic ideological changes in their environment in order to conserve an intellectual efficacy of unspecified character. It is all very well to say that ' . . . any system of differentiating features, provided that it is a system, permits the organisation of a sociological field which historical and demographic evolution are transforming . . .' [ibid., p. 75], but this remains an empty statement until we have specifications of the nature of, and interaction between, the particular 'system' and 'sociological field' involved. To these points it might be objected that we are asking too much of Lévi-Strauss. All that is demanded however, is substantive backing for claims which are ill-supported: the kind of backing moreover which would be able to provide a convincing analysis of a totemic system as one within a number of varied types of classifications making up the overall ideological domain of a society, as described by Worsley for example,[22] in the case of Groote Eylandt.

If we turn now, however, to the issue of 'transformation', we can return to certain misgivings which we expressed earlier on the overall way in which Lévi-strauss delineates the logical affinities which lie at its foundation in the case of the relationship between totemism and caste systems. It will be recalled that in his analysis there is an immediate endowment of priority to 'exchange function and structure', to 'conceptual basis', and to the 'natural or cultural content' of the features of the institutions considered, which furnishes the key points at which a comparison is effected. Now the imputation of 'logical inversion' or 'transformation' depends directly upon the validity of this comparison, which in turn itself is dependent on the preliminary demarcation and selection we have just mentioned. If this demarcation is insufficiently qualified or if it neglects important features specific to each pheno- menon, then the comparative analysis risks missing what is *essential* to the institutions considered by merely providing evidence for their correlation or concomitance at certain predetermined levels of gen- erality. Is this the case for Lévi-Strauss's analysis of totemism and caste organisation?

Unfortunately, in certain specific senses, we must say that it is. The problems with Lévi-Strauss's comparison of these two institutions begin with the fact that it is accomplished at such a level of generality as to render itself nearly devoid of any real analytical effectivity. The first plane of classification of each institution into, on the one hand, its 'ideological elements' and, on the other, its accompanying components of 'social organisation' is to begin with so schematic at each level that one is immediately suspicious. 'Social organisation', for example, is reduced to a reference to the systems of exchanges practised by totemic groups and occupational castes – we find no reference to the *detail* of the *jajmani* system which is fundamental to Indian caste organisation [23] – and to a vague set of hypotheses about the 'homogeneity of structure and function', while 'ideology' (upon which, to be fair, Lévi-Strauss concentrates because he is concerned with a 'theory of superstructures' (*The Savage Mind*, p. 117)) is in each case not a complex of representations, but a unified 'conceptual model'. The major difficulty, however, stems from the second level of classification: this time of these already vague components with respect to their putative natural or cultural basis. Here schematism becomes reductionism precisely beca- use the oppositional classification of the content of these components into either cultural or natural, which Lévi-Strauss relies upon for the establishment of an inversion between the institutions, is highly arbitrary. By assuming that what is important about these institutions is the position of their 'elements' with respect to a preconceived and highly inexact demarcation between nature on the one hand and culture on the other – each understood as rigidly distinct from the other – he sacrifices a more exact understanding of each institution in its social context, for a comparison between them which can show their 'transformational' interrelation only if it uses formal analytical distinctions (nature ↔ culture, homogeneous ↔ heterogeneous) *lacking any real rigour.* Accordingly the assertion of a transformational relationship between totemism and caste organisation relies upon proving a vague logical affinity at the cost of the loss of a more detailed analysis which would establish comparisons only after having attended to what is essential to each social institution considered in its context.

One final point must be repeated concerning the transformations which Lévi-Strauss generally tackles in his representation of totemism as homologous with other ideological phenomena (ritual, magic, food prohibitions, caste). The logical affinities which are suggested to be at the basis of this homology only really have full significance in terms of the common origin which is conceived to be at the basis of each set of phenomena. If transformations between different forms of classification (and as, we shall see shortly, different myths) are possible for Lévi-Strauss, then this is only because of the versatility of *expression* which is a property of 'the science of the concrete', the unitary basis of all primitive ideology. We shall see, in the final part of this Section, whether such a form of thought can be considered to exist: for the moment however, we must move on to Lévi-Strauss's theory of myth.

MYTHOLOGY

We can turn now, with a trepidation caused by the sheer bulk of the work and by the diversity of commentary it has occasioned, to Lévi-Strauss's analyses of primitive mythology. As is well known, in four massive volumes and in a series of smaller articles published over twenty years, he has provided the fruits of an exercise in the interpretation of empirical materials whose range and complexity are enormous, dwarfing the relatively more modest earlier treatments of kinship relations which we have discussed above. Now the true degree of detail of the myth analyses themselves cannot be adequately portrayed in this section of the book, but what can be attempted is a fairly close consideration of what must be considered as the theoretical anchor points of the set of analyses considered as a whole. This approach may leave unexamined a host of empirical issues which other authors have — quite rightly — considered important, but it ought to compensate by focusing on what is most essential to Lévi-Strauss's structuralist analyses of narrative texts. The latter have two general features and it is most important that these are not confused. They are, on the one hand, a set of conceptions about the general objects 'myths' themselves; and, on the other hand, a set of demonstrations (of relation, of equivalence, isomorphism, etc., between and within myths) embodied in the empirical analyses *in toto*.

What is the relationship between these two elements? This can be understood once a number of preliminary features of the empirical achievement of the *Mythologiques* are grasped. It is to reveal specific *types of order* in a vast range of myths drawn from selected South and North American primitive societies: this much can be stated without incurring the wrath of specialists in the cultures concerned who would dispute the justice of some of Lévi-Strauss's more cavalier manipulations of the data available to him. The forms of order constitute, however, only the skeletal outlines of the analyses, for it is in the simultaneous interpretation of this order according to distinct theoretical principles (some of which we have already glimpsed) that the true measure of the work consists. The forms, that is to say, are understood on the basis of concepts and theoretical presuppositions – some stated and others unstated – which pre-exist their excavation or abstraction. The interpreted orders do not thrust themselves upon Lévi-Strauss's gaze: by having from the start specific sets of ideas about the nature of myths and corpuses of myths (and derivatively of all systems of 'collective representations' in primitive societies) he progressively 'validates' his initial conceptions by the mode of presentation of 'successful' empirical demonstrations. It follows that although criticisms directed at Lévi-Strauss's handling of specific features in empirical analysis of myths have a not inconsiderable efficacy, they cannot be considered the most important: they question the existence of specific types of order within individual myths and in corpuses of myths, their character and primacy, but they do not question the principles which justify and guide the kind of search conducted for them in the first place upon which the whole enterprise reposes. The main issues of principle concern not whether Lévi-Strauss is correct to represent certain myths as governed by mediated oppositions between specific elements, and segments and complexes of myths as *ipso facto* quasi-algebraically related, but (a) whether this demonstration itself – given the empirical shortcomings which can doubtless be shown to exist – has the significance which the author claims for it, and (b), if this is not the case, whether the demonstration can be given a correct interpretation.

On Mythology: Preliminary Formulations

In a series of analyses written prior to the massive four-volume *Mythologiques*[24] we can see Lévi-Strauss preparing a set of preliminary conceptual tools for the analyses of myth which were to be so successfully developed in its construction:[25] proposals for the internal analysis of individual myths and suggestions about how to go about interrelating different versions of the same myth to show 'transformation'. Here theses are propounded on the interpretation of *individual* narrative texts and on the identification of the variants of what may be a unitary mythic message which different *versions* realise in different forms. If we begin by turning to the programmatic 1955 paper 'The Structural Study of Myth' we immediately discern on the one hand the outlines of a rough heuristic for the treatment of narrative texts and on the other hand a set of theses employing analogies with language (and to a lesser extent music) about the nature of myths as objects of analysis *per se*. Now the steps embodied in the heuristic technique have been discussed by so many previous commentators[26] in the context of Lévi-Strauss's discussion of the Oedipus myth but this analysis will not be heavily utilised here.[27] The intepretative principles which Lévi-Strauss proposes for the reading of individual myths and versions of myths can be established without reproducing yet again the matrix diagrams (the 'musical scores') the analysis uses.

We can say that there are four basic features of those principles which need to be emphasised. First, we have a preliminary methodological invocation to treat myths, as objects of analysis, as analogous in function and organisation to natural language. Second, we have the proposal to consider the given narrative texts of myths as composed of specific units – called by Lévi-Strauss 'mythemes' or 'gross constituent units' and regarded as provisionally analogous to linguistic phonemes – which consist of *bundles of relations between mythic elements* and which together have a definite structural interrelation. The elements of the mythic story will always, in principle, be susceptible to an ordering[28] which can reveal a small number of bundles of features in such a way that every element has a semantic position defined by its relation to one, and the 'meaning' of the narrative is the result of the specific *form* and *purpose* of the excavated interrelation between these bundles. Third, the *form* of the relationship between the bundles of features will define the 'structural law' of the myth and it will always be endowed with a *purpose*: to express an attempted resolution or palliation of a perceived contradiction. Socially felt contradictions (exemplified perhaps by those which may be 'seen' to exist between certain attributes of the natural and the cultural worlds, or between the content of a quasi-religious belief and actual experience)[29] are subjected in myths to a treatment which attempts to provide a solution of an original problem through concentration upon the solution of a related but derivative one.[30] For Lévi-Strauss this treatment will have a form in which each problem or contradiction is manifested in the interrelation of two of the bundles we mentioned above (say *a* and *b*, *c* and *d*) and in which the connection of contradictions is maintained by analogous *association* (giving an overall relation of 'mythemes' such as $a : b :: c : d$). Contradictions can always be palliated by means of logical *mediation*: an initial and seemingly absolute opposition can always be handled conceptually if its terms are translated by the myth into more familiar ones which are easily connected by opposition or correlation. In a form of algebra, the structured interrelation of 'mythemes' expresses the attempted palliation of a contradiction, the 'telos' of myth as a cultural form.

A fourth basic feature concerns the treatment of different *versions* of a myth. Lévi-Strauss considers it a defining feature of a myth that its basic meaning may become embodied in different forms: *a myth consists of all its versions* because each of these will express a common structurally invariant 'message'. If this is so, then any quest for a 'true', 'earlier' or 'privileged' variant of a myth is futile: apparently dissimilar narrative elements of these versions ought to be relatable to a constant structure which provides the *form* of the message they each manifest in slightly differing ways. On the basis of this hypothesis of a myth as a possible series of texts all 'realising' the same essence, Lévi-Strauss proposes that 'structural analysis should take them all into account', but, as he has decided from the beginning that all versions shall partake of a common foundation, the objection that appreciable differences between texts might indicate otherwise is dismissed out of hand for rather weak reasons. First because experience shows that any difference to be observed may be correlated with other differences, so that a logical treatment of the whole will allow simplifications . . . [ibid., p. 217]; and, second, because by recording a large enough (how large enough we are not told) number of versions it is possible to be reasonably sure that some common central core can be disengaged. Having decided on its presence Lévi-Strauss will then try by analysis – though he does not admit it – to eliminate all those differences between versions which fail to indicate it.

Further, however, if for Lévi-Strauss a myth is a summation or aggregate of all its different versions, it is at the same time 'a kind of permutation group' which possesses its own structural law stating an implicit relationship between them. First stated in 1955 but still claimed as valid much later,[31] this thesis proposes that a set of mythic versions must not only express a common meaning but also achieve this expression in such a way that a specific type of logical interrelation obtains between them. It is first outlined specifically in the 1955 paper, but attempts are also made to illustrate it in 'Four Winnebago Myths: A Structural Sketch' and in 'The Story of Asdiwal'. Essentially it states that structural analysis should make it possible

> to organise all the known variants of a myth into a set, forming a kind of permutation group, the two variants placed at the end being in a symmetrical, though inverted, relationship to each other [ibid., p. 223].

More formally however, it claims that

> every myth (considered as the aggregate of all its variants) corresponds to a formula of the following type:
>
> $$Fx(a) : Fy(b) \simeq Fx(b) : Fa - 1 \, (y)$$
>
> Here, with two terms, a and b, being given as well as two functions x and y of these terms, it is assumed that a relation of equivalence exists between two situations defined respectively by an inversion of *terms* and *relations* under two conditions: (1) that one term be replaced by its opposite (in the above formula a and a−1); (2) that an inversion be made between the *function value* and the *term value* of two elements (above, y and a) [ibid., p. 228].

The possibility of an historical or purely sociological connection between mythic versions is rejected in favour of a logical one which must express an asymmetry or inversion between extreme variants of the 'set'. Now because all versions to Lévi-Strauss must express a common message and because mythic message transmission *per se* requires (as we have seen) a specific type of logical interrelation of 'mythemes', it is quite consistent for him to claim that *some* logical relation must obtain between them. Versions must have in common at least a certain structural interrelation of a core of common mythemes.[32] But why must the relation take this particular algebraic form of asymmetry and inversion? In the three early papers which we have mentioned it cannot be said that this question is given a satisfactory answer. Two types of statement are made about it: first that it illustrates 'a fundamental process of mythic thought' which can be shown through *generalisations* from structural analyses; and, second, that it illustrates a form of 'distortion' of myth caused by the conditions of its transmission. The first type of statement fails however to show why this specific algebraic form should be regarded as canonical – generalisations from particular empirical analyses are in themselves not enough to give the formula a well-founded theoretical basis – and the second (expressed in the discussion of versions in 'The Story of Asdiwal'), as Douglas has acknowledged,[33] is formulated so schematically, using as it does a metaphor from optics without the least justification, that next to nothing is said about *how* social conditions must force mythic transmission into producing the kind of distortions referred to.

However, despite the difficulties briefly mentioned above, the theses mentioned in the previous pages form the basic stock of principles which, with slight refinement, Lévi-Strauss had elaborated before his embarcation on the massive journey of myth analysis which the *Mythologiques* embodies. Before we discuss its advances, however, two such refinements – made in 'The Story of Asdiwal' – must be mentioned.

The first concerns the nature of the relation between surface narratives, features called schemata or codes (at the 'mytheme' level) and the mythic message. To begin with, we have the specification that if the surface text (of chronological sequences) refers to different planes or orders of facts (for instance, 'geographical', or 'economic', etc., as loosely understood) then each order in turn will be structured by a 'schema'. Schemata themselves will embody axes, dimensions or scales with respect to which emphasised mythic elements are ordered and granted a 'value': examples which 'The Story of Asdiwal' provides are the geographical scales given by the relations of the cardinal points, the 'cosmological axis' Heaven – Earth – Subterannean World, the techno-economic scale afforded by variation in ecology and economic activity and the sociological axis of descent and residence rules in kinship. Within the myth-as-told, such schemata exist simultaneously and they may each encode definite attempts to resolve or palliate felt contradictions by using mediating terms appropriate to their level. Lévi-Strauss is able to show that 'The Story of Asdiwal' *in all its versions*, has five pertinent codes governing its narrative sequences and that these are superimposed or compounded in such a way as to permit the excavation of a unified code in the myth which is that schema of oppositions produced by an integration of its five constituent ones.[34] Second, however, we have the implicit conception that despite this plurality of coding, the overall mythic message will be mainly concerned with *one specific* order of facts and with one specific contradiction, which will dominate the meaning conveyed. In the Asdiwal myths, for instance, it is a *sociological* contradiction (of kinship organisation) which is accorded semantic priority so that it is proposed that

> All the paradoxes conceived by the native mind, on the most diverse planes: geographic, economic, sociological and cosmological, are, when all is said and done, assimilated to that less obvious yet so real paradox which matrilateral cross cousin marriage attempts but fails to resolve. But the failure is *admitted* in our myths and there precisely lies their function ['The Story of Asdiwal', p. 28].

But why is a *kinship* contradiction given a privileged place within this diversity? Lévi-Strauss asserts that it is because of the ideological dominance of kinship problems in the societies concerned, but with Douglas and Kirk we must note that his reasons are unconvincing,[35] and also (a point not emphasised by the two commentators) that this is because he fails to elaborate generally on what is the *mechanism* which determines which particular coded order of facts will dominate a mythic 'message'.

Leaving this point aside for the moment, however (we shall return to it later), we must briefly mention a *second* refinement, this time concerning what Lévi-Strauss understands as 'the relation of myth to reality'. His essential point is that there is never a full correlation (*viz.* a simple 'reflection') between mythic content and cultural reality — *contra* Boas — but more often than not a distortion or transformation of the latter by the former. Myth accordingly, ' . . . is certainly related to given (empirical) facts, but not as a *re-presentation* of them. The relationship is of a dialectic kind, and the institutions described in the myths can be the very opposites of real institutions' [ibid., p. 29]. Now although the nature of this 'dialectic' is not elaborated in the text[36] — where it is suggested mainly as a way of supporting the idea that myths may well present a distortion of reality, which is an *inversion* — its importance must be indicated. It points to Lévi-Strauss's notion that 'mythic thought' is a particular type of ideological distortion (and probably misrecognition) of reality and highlights his general conception of ideology, which we shall come to in the next section. For the moment, however, it is enough to note some of the limitations and difficulties involved in many of Lévi-Strauss's earlier (pre-*Mythologiques*) formulations on the theory of myth.

It would be wrong to make too much of their schematism and conceptual looseness, however, when the massive bulk of the *Mythologiques* lies beyond them as another phase of development of Lévi-

Strauss's analytical ideas. It should be understood, however, that some of the problems indicated above do recur in the specifications which they provide.

The Mythologiques: *Basic Principles*

Now these problems cannot be dealt with exhaustively here – this would constitute a whole work in itself[37] – but we can approach them by suggesting that the *Mythologiques* provides, within the context of an exhaustive empirical analysis of hundreds of North and South American narratives, a framework of three central interpretative developments. These developments cover the following essential areas:

(a) developments of the conception of *myths* per se *as a distinct genus of cultural objects* among others, fulfilling certain functions and deploying specific internal mechanisms;

(b) interrelation of sequences, versions and corpuses or 'sets' of myths *on the basis of putative common mechanisms and traits,* establishing different types of 'transformations'; together with the suggestion that these transformations reveal a unitary space of myths *governed* by an algebraic interconnection between empirical categories.

(c) the suggestion that this logic of empirical categories can be regarded as the product of a unitary 'mythic thought' and some of the cultural conditions of its exercise and transmission.

Each of these areas will be considered in what follows. To begin with, however, it is necessary to establish certain points about the nature of (b), the network of connections between myths which the *Mythologiques* establishes through its four volumes.

1 Mythologiques: *a Network of Transforms in Construction.* It is on the first page of Volume I that Lévi-Strauss states:

> I intend to carry out an experiment, which, should it prove successful, will be of universal significance, since I expect it to prove that there is a kind of logic in tangible qualities and to demonstrate the operation of that logic and reveal its laws [*The Raw and the Cooked*, p. 1].

The culmination of this 'Gedankenexperiment' is a demonstration – composed of hundreds of pieces of individually complex analyses of myths and sets of myths, which are progressively interwoven – of the existence of an overall pattern within the vast complexity of the native mythologies of the New World. The nature of this pattern is somewhat akin to that of a complex web (with individual myths in between, as well as at the junction of strands) and if here we cannot outline its finished form, we can at least sketch exactly how (specifically with what means) certain of its elements are constituted by Lévi-Strauss. By considering certain moments in the progressive construction of the webbed pattern (a 'nebula', a 'multi-dimensional body', as Lévi-Strauss calls it) we should be able to discern *the dominant techniques of comparative analysis and the guiding principles which are supposed to legitimate them*: in order to assess the stability of a building we need to know about the soundness of the principles which have governed certain aspects of its construction. Such *guiding principles* are all-important precisely because (through their coherence or incoherence) they impose limits upon the degree of intrusion of the arbitrary and the purely intuitive or speculative, into all analysis whose aim is causal explanation; already we have outlined certain ones referring to the correct mode of reading individual myths and their interrelating versions.

The *Mythologiques* relies, however, as we have stated, on a more expanded type of comparison than that limited to mythic versions: it utilises sequences of individual myths (which at first sight appear to have no connection), dissimilar myths, rites, and whole 'sets' of myths to build up an overall pattern. Thus at the outset it is stated that

> it must not be considered surprising if this work, avowedly devoted to mythology, draws unhesitatingly on material provided by folk-tales, legends and pseudo-historical traditions and frequently refers to ceremonies and rites. I cannot accept over-hasty conclusions about what is mythology and what is not; rather *I claim the right to make use of any mental or social activities of the communities under consideration which seem likely to allow me to complete or explain the myth, even though it may not constitute an obligato accompaniment to the myth* [ibid., p. 4; my emphasis].

Putting aside for the moment the important question of the criteria involved in this 'making use' (and in the assessment of the 'completion' and 'explanation' of myth) we must note that this is held to be necessary because ' . . . *the analysis itself, as it progresses, demands that use be made of myths originating in more remote regions* . . .' [ibid.; my emphasis]. There are, that is, qualities inherent in the nature of mythology itself as an object of analysis which require what can, it seems, be either a local or a more expansive search for factors which illuminate each of the different features of a specific myth. The above passages refer to two such qualities: first, the 'dialectical' interaction between myth and ritual suggested by Lévi-Strauss since 1956; and, second, the 'endless' nature of the mesh or web which constitutes the semantic space of all mythology. While the first, if it is accepted, legitimises Lévi-Strauss's recourse to local *rituals* to fill in a gap in the analysis of a myth (as in his discussion of a Pawnee myth in relation to the rituals of neighbouring Plains Indian tribes in 'Structure and Dialectics'), the second authorises 'an analysis without end' (as in the *Mythologiques*) where – provided we have sufficiently rich material –the analyst can go on and on because there is

> no hidden unity to be grasped once the breaking down process has been completed. Themes can be split up *ad infinitum*. Just when you think you have disentangled and separated them, you realise that they are knitting together again in response to the operation of unexpected affinities [ibid., p. 5].

The 'interminable' exploration in the *Mythologiques* is thus supposed to show *how* mythological space is endless by faithfully reflecting – in its helical progressions – its true characteristics. Using this argument Lévi-Strauss can attempt to justify his most ambitious comparisons between narratives that are widely spaced temporally, geographically and thematically.

What main analytical means will the 'exploration' use? We have already seen above how Lévi-Strauss – in his earlier treatments of myths – proposed the abstraction from individual narratives of an underlying opposition of invariant elements which encode a message, and how, after having done this, he proposed an interconnection or transformation between narratives (which are in fact versions of one myth) on the basis of their common realisation of the same message. Now, in the *Mythologiques* the establishment of interrelations between myths on this basis is continued but it is supplemented by a process of 'superposition' of myths and segments on to one another, which becomes a dominant heuristic technique.[38] Having been told in the 'overture' that 'mythological patterns are absolute objects' all of whose aspects change when external influences produce transformations, the comparative technique is described thus:

> if one aspect of a particular myth seems unintelligible, it can legitimately be dealt with, in the preliminary stage and on the

hypothetical level, as a transformation of the homologous aspect of another myth, which has been linked with the same group for sake of argument, and which lends itself more readily to interpretation. This I have done on more than one occasion: for instance by explaining the episode of the jaguar's closed jaws in $[M_7]$ by the reverse episode of the wide open jaws in $[M_{55}]$ . . . The method does not, as one might expect, create a vicious circle. It merely implies that each myth taken separately exists as the limited application of a pattern, which is gradually revealed by the relations of reciprocal intelligibility discerned between several myths [ibid., p. 13].

The whole of the edifice of the *Mythologiques* does in fact depend upon the progressive utilisation of this technique of reading two or more myths together simultaneously and extracting from them a logical affinity at one or more levels. Many, many examples could be given apart from the one mentioned by Lévi-Strauss in the above passage, but the problem for the interpreter of the *Mythologiques* consists in the fact that (a) there is a considerable variation in the quality of the different comparisons which form the basis of its analyses, and (b) there are hardly any explicitly stated criteria (as we mentioned above) for what can or cannot be utilised.

The problem of the variation in quality is implicitly bound up with the whole character of the progression of Lévi-Strauss's analysis: once a number of South American myths – most of which have a great richness of content – are each considered in the structural manner as planes of different orders of facts expressing oppositional relations, then it is obvious that, provided certain thematic similarities are present, a field of enormous complexity can present itself to the analyst intent on elucidating or 'interpreting' by comparison and contrast themes and elements present in these myths. It is also likely that there will be a number of possible paths across this complexity once the 'search' for comparisons is begun: there will probably always be certain sequences and episodes of the myths of known communities which can only be contrasted with others on condition that an appropriate myth is found in another – and possibly far-flung – community. It follows that, in analyses where the contrast of themes and sequences is pushed to its limits, as it is in the *Mythologiques*, there will be the generation of a whole spectrum of types of contrast. Some will deal with features of myths of neighbouring communities while others will utilise for comparative purposes features and sequences from myths of disparate cultural and geographical origin. At the same time, because the preliminary conception of the nature of myths decrees that comparisons may be at any one or more of a number of levels – relating to the coded values of common elements, to the contrast of elements, or to a shared message – the number of variables available to comparative analysis becomes gigantic. Lévi-Strauss's great achievement is in the *manipulation* of the variables to reveal specific types of affinities; what concerns the interpreter of this achievement, however, is the significance and justification of this manipulation, and to make some points about this we need to present a number of representative comparisons from the *Mythologiques*.

Let us begin by considering the assertion of an 'isomorphism' between an important set of myths, from Ge tribes, on the origin of fire [M_{7-12}] and another set [$M_{15, 16, 18}$] on the origin of wild pigs, in *The Raw and the Cooked*. Myths [M_{7-12}] (in what follows M_1, M_{15}, M_{21} etc. refers to specific myths used by Lévi-Strauss in the *Mythologiques*, M_{7-12} etc. to sets of myths.) have been shown to constitute a set in the sense of sharing certain common elements and realising them in various modes: while each individual narrative contains episodes peculiar to itself, all have the same aetiological content (explanation of the origin of fire), and all feature two men (a sister's husband and a wife's brother, the first older than the second) between whom a quarrel develops, after the younger (the hero), is sent bird-nesting, resulting in his being stranded, having to suffer various indignities and eventually to enter into various relations with a jaguar and its wife, from whom finally, and by various means, fire is obtained by man. By selecting as basis for comparison the attitudes of the common protagonists in the myths (the hero, the jaguar, etc.) Levi-Strauss categorises each of the myths on a common scale in so far as attitudes are strong $(+)$, weak $(-)$ or absent (0).[39]

The analysis proceeds from here, however, by a selective concentration upon the nature of the kinship relations expressed in the myths: in the Ge myths (as in [M_1], the key myth, and other Bororo myths [M_{1-5}]) there is a curious indifference to incest (expressed in the relation of the jaguar and its wife) and this attitude is explained through the introduction of another myth [M_{14}] of the Opaye which develops the same theme more clearly; a jaguar providing 'culinary satisfaction' (*viz.* fire for cooking in the Ge myths, or grilled meat in [M_{14}]) which humans can enjoy safely only on condition that its wife is eliminated, a necessity which it accepts indifferently. According to Lévi-Strauss this necessity springs from the crucial role of the jaguar's (human) wife as an agent for the establishment of a relation between man and jaguar who are in a twin sense (one eats raw meat, the other cooked meat; jaguar eats man but man does not eat jaguar) totally opposed and devoid of reciprocal relation: so that man may obtain his present possessions from the jaguar, its wife must intervene to establish the required connection. Once this is accomplished she must be removed because she has fulfilled her only function, and because her survival would contradict the situation of the absence of reciprocity.

The introduction of three myths about the origin of wild pigs, $[M_{15}]$ Tenetehara, $[M_{16}]$ Mundurucu and $[M_{18}]$ Kayapo-Kubenkranken, adds an additional dimension to the analysis however: first these are used to clarify the semantic position of the species queixada and caititu which have significant positions in $[M_{14}]$ and in one of the $[M_{7-12}]$ myths ($[M_8]$ Kayapo); and, second and most importantly, their patterns of kinship relations are shown to have a logical affinity with those of $[M_{14}]$, $[M_{7-12}]$, $[M_1]$ and with two other Bororo myths, $[M_{20}]$ and $[M_{21}]$. Both $[M_{15}]$ and $[M_{16}]$ suggest conflicts between brothers-in-law ($\Delta \overset{\prime\prime}{\frown} \bigcirc = \Delta$), as do $[M_{7-12}]$, $[M_{14}]$ and the Bororo myth $[M_{20}]$ on the 'origin of manufactures', which Lévi-Strauss introduces at this point. Others, however – $[M_{18}]$, the key Bororo myth $[M_1]$ and a second newly introduced Bororo myth $[M_{21}]$ on the 'origin of wild pigs' – are each represented by Lévi-Strauss as entailing conflicts between spouses ($\bigcirc \neq \Delta$). By utilising these contrasts, and relating them to the contents of different myths Lévi-Strauss is able to suggest various logical affinities: for the moment, however, we must consider that between $[M_{7-12}]$ and $[M_{15,16}]$.

In both $[M_{14}]$ and $[M_{7-12}]$ the jaguar, 'master of fire', is an affine and an animal brother-in-law (a 'taker of women') who protects and feeds a human hero personifying the group of affines. On the other hand, in $[M_{15}]$ and $[M_{16}]$, we have a conflict between one or more superhuman heroes (which are relatives and demiurges) and their human brothers-in-law (sisters' husbands) who refuse to give them food, and as a consequence of which are changed into wild pigs (providing their origin as meat, *par excellence*). The concentration on affinal relations enables Lévi-Strauss (on p. 21 of *From Honey to Ashes*) to set out certain logical affinities of $[M_{7-12}]$ and $[M_{15,16}]$ as follows:

as we move from one group of myths to the next we see that they depict either a human hero and his relation (by marriage): the jaguar, the animal master of cooking fire; or superhuman heroes and their relations (by marriage): human hunters, the masters of meat. The jaguar, although an *animal* behaves *courteously*: he gives food to his human brother-in-law, protects him from his wife's spitefulness and allows the stealing of cooking fire. The hunters, although *human*, behave *savagely*: they keep all the meat for their own use, and indulge in unrestrained intercourse with the wives they have been given, without offering any gifts of food in return:

(a) [Human/animal hero] ⇒ [Superhuman/human heroes]

(b) [Animal, courteous brother-   [Humans, savage brothers-
    in-law → eater of raw   ⇒ in-law → eaten cooked]
    food]

This double transformation is repeated on the aetiological level since one of the groups deals with the origin of cooking of food and the other with the origin of meat; the *means* and *matter* of cooking respectively:

(c) [Fire] ⇒ [Meat].

Thus is a symmetry and, as Lévi-Strauss would have, a 'dialectical' relationship[40] established between the myths.

Other relationships between myths are also suggested by using the axis of affinity as a means of comparison. Myth $[M_{20}]$ of the Bororo, for example, is suggested to discuss relations between brothers-in-law in much the same way as the myths $[M_{15, 16}]$ on the origin of wild pigs but by an 'inversion of contents'. Whereas the latter identify the wife-givers with bird-hunters who imprison married people – sisters and brothers-in-law – in a building of feathers to suffer under a curse, the former regards its wife-givers *as* birds which themselves inhabit feather huts. Further, where $[M_{16}]$, for example, contains a reference to wild sexual activity by the wrong-doers (prior to their transformation into pigs) after the wife-givers – expecting gifts of meat and honey from these 'takers' – had been denied these rights, $[M_{20}]$ presents an opposite pattern. Here,

sexual activity, forbidden during the collecting of honey, involves what is tantamount to a refusal of a gift (since the latter consists of inedible honey), followed by a transformation of the victims (not the guilty) first of all into culture heroes who invent ornaments and the technique of producing them; then, through an auto-da-fé, into birds of brighter and more beautiful colours (therefore more suitable for ornaments) [*The Raw and the Cooked*, pp. 93–4].

Along with these inversions there is also of course a change in aetiological content. Where $[M_{15, 16}]$ are supposed to explain the definitive origins of one species (wild pigs) providing food, $[M_{20}]$ is concerned with those of *varieties* of birds and plants (it refers to red and yellow macaws, falcons, egrets and to urucu, cotton and colabashes) which in the myth become available to specific clans, who use them for adornments (non-food) in various ways. As a result of these comparisons, Lévi-Strauss suggests that the three myths develop 'contrapuntally', exhibiting an identity at the level of the *coding of certain invariant elements* (which Lévi-Strauss now calls the *armature* of one or more myths)[41] – seen in the common pattern of disjunction between brothers-in-law – but a distinction at the level of the *message* transmitted. In his own shorthand, for a non-varying armature ($\Delta \overparen{\quad}^{/\!/} O = \Delta$), 'we have the transformation

Mundurucu $[M_{16}]$
Tenetehara $[M_{15}]$ $\Big\}$ (origin of meat (*matter* of cooking)) $\Rightarrow$ Bororo
$[M_{20}]$ (origin of adornments (*anti-matter* of cooking)),

whose details can be set out in tabular form.[42]

A comparable transformational relationship is suggested for another Bororo myth $[M_{21}]$ which this time has the same *message* as $[M_{15, 16}]$ – it explains the origin of wild pigs also – but contains a different disjunction in the pattern of affinal relations it describes: like $[M_1]$ it entails a conflict between spouses ($O \neq \Delta$). It uses, for Lévi-Strauss, a modified code to transmit the same message. Here then we have

Mundurucu $[M_{16}]$
Tenetehara $[M_{15}]$ $(\Delta \overparen{\quad}^{/\!/} O = \Delta) \Rightarrow$ Bororo $[M_{21}]$ ($O \neq \Delta$),

for a constant message.[43] There is also a second comparability, however. In $[M_{15}]$, $[M_{16}]$ (and $[M_{18}]$) the means used to transform the wrong-doing brothers-in-law into pigs have an affinity: for $[M_{15}]$ it is the suffocating effect of feather smoke, for $[M_{16}]$ that of tobacco smoke and for $[M_{18}]$ a charm made from feathers and thorns. Lévi-Strauss suggests that here we have a series based on the axis of devices: ^{T}(humans $\rightarrow$ pigs) = f^1(tobacco smoke $[M_{16}]$), f^2(feather smoke $[M_{15}]$), f^3(feather and thorn charm $[M_{18}]$) and attempts to consolidate this somewhat tenuous link by introducing a Cariri myth $[M_{25}]$ which explains the origins of tobacco *and* wild pigs using as means tobacco itself posited as quasi-divine (*RC*, p. 101). At the same time $[M_{20}]$ is linked on the same axis as a weak variant of the series – here it is the *thorns* of fruits which are used by insulted wives to obtain vengeance by turning their husbands into wild pigs.

If we now take stock of the situation, we see that Lévi-Strauss has linked myths about the means of cooking (fire) to myths about the substance for cooking (meat) and, secondly, myths about the substance of cooking to myths about the 'anti-matter of cooking' (adornments), (Lévi-Strauss here rather stretching a distinction into an opposition as we have seen). By sketching one more transformation, this time between $[M_1]$, the key Bororo myth, and $[M_{7-12}]$ on the origin of cooking fire, we shall be able to present one aspect of the synthesis Lévi-Strauss presents in the first half of *The Raw and the Cooked*.

Having noted that the key myth on 'the macaws and their nests' appears to have little in common with the Ge $[M_{7-12}]$ save the episode of a marooned bird-nester, Lévi-Strauss resists the temptation to interpret the former as 'a collection of odds and ends' and concentrates on interrelating the apparent divergences of the myths. The most serious distinction – (on the aetiological level, $[M_{7-12}]$ are about the origin of cooking fire but this element appears to be lacking in $[M_1]$) – is tackled to begin with by the suggestion that the latter is about the origin of storms and rain, or, as Lévi-Strauss would have it, about the origin of 'anti-fire'. The preliminary evidence for this is threefold: first, although the second published version of the myth excludes a 'sentence' with this aetiological import, it *is* present in the first version; second, the natives themselves interpret the myth in this manner; and, third, through being alone in having fire (after a storm) in the village in which he has taken refuge, the hero of $[M_1]$ appears to be analogous to the jaguar in $[M_{7-12}]$ in being 'master of fire'. Other distinctions are turned by Lévi-Strauss into oppositions also – contrasts in relations of kinship and in family attitudes are represented as inversions of contents between the different myths[44] – but we should note the supplementary evidence which he uses to consolidate the thesis of an aetiological inversion. This is based on a recourse to *other* myths, $[M_{65-8}]$, on the origin of fire which belong to a linguistic family (Tupi-Guarani) quite different to the Bororo and Ge: Lévi-Strauss considers that a comparison between the episodes of the key myth and these other new narratives (also, like $[M_{7-12}]$ on the origins of fire), provides an even stronger case for the existence of an inverted aetiology in the former. Apart from superficial similarities, the main point concerns the fact that '. . . one detail of the Bororo myth is incomprehensible until it is interpreted as a transformation of the corresponding detail in the Guarani myth' [ibid., p. 141]. Both myths contain reference to a hero, changed into or covered in carrion, who attracts the attention of hungry vultures (urubus). The crucial issue for Lévi-Strauss is that the action of the vultures in the key myth, in ceasing to devour the hero/victim (upon whom they are feasting) in order to save him, is only intelligible if it is regarded as a reversal of their action in the Guarani myth, where, claiming to be healers, they cook the hero/victim as they pretend to revive him, and fail to eat him. The fact of this reversal in the content of a sequence of the key myth in another sequence drawn from a myth on the origin of fire is confirmation for Lévi-Strauss that $[M_1]$ is about the origin of 'anti-fire' (rain and wind) and, consequently, linked aetiologically to $[M_{7-12}]$.

At this point we can pause and set out a summary of the transformations we have sketched in order to bring together a portion of Lévi-Strauss's synthesis in the first part of *The Raw and the Cooked*. He considers that, taken together, the three major ones show discrete sets of myths to be related about a circular axis concerned with the origin of cooking:

(a) Ge [origin of cooking (fire)] $\Longrightarrow$ Bororo [origin of anti-cooking (fire) = water]

(b) Ge [origin of cooking fire (= *means*)] $\Longrightarrow$ Tupi [origin of meat (= substance) for cooking]

(c) Tupi [origin of meat (cooking substance)] $\Longrightarrow$ Bororo [origin of adornments (*anti-matter* of cooking)]

The 'cyclical character' of the group of myths stems from the result that: 'The initial contrast between the means [of cooking] and its opposite, has . . . simply been transformed into a contrast between the substance [for cooking] and its opposite' [*From Honey to Ashes*, p. 27]. By conducting an analysis which follows a path from group to group and which concentrates on logical affinities about a specific axis, Lévi-Strauss is able to provide a plan of their overall integration about the central parameter of culinary activity as a mediator between the natural and the cultural domains.

Our outline of this partial syntheses would have no meaning, however, if we did not stress its *exemplary* character. Although the *Mythologiques* as a whole is a patchwork of such syntheses and contains the development of many dimensions and elements, not only of the integration we have sketched but of quite distinct cycles of analysis, the fact remains that the portion of investigation we have expounded is typical of what takes place in the work as a totality. By a procedure which seems intuitive and arbitrary, myths and sequences of myths are set beside one another for comparison when it is conceived that this procedure can 'illuminate' some episode, theme, aetiological reference or set of elements which they appear to have in common. In the small illustration we have given above, moreover, we have already seen ample evidence of the variation in the application of this procedure which we sought to emphasise earlier on. Once an attempt to trace logical affinities between myths (or sets of myths) was started, we saw a variety of means used to this end: a concentration upon a particular axis or level at which narratives appear to share a common pattern of elements (for example, kinship relations in $[M_{7-12}]$ $[M_{15, 16}]$, etc.; the devices used to transform men into pigs in $[M_{15}]$, $[M_{16}]$, $[M_{18}]$ and $[M_{25}]$; the sharing of a common explicit aetiology, etc.) and/or an introduction of one narrative or set of narratives to provide a missing link or pattern in the comparison (for example $[M_{14}]$ and $[M_{25}]$ used individually, and $[M_{65-8}]$ used as a set, in 'confirming' $[M_{7-12}] \Rightarrow [M_1]$). Having sketched this variety of comparison, we now face the central question: namely, that of its *theoretical justification and significance*.

2 Comparisons, Transformations and the Nature of Mythology. There are in fact two major methods which Lévi-Strauss uses to justify his comparative modes of approach. First, by pointing out that they do in fact achieve a degree of empirical success, and, second, by suggesting that they are required by the nature of mythology as an object of analysis. It is important to realise, however, that the first is in fact subsidiary to the second. The *fertility* of the comparative procedures Lévi-Strauss uses cannot be doubted on the formal level – they do, when used shrewdly, reveal levels of abstract organisation in the material[45] – but this formal achievement only has a significance in relation to a substantive conception of *what* this organisation is which analysis reveals.[46] It is quite clear that for Lévi-Strauss it is the *quasi-linguistic* constitution and function of mythology considered as a 'space' or 'field' (which produces its quality of 'endlessness', which we referred to above).[47] Accordingly the main mode of justification Lévi-Strauss offers is based on the thesis that mythology is a semiological phenomenon: its investigation (as supposedly set out in the *Mythologiques*) must proceed by isolating those aspects of its constitution which are formally analogous to the *syntagmatic* and *paradigmatic* dimensions of natural languages.[48] The following long passage makes explicit the semiological justification: occurring in the context of a discussion of the problem of interpreting the significance of 'mythic syntagms' – which considered alone seem to be meaningless – it advocates only two procedures for grasping their meanings:

> One consists in dividing the syntagmatic sequence into superposable segments and in proving that they constitute variations on one and the same theme [At this point there is a reference to 'The Structural Study of Myth' and 'The Story of Asdiwal']. The other procedure, which is complementary to the first, consists in superposing a syntagmatic sequence in its totality – in other words, a complete myth – on other myths or segments of myths. It follows that on both occasions we are replacing a syntagmatic sequence by a paradigmatic sequence; the difference is that whereas in the first case the paradigmatic whole is removed from the sequence, in the second it is the sequence that is incorporated into it. But whether the whole is made up of parts of the sequence, or whether the sequence itself is included as a part, the principle remains the same. Two syntagmatic sequences, or fragments of the same sequence, which, considered in isolation, contain no definite meaning, acquire a meaning simply from the fact that they are polar opposites . . . The meaning is entirely in the dynamic relation which simultaneously creates several myths or parts of the same myth, and as a result of which these myths, or parts of myths, acquire a rational existence and achieve fulfilment together as opposable pairs of one and the same set of transformations [*The Raw and the Cooked*, p. 307].

Here both the techniques advocated for the analysis of individual narratives (in the earlier texts, see above) and those propounded (in the *Mythologiques*) for their interrelation are broadly justified with the same semiological metaphor. Segments of an individual text and whole myths together *must* be set into interrelation if the 'syntax' at the basis of the putative language of mythology is to be reconstructed by the analyst. But if this explains why *some* comparison in general is necessary, at the same time it says nothing about the particular forms which it should take and the guiding constraints under which it should operate. To be consistent Lévi-Strauss ought to be able to suggest that comparisons can only be undertaken when specific conditions, relating to the nature of the narratives considered and demarcated in terms of their *mechanisms* (armature, code and message), are operative. That he cannot do this is particularly evident in the case of the second procedure mentioned in the previous quotation. The *Mythologiques* is full of examples of the 'explanation' of the significance of seemingly unintelligible sequences of myths through reference to quite distinct narratives whose sequences 'complete' the former by a 'paradigmatic' comparison,[49] but it seems that there are no constraints on what can qualify as a 'paradigm'. This is clear in Lévi-Strauss's attempt, in *From Honey to Ashes*, to explain a gap in an Apinayé myth [M_{142}] by comparing it ('paradigmatically') with a similar but more precise Kraho text [M_{225}]. He justifies this procedure (having noted that it seems to contradict the rule of structural analysis to attend primarily to one text – see p. 127) by the assertion that this is analytically legitimate when the myths we are dealing with transmit the same message. Lévi-Strauss answers the next crucial question himself, however:

> When and how can we decide whether they represent identical messages, differing only in respect of the quantity or quality of the information transmitted, or whether they are messages conveying irreducible information and cannot be used to complete each other? The problem is a difficult one, and there is no hiding the fact that, in the present state of both theory and method, it is often necessary to settle the matter empirically [p. 128].

On the one hand it is stated that asserting a 'paradigmatic' relation requires two myths to transmit the same message, while on the other it is acknowledged that there are no satisfactory conceptual means for assessing whether the latter is in fact the case. It is hardly surprising then that in the *Mythologiques* 'paradigmatic' groups or sets are often set up on the rather simple basis (a) of the presence in constituent myths of a similar set of elements in one sequence (an 'armature') which may or may not have the same 'values' (encoding) – we have given ample demonstration of this above in Lévi-Strauss's use of the different patterns of kinship relations present in different myths – or (b) of the common presence of a vague aetiological message. In both cases the absence of a real *specification* of conditions governing the formation of 'paradigms' leaves a vacuum in the analysis which can only be filled by the arbitrary and the intuitive.[50] The difficulty, then, with the plethora of comparisons out of which the patterns of the *Mythologiques* are built – and this explains why their mode of construction is so difficult to assess – is one of theoretical underdevelopment.[51] There is a rift between, first, the semiological invocation to search for the syntagmatic and paradigmatic planes at the basis of the putative 'syntax' of mythology, and, second, how, in terms of the mechanisms attributed to myths, this is to be achieved.

But if there are distinct problems with the comparative procedures Lévi-Strauss uses to construct the patterned transformations between myths in the *Mythologiques*, and with his *justifications* of them, the fact remains that he *has* shown such patterns to exist, and we must confront the issue of their *significance*. For Lévi-Strauss himself, the demarcation of these patterns decisively *confirms* four main theses on the constitution and foundation of myths and mythology. They are as follows:

(1) that the myths of a society are like its speech, and that there exists a corresponding language which this mythic discourse articulates, the patterned transformations between myths expressing its 'syntax';

(2) that if myth is like speech, then the transmission of this speech has certain specifiable characteristics;

(3) that myth and music have certain logical affinities;

(4) that at the causal foundation of the 'syntactical' patterned transforms between myths lies the operation of a 'mythic thought' ('the science of the concrete') and, derivately, of the unconscious mind.

All these ideas are closely linked in the *Mythologiques*, but we can perhaps start to assess them if we begin by looking at the theoretical function of the general analogy of myth with language. It is quite clear, from what we have said above, in Part One, that the basic source of Lévi-Strauss's postulate that systems of collective representation (like myth) are quasi-linguistic in constitution lies in his implicit preliminary theory that the type of order manifest in language must be present in other types of 'symbolic' form because both the former and the latter are at basis expressions of a common and constant structuring origin (the unconscious mind). It is also clear from what we said, however, that this theory is untenable in the way Lévi-Strauss presents it. The implications of this for his analyses of myth are far-reaching because it now means that the aspects of myths he refers to in analysis as 'codes' and 'messages' or as 'syntagms' and 'paradigms' cannot be understood as comparable to those aspects of language to which linguistics refers when *it* uses these terms. The pseudo-linguistic terminology actually hides an underdeveloped demarcation of what is specific to mythic mechanisms and, importantly, actually hinders the achievement of a correct comprehension of them.

In this respect, and despite the fact that he does not really get to the roots of the basis of the linguistic analogy in Lévi-Strauss's work, Sperber highlights one of the deficiencies admirably by *showing* that what Lévi-Strauss calls the 'syntagmatic' and 'paradigmatic' levels of mythology actually bear little comparison with these orders as precisely defined in linguistics.[52] The linguistic concept of paradigm specifies an inventory of elements (entertaining certain affinities) which can be substituted one for another in the same invariant syntagmatic chain, but as far as mythology is concerned Lévi-Strauss (a) does not know what the syntagmatic chain is in which *whole* myths (which are supposedly 'paradigmatically' interrelated, as we have seen) have a place, and (b) cannot show how 'paradigmatic' elements within *single* myths can be substituted in the same invariant chain.[53] Lévi-Strauss uses the labels 'syntagm' and 'paradigm' but their connotation for mythology has little in common with the linguistic concepts.

The same must be said about the claim that the orders revealed in the *Mythologiques* demonstrate the syntax of a mythic 'language' spread across North and South America and 'spoken' by quite hetergeneous communities. On pp. 565–6 of *L'Homme nu*, Lévi-Strauss replies to the objection that there is a contradiction between his assertion that myth is 'endless' and his suggestion that the myths examined in the *Mythologiques* form a closed system by differentiating between

le discours mythique de chaque société, qui, comme tout discours, demeure ouvert – une suite peut être donnée à chaque mythe, des variantes nouvelles peuvent apparaître, des mythes nouveaux voir le jour – et la langue que ce discours met en oeuvre et qui, à chaque moment considerée, forme un système [the mythic discourse of every society, which, like all discourse remains open – each myth itself can develop, new variants can appear, new myths are born – and the language which this discourse sets to work and which, at each moment considered, forms a system.]

And he goes on to suggest further that

C'est par rapport à elle-même, et envisagée selon l'ordre de son discours déployé dans la diachronie, qu'une mythologie n'est jamais close. Mais l'ouverture de cette parole, au sens saussurien du terme, n'exclut pas que le langue dont elle rélève soit close par rapport à d'autres systèmes aussi aperçus dans la synchronie un peu comme on le constaterait d'un cylindre surface close et qui restrait telle même si elle s'allongeait indéfiniment au cours du temps par une de ses bases:

l'observateur pourrait pretendre en avoir fait le tour et determiner la formule permettant a chaque instant de calculer le volume inclus, même s'il ne reussissait jamais à la parcourir en long. [It is in relation to itself, and considered according to its discourse drawn out diachronically, that a mythology is never closed. But the openness of this speech, in the Saussurian sense of the term, does not eliminate the possibility that the language upon which it depends might be closed in relation to other systems also perceived synchronically, in the same way as it would be seen that a closed cylinder would remain so even if it was indefinitely elongated through time by one of its bases: the observer could ascertain the circumference and determine the formula enabling him to calculate, at each moment, the volume included, even if he could never succeed in assessing its length.] [Ibid., p. 566.]

What we must note, however, is that this 'deduction' of the mythological 'language' from a knowledge of fragments of its putative realisation in single mythologies ('speech') cannot be taken literally. The pattern of Lévi-Strauss's analysis in the *Mythologiques* does not compare favourably with that elicited by a rigorous deduction in linguistics of the syntax of a language from fragments of speech: logical affinities are indeed sketched in the former, but these do not reveal a transcontinental mythic grammar validating the preliminary thesis of an identity of causal foundation of language and myths. The latter theses cannot, as we have seen, be supported and the orders in myth do not compare rigorously with those in natural languages. Lévi-Strauss's comparison between myth and language should in the last analysis be regarded only as a fairly useful but limited metaphor pointing to certain features which these domains, as 'discourses without subjects', share.

Are similar remarks apposite for Lévi-Strauss's metaphorical recourse *to music*? To consider this we need to examine his set of general postulates on the overall comparabilities of myth, music and language when each is considered as a particular type of system for the expression of a communication or signification. These highly suggestive and interesting comparisons suggest a number of things about the nature of mythology – and not merely two as Pettit contends[54] – most of which relate essentially to the conditions understood to govern the *transmission, reception* and *effectivity* of its particular type of communication.

Certain preliminary comparisons in *The Raw and the Cooked* posit a provisional connection between myth and music: both operate on the basis of an articulation of an 'external' or cultural 'grid' with an 'internal' or natural one, as a result of which effective communication is achieved. The natural grid concerns factors internal to the human subject, factors 'situated in the psycho-physiological time of the listener, the elements of which are very complex . . . the periodicity of cerebral waves and organic rhythms, the strength of the memory, and the power of the attention' [p. 16]. Music has a cultural external grid composed of the culturally selected systems of sounds making up the scale, and mythology one built out of the particular stock of historical and social incidents which societies select for use in mythic stories. In each case these factors are articulated with different specific capacities of the human subject which Lévi-Strauss understands to be particularly important for the reception and appreciation of each type of discourse: for music these are 'visceral and organic', whereas in mythology they are 'neuro-mental' ones which enable listeners to grasp the back references and parallels which narratives exploit. The efficacy of musical and mythic communication depends on the quality of the fusion which a specific organisation of the external grid entertains with these particular capacities of listening subjects. Music, through a highly systematic means of transmission (voice and the ensemble of instruments) is effective by making the individual 'conscious of his physiological rootedness' and mythology, through less systematic means (singing, chanting or other verbal elaborations) makes the individual 'aware of his roots in society': 'The former hits us in the guts, the latter, we might say appeals to our group instinct' [ibid., p. 28].

These basic comparisons are elaborated and modified in the finale of *L'Homme nu*, however, where the notion of a provisional 'symmetry' between language and mythology is re-examined and clarified. To begin with, certain basic similarities are reiterated – mythic transformations are compared with transcriptions of melody into homologous forms, for example – but then more important *structural affinities* are restated in a slightly different form by placing music and mythology, along with mathematics and language, on a common scale according to the degree of importance of sound and 'meaning', within these discourses. Myth and music are both regarded as structurally derivative in relation to language, for while both *require* elements of sound and meaning (which in language have equal importance) music has a structural dominance of sound, and myth a corresponding dominance of 'meanings'. Music is language without meaning and the listener feels himself compelled to supply the absent significance in the reception of the musical communication. Myth, for its part, becomes *almost* purely semantic: the significations of narratives are far less bound up with the structures of the supporting language in which they are transmitted than are those of speech.

At the same time, however, while music '*n'emprunte au langage naturel que l'être du son*', myth requires the *whole* of language for its transmission, and has its 'deficiencies' in relation to sound made up for by variations in the mode of narration just as the semantic deficiencies in music are compensated by meanings 'invested' by the listener. Vocal effects, alliteration, gestures, chanting and theatrical representation embellish the telling of stories so that

> le mythe, système de sens, s'accommode de la serie illimitée de supports linguistique que ses narrateurs successifs peuvent lui prêter, de la même façon que la musique, système de sons, s'accommode de la serie illimitée de charges sémantiques dont ses auditeurs successifs se plaisent a l'investir. [myth, a system of meaning, makes the best of the boundless series of linguistic supports which its successive narrators can lend it, in the same way that music, a system of sounds, makes the best of the limitless series of semantic charges which successive listeners invest in it.] [*L'Homme nu*, p. 580.]

The messages of myth can always be expressed meta-linguistically ('above' language) whereas those of music can never be manifested adequately in a verbal form (it signifies 'below' language). Communication for both is achieved through an indirect exchange of monovalent molecules of sound and imagery for those of meaning, in contrast to language (speech) which effects a direct exchange of bivalent units of both sound and meaning. (See *L'Homme nu*, pp. 585–6).

However, the same text also introduces a specific modification of the comparison of myth with music: it now appears that a symmetry can only be posited between mythology and a *specific form of music*. This form is exemplified in classical music of the sixteenth to eighteenth centuries and finds its highest expression in the figure of the fugue (p. 583). What takes place in this period is the growth of the sciences, the decline of mythology and the gradual transmutation of the characteristics of the latter into other discursive forms in literature as well as music. The 'structural heritage' of myth is divided between romantic music and the novel – while the former takes on a quasi-mythic structure the latter constructs free narrative out of 'deformalised residues' of mythic materials by freeing them from symmetry (idem.). Should this comparison of myth with the constitution of the fugue be regarded as important? What we should note is that the onus of Lévi-Strauss's discussion is not on proving the former to be like the latter, but quite the reverse. His attempt to show that Ravel's *Bolero* (which is represented as fugue-like) has a structure which is in some degree comparable to that of myth as he understands it[55] – in setting into play a complex series of oppositions which the text as a whole attempts to resolve – is dedicated to precisely this end. We cannot assess the value of this demonstration here, but it must be pointed out generally that the cross-reference to the musical fugue specifies little about the *nature of myth*, while it restricts significantly the scope of the thesis of an overall symmetry of music and mythology.

Any value that Lévi-Strauss's comparison of myth and music may have, however, does not lie in its positing of symmetries between them (which different parts of the *Mythologiques* are supposed to reflect), but in its specifications on the nature of mythic communication. In this respect it makes certain important points which link up generally with Lévi-Strauss's overall understanding of what the patterns in the *Mythologiques* confirm about the origins, structure and communication of myths, and their reception and ideological effects.

To begin with, the reference of the music analogy to myth as constituted out of a stable 'cultural/external' grid of representations of social incidents is linked to a general set of three constraints on the origin and structure of mythology which Lévi-Strauss posits. Two of these constraints concern psychic and ecological determinisms, to which he considers all systems of representation to conform,[56] and the third concerns the suggestion that all myths are only ever *born*, *developed* and *eroded*[57] in accordance with transformational processes. The sequences of empirical transforms reflect this internality of mythological developments while at the same time revealing how mythic versions necessarily accommodate ecological or 'infrastructural' factors peculiar to specific types of societies by subjecting them to an incorporation which depends on the organization of narrative structures (we have already seen this in the case of 'The Story of Asdiwal').

All mythological development is regarded as a 'process without a subject' depending principally on supra-individual structures just as is mythic *transmission*. Lévi-Strauss does posit a specific role for the individual subject in oral transmission, but one which is essentially subordinate to specific structural conditions. Because myths are *told*, certain 'probabilistic' elements enter into their communication which have two sources: on one hand the inescapable idiosyncrasies of different narrators, and on the other (and more significantly) those variations in the embellishments of the language used to transmit the story which are the inevitable effects of an attempt to compensate for the 'deficiencies' in the means available to mythology to express an abundance of meaning. However, this 'probabilistic' variation represents only the surface of oral tradition – the process of transmission will itself tend to separate out stable common structures for the expression of particular messages and the instabilities of individual 'embroidery' will be eroded (*L'Homme nu*, p. 560). Stable structures for Lévi-Strauss thus come to have primacy in mythic origins and transmissions, and the patterns of the *Mythologiques* to represent in *some degree* the latter's traces and trajectories.

If we cannot accept the idea of a mythic 'language' we *can* consider, then, Lévi-Strauss's understanding that the transformations he unravels represent the traces of a number of developments in 'mythic space': (1) the origins of myths, (2) the distortions of myths in transmission within and between communities, (3) the varied expressions of particular messages in different structural form, and (4) the erosion and gradual deterioration of myths. There are very great difficulties with these conceptions, which stem from constant ambiguities in Lévi-Strauss's specifications on the forms of constraint and determinism to which mythology, as a social phenomena, is suggested to be subject. These ambiguities stem from the notion that mythology is on the one hand more or less devoid of constraint and free to develop in accordance with purely internal necessities, yet on the other hand subject to the influences of other ideological and social phenomena, (We have in fact seen Lévi-Strauss state it as legitimate to explain myth by drawing on any type of extra-mythic material). This tension is expressed in the following passage from *The Raw and the Cooked*:

the mythological system is relatively autonomous when compared with the other manifestations of the life and thought of the group. Up to a point all are interdependent, but their interdependence does not result in rigid relations which impose automatic adjustments among the various levels. It is a question rather of long term pressures, within the limits of which the mythological system can in a sense argue with itself and acquire dialectical depth: that is, be always commenting on its more direct modalities of insertion into reality, although the comment may take the form of a plea in favour of a denial [p. 322].

Now, if we accept for the moment that they are empirically well-founded, we can state that Lévi-Strauss's transformations in myths are in fact the ideological results of a kind of *complex causality* such as that which he is trying to express here as a 'relative autonomy' and a restricted 'interdependence'. The patterns of the *Mythologiques* are represented as the outcome of interplays between factors both internal and external to mythic systems but we must note that in trying to understand this complicated interplay Lévi-Strauss gets into some difficulty because of the confused way in which he blends together psychic, 'ecological' and ideological determination.

Myths as ideological systems of representations refer to the social as part of their *content* and are subject to a double determination caused by the fact of their communication in a specific *'infrastructural'* and ideological context. *Ideological* constraint is due to the influence on myth of other representational systems, including other myths, which are present in society, but Lévi-Strauss is extremely vague over what can or cannot be regarded as constraint and when it will or will not be effective. Sometimes we are told that myth can 'argue with itself' to achieve 'dialectical depth' (in the anagrammatic fashion of all semiological systems (*L'Homme nu*, p. 581)), but at other times that other myths, rituals, etc., necessarily impose ideological influence. Sometimes this influence is regarded as appreciable and at others it is not. There is little consistency in his reflections on the constraints placed upon mythology by an ideological context. The 'infrastructure' (or 'techno-economic conditions', as they are called) appears to be effective in mythology in two ways: by being ideologically appropriated to provide part of the narrative content, and by constituting a set of social conditions which are supposed to restrict the effective communication of a myth and produce distortions. The second point suggests that what we calls 'differences of language, social organisation or way of life', can disturb a myth in the process of its transmission in such a way as to modify its internal organisation (it can become 'impoverished' or 'confused' or even obliterated). In both aspects of the intervention of ecology Lévi-Strauss assumes that a set of given empirical conditions, which can be simply specified, has an influence in mythic communication which is quite straightforward. Nothing could be further from the truth, however. To begin with, the way Lévi-Strauss understands 'the real' to be effective in mythic content is full of difficulties, and second, this has definite implications for his conception that distortions and modifications in myths can be shown to be the results of factors of social organisation, etc., whose function and effectivity in relation to ideology are clear.

Lévi-Strauss's theory of the role of real ecology or social organisation in mythology is in fact untenable. In this theory myth is a particular 'image of social reality' (*The Raw and the Cooked*, pp. 332–4) which is not a 'representation of empirical facts' (see above, page 122) but an ideological commentary on them as they are 'given' to the minds of individuals in a particular society. What we should note, however, is that (as we stressed in our discussion of totemism) this idea of the 'givenness' of reality to a primordial perception is without foundation. Myths do not 'ideologise' basic perceptions of ecology and society but work on distinct categorisations which are themselves already ideological: myth is an ideological reorganisation into narrative form of elements from other ideological systems. It follows that it is not distinctive features of ecological or social *reality* that are selected for use as mythic material, but distinctive classifications and associations which are *already* part of native ideologies and knowledges.

If this is the case then it is a simplification to suggest that changes and distortions in mythology can be regarded as straightforward products of a 'reflex action' of native thought touched off by its 'perception' of ecological changes. This thought has a structure which cannot be based on such a perception and so it cannot be said that a 'given' ecology is active in mythology through one. Native ideologies may have an ecological reference but this is not to say that they are based on a (collective) perception of ecological reality. Accordingly, it is not real ecologies which are active in mythic distortions, but on the contrary ideological representations. When Lévi-Strauss discusses what *causes* such modifications he should therefore always remain at the level of *ideological* constraints.

The notion of mythology as grounded in a 'collective perception' brings us to the *psychic* determinisms which Lévi-Strauss posits. If myths exist as selective combinations of representations, if the order of this combination can be shown to be rigidly structured and if the development, distortion and even deterioration of myths can also be revealed as structured, then this is so only because of the action of the unconscious mind in *directing* these processes of combination and structural ordering in a specific fashion. We have already seen aspects of Lévi-Strauss's portrayal of the operation of this mechanism in Part One, but what we must emphasise now is its role alongside ideological and ecological determinism in the foundation of mythic structures and transforms. Distortions, developments and interconnections of myths which transformations are supposed to represent have a *quasi-algebraic* form[58] not because of the action of ideological and ecological influences, but because l'ésprit travaillant inconsciemment sur la matière mythique, ne dispose que de procédures mentale d'un certain type: sous peine de détruire l'armature logique qui supporte les mythes, et donc de les anéantir au lieu de les transformer, il ne peut leur apporter que des changements discrets, au sens mathématique . . . [the mind, working unconsciously on mythic material, only has mental procedures of a certain type: under threat of destroying the logical armature which supports myths, and therefore of annihilating them instead of transforming them, it can only impose upon them discrete changes, in the mathematical sense . . .] [*L'Homme nu*, p. 604.]

The constantly affirmed idea that the patterns of *Mythologiques* express stable structures of the mind, 'experimentally verifying' the postulate of their action,[59] has at its basis this endowment of causal primacy to the psychic.

But where Lévi-Strauss presents this as an absolute theoretical necessity (the *sine qua non* of accounting for the transformational patterns· in mythology), we must on the contrary reject it. We have already seen in Part One that his thesis of the immutable effectivity of the unconscious in culture cannot be supported and this must mean that the *Mythologiques* cannot rely upon its putative quasi-mathematical psychic determinism to ground theoretically the results of empirical myth analyses. Lévi-Strauss uses this psychic determinism to present a rounded and complete picture of the composition of the forces making up the complex causality of which mythic transformations are the products, but from what we have seen of his representation of the function of ecology and ideology we must now conclude that his picture is deficient. Each constituent force – psychic, ideological and ecological – is characterised in a manner which is vague and redolent of a theoretical reductionism. Lévi-Strauss may defend himself against charges of 'mentalism' and 'Hegelianism'[60] which certain critics have levelled against him,[61] but both the defences and the criticisms miss the essential point: it is at a *number* of levels that his understanding of the basis of mythological patterning is inadequate. The mechanisms of psychic and ecological factors being unfounded, Lévi-Strauss presents an erroneous theory of what the ideological processes are that produce the rigid organisations and interconnections in and between myths which his empirical analyses had so painstakingly revealed. His interpretation of their significance cannot, accordingly, be accepted.

How then can they be understood? The hundreds of unanswered analytical questions posed by the huge advances of the *Mythologiques* cannot be examined here, but at least we ought to sketch some of the paths which might be followed in areas which have been left in a relatively underdeveloped conceptual state in spite of this 'empirical' progress. To begin with there are many difficulties of definition and specification relating to myths and their internal mechanisms. Apart from concern with the whole preliminary issue of the definition of myths *per se* as ideological objects (about which Lévi-Strauss is somewhat offhand (see *The Raw and the Cooked*, p. 4)) what is needed is a reworking of the notions of the 'mytheme', 'armature', 'code' and 'message' – outside a reliance upon a neo-linguistic terminology – in such a way as to make more specific the interconnection between the various graded valuations of different types of representations in the narrative (the 'encoding' which Lévi-Strauss usually, but not always,[62] presents as binary) and a clarification of the thesis that it is one particular such valuation which dominates the overall significance of the text (its 'message'). This would combat arbitrariness in the reading of myths and militate against viewing them as simple realisations of a central *pre-given* message which it is their purpose to resolve by means of a dominant mediation. Only on the basis of such a clarification of the internal mechanisms of myths could the issues of the 'empirical successes', and of the varying degree of applicability of the structuralist technique of text analysis in different domains, be examined. Instead of taking this mode of textual analysis to its extremes in domains where it seems to have a perfect object (as in Lévi-Strauss's analyses of Amerindian texts in the *Mythologiques*) or of simply asserting the universality of its applicability and proceeding with empirical analysis unhesitatingly (as does Leach),[63] attention would be focused upon providing more specific information on mythic mechanisms and how they interact with different types of ideological environments in detail. This would direct research to the specific mythologies of single and neighbouring communities and to the acceptance of only those comparative affinities between myths which are statable in precise relation to their mechanisms and to predominant characteristics of shared ideologies and narrative cultures. Those 'transformations' which were established would represent neither segments of a transcultural 'language' nor traces of the 'architecture of the mind', but constants of narrative representation characteristic of primitive societies at a particular level of ideological development. There being no *theoretical* justification for rooting this constancy and correlation of myths in psychic exigencies, theory would have to seek causes wholly internal to the fields of ideology of the societies concerned.

This is the path which any attempt at reinterpreting the significance of the various types of logical affinities in the *Mythologiques* would have to take, and there are signs that certain authors are giving this task precedence over further structural analysis. Sperber for one accords causal primacy (at the root of transforms) to 'borrowing' by different communities from each other of stable matrices of representations which are the putative raw materials of mythic production. The matrices have a *structural* form because it is that which makes them 'collectively memorable' throughout the process of transmission and internalisation (by native subjects) and the borrowing community constructs its own distorted narratives from them by clothing them with an additional content furnished by the features of its own particular ideologies. Unfortunately, however, this is essentially a repetition of Lévi-Strauss's own position on oral transmission, with the difference that where he accounts for the persistence of stable structures by recourse to constraints of the unconscious mind, Sperber seems to posit the operation of a *collective memory* in society which — from the narrative material available — selects and preserves only a rigidly structured 'psychologically salient' and memorable core. This is an unnecessary step backwards: by attempting to avoid Lévi-Strauss's notion of the action of the mind as being at the basis of mythic homologies and inversions, Sperber falls back on a (Durkheimian) conception of society as a 'collective subject' (endowed with mental states, will, memory, etc.) which really faces the same types of theoretical difficulty. Both ground what is structurally stable in mythology in psychic agencies of obscure characteristics when this is quite unnecessary: the true issue concerns those conditions *within* the body of a particular society's different *ideological discourses* which require narratives to have such a structure and fulfil a specific signifying function. Appealing to 'collective memory' or to the unconscious leads research away from analysis of solely ideological conditions.

Having offered these schematic proposals, however, it is necessary to conclude this examination of Lévi-Strauss's theory of myth. Throughout a long discussion it can be said that we have focused upon two main sets of problems endemic to it. *First*, we have concentrated on those difficulties confronting Lévi-Strauss in giving a firm and well-justified foundation to the analytic and comparative procedures which his theory evolves; and, *second*, we have concentrated on associated problems arising from inadequacies in Lévi-Strauss's own interpretation of the precise significance of the structured results (mythic structures, affinities, transformations) of these procedures in terms of the concepts of the mechanisms of myths he advocates. The paradox of Lévi-Strauss's work on mythology is not only – as Sperber has noted – that it does not demonstrate that myths are quasi-linguistic in any rigorous sense, but also that in its extension into empirical analysis (in the *Mythologiques*) it confounds both its own and all other existing schemes of interpretation with a whole set of new and unsolved problems. In many ways this is at the same time a measure of its weaknesses and of its strengths.

II The 'Science of the Concrete' and the Unity of Ideology

Behind the diversity in the different segments of Lévi-Strauss's analyses of varying types of primitive representations which we have been examining, there lies, as we noted at the beginning of this section, the conception of an essential unity to primitive ideologies: 'mythic thought', or 'the science of the concrete', as he calls it. This form of thought is understood as characteristically dominant in *primitive* societies – where its parameters as 'expressed' not only in totemism and myths, but also in ritual, magic, sacrifice, etc. (see my comments on pp. 110–11); and yet at the same time denied any *historical* priority in relation to philosophy and the sciences.[64] Just as Lévi-Strauss is opposed to an evolutionary classification of societies, so he is equally opposed to one of forms of thought and representation. If 'mythic thought' has any relation to philosophy and the sciences it must be logical and not temporal, discursive not historical.

This brings us to a suitable starting point for a brief examination of how Lévi-Strauss characterises the 'science of the concrete':[65] his polemical discussion in *The Savage Mind* – doubtless directed against any thesis of a 'pre-logical' native mentality – of the complexity and detail of systems of thought in primitive societies. We have already had ample enough demonstration of this, so all we need to examine is Lévi-Strauss's thesis of its unity. One of its basic points of reference is a contrast of primitive representations with another putative discursive unity: 'modern science' or the 'science of the abstract'. The *order* which magical and ritualistic thought require serves as a symptomatic starting point for this contrast – both their precision and determinism indicate for Lévi-Strauss an 'anticipation' of scientific thought which bases itself, unlike the latter, on a systematisation of 'what is immediately present to the senses'. This leads to the conception of a parallelism of two general modes of acquiring knowledge which primitive magic and the modern sciences exemplify in turn. Thus

> there are two distinct modes of scientific thought. These are certainly not a function of different stages of the development of the human mind, but rather of *two strategic levels at which nature is accessible to scientific enquiry: one roughly adapted to that of perception and the imagination: the other at a remove from it.* It is as if the necessary connections which are the object of all science, neolithic or modern, could be arrived at by two different routes, one very close to, and the other more remote from, sensible intuition [*The Savage Mind*, p. 15; my emphasis].

The first route is that of the science of the concrete, an 'exploitation of the sensible world in sensible terms', an 'intellectual bricolage' which for Lévi-Strauss is pursued by the constant utilisation of 'elements half-way between sensation and intellection' (images and concepts): signs (understood in the Saussurian sense). It is posited therefore that the science of the concrete is a unitary process of the manipulation of elements already given in a culture into structured sets endowed with an injected *significance* – it 'makes do' with pre-constrained aspects of culture to which it grants a new positional meaning. Indeed, these 'aspects of culture' are anchored to images and perceptions of reality in which the processes of signification of the science of the concrete are assumed to be 'imprisoned'. If for Lévi-Strauss this 'science' can be regarded as having any real existence as a specific complex of types of interpretation, it is in the sense of having at its disposal a plethora of intellectual possibilities for the establishment of symbolic affinities among the diversity of natural and cultural images presented to the human subject in the 'closed' world of the primitive society. Of course, we already know how Lévi-Strauss conceives this field of possibilities as centred on a symbolic framework whose model is semiological: if ' . . . attentive, meticulous observation turned entirely on the concrete finds both its principle and its result in symbolism' [ibid., pp. 222–3], then it is because savage thought unifies observation and interpretation of the natural and cultural worlds just as speakers of a particular language unify these acts in the process of discourse. It follows that the foundation and source of the diversity of the science of the concrete lies, like language, in its metaphorical and metonymical discursive processes (particularly the former):

The savage mind deepens its knowledge with the help of *imagines mundi*. It builds mental structures which facilitate an understanding of the world in as much as they resemble it. In this sense savage thought can be defined as analogical thought [ibid., p. 263].

Now, having sketched some of the characteristics of the science of the concrete, we need to address ourselves to two types of question which will enable us to assess whether Lévi-Strauss's notion makes a valid contribution to the perennial anthropological question of whether there is a specifically unified 'traditional' or 'primitive' thought with the constitution he suggests, entertaining specific types of relation (logical or historical) with other and more contemporary discourses. First, there is the question of the overall adequacy of Lévi-Strauss's understanding of the processes of representation at the basis of the science of the concrete; and, second, that of the acceptability of its putative relations to philosophy and modern science.

If we begin with the second question, we can immediately register difficulties in Lévi-Strauss's whole mode of utilisation of modern science (the 'science of the abstract') for comparative purposes. These begin with his assumption that there does exist a *unity* of thought which can bear this name and to which primitive thought can be simply compared at a number of specific levels. Now this is not an uncommon thesis (most comparisons of 'traditional thought' with 'science' propose it in various ways)[66] but we should note that it rests upon the erroneous idea that it is possible to simply demarcate, in a number of paragraphs, a number of central conceptual features to which all modern science can be 'boiled down'. Indeed, as we claimed in our discussion of Lévi-Strauss's epistemology in Part One of this book, the complexity of the different forms of conceptualisation, classification and experimentation in the sciences cannot be reduced to an essential 'scientific method' which they all manifest, and so any attempt to use such an apocryphal body of principles as a yardstick against which to judge primitive forms of representation must be regarded with suspicion. Such comparisons do have an important effect in stressing – quite rightly – the varying levels of abstraction in primitive representations, but they cannot establish *logical* connections between the latter and 'modern science' considered as a whole. In particular, Lévi-Strauss's contrasts between the two bodies of thought should be regarded as restricted. His suggestions that the science of the concrete uses signs and not (solely) concepts like the science of the abstract, that it builds up structures using the remains of events instead of creating means and results in the form of events by using structures (hypotheses and theories) and that its objects are closer to sensible experience than those of modern science (ibid., pp. 19–22), do *not* succeed in establishing a rigorous logical connection where Comte and others had posited a spurious historical one, precisely because the vaguely sketched yardstick which 'the science of the abstract' provides has little to do with the real complexity of the sciences. Rather, they provide a set of assertions about the unitary rigour and 'rationality' of a diversity of thought which for long was regarded as quite the reverse: Lévi-Strauss has done more than anyone else to rescue the analysis of primitive ideologies from ethnocentrism and reductionism.

Having said this, however, we must now show that his notion of the science of the concrete cannot be upheld because it has at its centre *two* main errors relating to the processes of ideological representation in primitive thought. The first error concerns the origin of the rigidly structured quality of native ideologies and symbolisms. We have seen Lévi-Strauss account for this characteristic through constant recourse to a *semiological* insistence on the invariance of metaphorical and metonymical discursive processes, and a 'rationalist' insistence on the operation of the unconscious at the foundation of this invariance, but we now know that neither of these assertions has an adequate foundation. Together they make up what Godelier calls the 'effect of analogical thought on its content',[67] but in the course of this book we have demonstrated, on the one hand, that the structured orders Lévi-Strauss shows in various fields of primitive thought are really not quasi-linguistic in any rigorous sense at all, and, on the other, that any attempt to ground them in the mysterious activities of an unconscious is both impossible and unnecessary. The second error – to which we referred when discussing totemism and mythology – centres on what has aptly been called (again by Godelier) 'the effects in consciousness of the content of the historical relations among men and between them and nature', and concerns that particular version of the 'neo-Marxist' theory of ideology as 'a distorted representation of the real' which Lévi-Strauss and his followers[68] have advocated. We have already seen Lévi-Strauss present the elements of this theory in his discussion of the relation between myth and the social (and ecological) domain: reality is given to human subjects in the form of social and natural conditions which they experience; the thought of these subjects, governed not by the will nor by conscious intention (Lévi-Strauss is of course rigorously anti-humanist), but by unconscious structures, selects specific elements from this reality and transforms them into an imaginary representation of it. Authors such as Godelier and Sebag are quite right in suggesting a link between this conception of ideological thought and that of Marx in his early works and in *The German Ideology*,[69] but quite wrong in assuming that this entails the presence of a correct theory of ideology. Both these conceptions present ideological thought as based on a process in which some given reality – independent of the process – is refracted or distorted in the process of being represented in thought, to an extent which can in principle be determined by a simple comparison of the real and its representation. For example, in Lévi-Strauss's theory, mythology '. . . provides a particular image of reality: social and economic relations, technical activities, relation to the world etc.; *and ethnographic observation must decide whether this image corresponds to the facts'* [*The Raw and the Cooked*, pp. 333–4; my emphasis].

As we have seen, what is specific to Lévi-Strauss's position is the thesis that all systems of representation must have a necessarily algebraic or structural form because of the activity of the laws of the unconscious: all ideological reflection has a quasi-mathematical quality.[70] This gives a position which can be expressed dragrammatically, as in Figure 19.

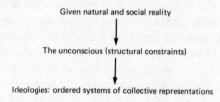

Given natural and social reality

↓

The unconscious (structural constraints)

↓

Ideologies: ordered systems of collective representations

FIGURE 19

A simple embellishment of the terms of this diagram brings us to the whole secret of the unity of Lévi-Strauss's science of the concrete. As Godelier notes, the latter has a specific set of metaphorical trajectories which

> can theoretically develop in four different directions: from Culture to Nature (I), from Nature to Culture (II), from Culture to Culture (III) and from Nature to Nature (IV) . . . Starting from these four basic axes, numerous analogous links can be deployed and combined in a kind of vectorial algebra of the imagination, which confers on mythical discourse and mythical thought their inexhaustible polysemia and symbolic richness [1971, p. 8].

Despite the fact that Godelier neglects the *metonymical* process which for Lévi-Strauss is just as essential as the metaphorical or analogical one, this spotlights the fundamental point: for Lévi-Strauss the essence of all primitive thought is enclosed within *four* directions of conceptualising *two* real domains (nature and culture) by means of *two* combined and constant classificatory processes (metaphor and metonymy). The complexity and diversity of primitive ideologies is acknowledged, but only on condition that each system is regarded as some combination of these few elements which make up the schema of the science of the concrete.

Now one central problem with all this is that the representational process illustrated in Figure 12 above is implicitly *empiricist* in that it presupposes that that which is represented in thought is a reality *given* to the experience of a subject. Ideological knowledge is a refracted image of this reality, and the extent of the distortion of the latter by the former can be assessed by a proper non-ideological knowledge of reality, achievable – as we have seen Lévi-Strauss say – simply by observation. Unfortunately, however, neither of these points can be maintained. As we have seen above in Part One in a discussion of 'empiricist' epistemology, Althusser and his followers have effectively demonstrated that the theory that knowledge is the product of an abstraction by an epistemological subject, from a 'given' reality, independent of thought, is untenable and this must apply to Lévi-Strauss notion that ideology is an 'appearance' of an essential reality given to observation. On the one hand ideologies are not images of a given reality achieved through the empiricist process of the construction of knowledge, and on the other the degree of their distortion or versimilitude cannot be assessed by simply comparing them with a 'true' empiricist knowledge of this reality achieved by direct and unproblematic observation.[71]

This brings us to a final critical comment which is implicit in what we have already said. The whole way in which Lévi-Strauss conceives of ideology *per se* on the one hand, and of the science of the concrete on the other, imposes definite limitations on what can be said analytically about the diversity of primitive thought systems. To begin with, because ideological representation must always for him be the direct effect or expression of a discrete (in the mathematical sense) structured *refraction of reality* – the unconscious producing the algebraic quality of this refraction – the conditions and means of representation cannot be granted any autonomy and cannot be analysed on their own terms as socially effective in ideological formations. We have already seen this in Lévi-Strauss's analyses of mythology: within the framework of his theory he can never specify the ideological conditions governing mythic transmissions and distortions and always oscillates between a reference to the purely internal teleological necessities of mythic messages on the one hand, and the external role of ecology (directly expressed in myth) on the other. His compound of these two types of factors reflects an incapacity to tackle the analysis of ideological conditions surrounding the means of production of mythic messages. At the same time, because of the conception of the structure of the science of the concrete, we should note that Lévi-Strauss can explain and analyse primitive ideological diversity only in so far as it must at all times be regarded as the result of a combination of a few basic elements operative within it, which we have sketched above. The complexity of ideology is acknowledged, but the particular way in which it is understood as founded upon a conceptual unity sets definite limits to what can be achieved in its analysis.

However, from what we have said so far, we can claim to have shown that the operation of this unitary schema cannot be supported. Lévi-Strauss's conception of the science of the concrete contains within it a number of important assumptions and theses which cannot be accepted and we must conclude by endorsing the suspicions of other authors[72] with a rejection, and say that in having furnished a wholly welcome stress upon the diversity and complexity of primitive ideologies he has at the same time, through the peculiar content of his basic concepts, postulated its foundation upon a spurious unity. The science of the concrete, or 'mythic thought', is as much an illusory unity as its companion the science of the abstract, and the analysis of ideologies has no need for the thesis of its existence.

III Conclusion

To conclude Part Three of this book, it is important to emphasise, over and above the critical points we have sought to stress in each of its Sections, the enormous value of the kinds of investigations into the structure of ideologies which Lévi-Strauss has conducted in his major works. Demonstrating time and again the constant complexity in organisation of systems of ideological representation, they have succeeded in raising the level of approach to such phenomena to an elevation from which anthropology and sociology can only benefit. If we have laboured to demarcate what is essentially weak in the constituent concepts making up this approach, it is only from the conviction that the structural analysis of ideology has reached something truly essential in its exercise, that it is only by an elimination of weaknesses that strengths can be consolidated and that in order to face the challenge posed by its demonstration of precise forms of order in societal discourse more rigorous interpretative concepts must be elaborated where those of Lévi-Strauss can be found wanting.

Conclusion

Having come to the end of our discussion of the content and rigour of Lévi-Strauss's major concept in social theory, it is time to recall the conclusions of each of the three principal divisions of the text – Parts One, Two and Three – and to say something about the possible general implications for future social theory.

What we attempted to show in Part One was the ultimate incoherence of the formulations Lévi-Strauss provides (in a far from systematic manner) to justify a 'semiological' science of social forms. While on the one hand we showed that these formulations have a conceptual structure which is both *substantive* (in advocating a specific idea of the nature of the social) and *epistemological* (in advocating a thesis on the appropriate means to achieve a knowledge of this reality), on the other we demonstrated that each of these elements of the structure was theoretically incoherent in its own specific manner. The conclusion had to follow that, for both substantive and epistemological reasons, Lévi-Strauss's proposals for a scientific semiology were ultimately unacceptable.

In Part Two, we tried to problematise the basis of Lévi-Strauss's theory of social organisation by demonstrating internal difficulties in the concepts constructed within his work to theorise, first, the constitution of primitive societies as distinct and complex social forms; second, the mechanisms *and* effects of kinship phenomena within these forms; and, third, the nature of the relation between social forms and the process of history. An attempt was made to show the different *levels* of conceptualisation in this area of Lévi-Strauss's thought and to supply, correspondingly, distinct levels of critique.

Lévi-Strauss's work on systems of representation (*viz.* totemism and mythology) formed the subject of Part Three. Particular attention here was placed upon analysing the coherence and adequacy of the specifications of the concepts and forms of explanation utilised in the analysis of totemic and mythic phenomena. Further, however, we saw it necessary to scrutinise two sets of theses providing the foundation and logical support of these analyses: on the one hand theses on the form of 'primitive' representation called 'the science of the concrete', and on the other theses on the *general* characteristics of all symbolic and ideological representation. By tackling these conceptions – which provide the whole of Lévi-Strauss's analytical effort with its grounding and unity – our final purpose was to establish what was acceptable and what was not acceptable for a social theory seeking to build upon their contribution.

SEMIOLOGY, 'MEANING' AND THE NATURE OF SOCIAL ACTION

Now, however, having provided a basic summary of the content of each of the main parts of the book, there is an opportunity to highlight one particular aspect of Lévi-Strauss's structuralism which was mentioned in this content but not explored fully; the general concept of action which emerges in his semiological orientation. The structure of this conception has already been outlined elsewhere (see Part One, Section I) but, to recapitulate, we can recall that for Lévi-Strauss, as for many other social theorists, the unique distinguishing feature of the socio-cultural domain is its peculiar *fusion* of natural elements with others of a quite distinct origin which can be called 'ideal' or 'meaningful'. The major distinguishing feature of Lévi-Strauss's own position, however, is his understanding of the mechanism through which this takes place and through which, as a consequence, social reality is made possible. Unlike theorists who stress the paramount role of the individual subject in clothing reality with meaningful intentions, for Lévi-Strauss prime place must be given to a *supra-individual* mechanism – the unconscious – whose activities are not reducible to those which are present to human consciousness. This distinctively anti-humanist position is a constant in Lévi-Strauss's work and is most explicit in his polemical confrontations with critics inspired by precisely the kind of 'subjectivist' orientation (e.g. existentialists, phenomenologists, Weberians) to which the substance of his basic concepts is opposed.[1]

Now, a recourse to *language*, as we have seen, plays a crucial rôle in Lévi-Strauss's anti-humanism, in providing a prime example in social life of the determinacy of unconscious processes and structures through which 'meanings' are sedimented. The whole basis of the Saussurian conception of linguistic signification, in specifying a process of the unification or 'matching' of a system of sound images with a system of meanings or ideas, appears to demonstrate perfectly admirably the overall process of the synthesis of 'meanings' with natural elements which is the putative characteristic of the cultural realm in general. This type of argument is one of the main features of all semiology and it is quite easy to see how it comes to be propounded by a theoretical 'slide' from one distinct issue to another, culminating in their eventual conflation.

On the one hand we have the issue of the specific structures of language, considered phonologically, syntactically and semantically, as they are established by the science of linguistics. Here what is called 'meaning' has a precise specification wholly in terms of the concepts of the structures of words and sentences: unities wholly internal to language considered as a highly specific mode of discourse.[2] On the other hand, however, we have the issue of 'the speech act' – in which takes place the realisation of linguistic structures in a social context – whose consideration (by linguists themselves, by social scientists and philosophers) tends to operate with a concept of meaning which is more vague and ambiguous than the previous one. This distinction of issues parallels that between linguistic 'competence' and 'performance' popularised by linguistics itself: thus for Katz,[3] for example,

A theory in linguistics explicates linguistic competence, not linguistic performance. It seeks to reconstruct the logical structures of the principles that speakers have mastered in attaining fluency. On the other hand, a theory of performance seeks to discover the contribution of each of the factors that interplay to produce natural speech with its various and sundry deviations from ideal linguistic norms. Thus it must consider such linguistically extraneous factors as memory span, perceptual and motor limitations, lapses of attention, pauses, level of motivation, interest, idiosyncratic and random errors etc. (Katz, art. cit., p. 107).

Now there is often, of course, in this concern with 'performance' and the 'speech act', a tendency to assert the dominance of the *intentionality* or *intentional meaning* of the speaking and acting subject[4] (this purporting to explain his linguistic choice) but there is also no shortage of attempts to expand the analysis of 'performance' *beyond* this into a general theory of social action.[5] However, we should note that the drawing of specific subjectivist conclusions about the necessarily 'rationalistic' quality of social reality (despite lip service to its objectively structured foundation) from the concept of linguistic performance is not justified simply by the fact of the wholehearted assent of certain schools of linguistic science.[6] Other theoretical arguments must have their say, and it is particularly interesting in this respect to confront these extrapolations from linguistic theory into social action with certain recent criticisms of all social theories which conceive of the social domain as founded upon some 'rationalist' process of the expression of intentions or meanings in reality,[7] a domain which, to be explained, must be 'understood'.

The central platform of these criticisms concerns an attack on the coherence of the general understanding of the three constituent elements usually engaged in this process – a domain of ideas or meanings, natural reality and a mechanism for the realisation of the former in the latter to produce the 'meaningful' characteristics of the socio-cultural domain.[8] To begin with, there are two consequences which the process itself must necessarily imply: first, there is the requirement that the mechanism for the expression of ideas has a capacity for recognition and selection among the resources of the ideal realm and for the registration of whether its purpose has been achieved (we have already seen this with Lévi-Strauss's concept of the unconscious – he understands it to be selective and teleological in its structuring action); second, there is the requirement that ideas *govern* and constrain social action through the mechanism of their expression, which is also subject to natural determinations. There are difficulties for 'rationalist' theories of action in each case. As far as the first is concerned problems centre on a general lack of specification of the principles by which recognition and selection operate: whether it is understood to take place at an individual level (as in theories attributing primacy to free will) or at a supra-individual one (as for example in Lévi-Strauss's representation of the unconscious) the real modalities of its action can only appear in the last analysis as mysterious. The second point is more important, however, for it immediately entails that the mechanism of expression of ideas must be subject to a *double determination*, in being governed by both natural *and* ideal elements. In so far as the mechanism must effect a fusion of ideal and natural factors (to produce the social domain) it must operate at the interface, so to speak, of each realm and thus to some extent in accordance with the dictates of both. On the one hand, because social action is understood to conform to ideas (the latter exclude actions which conflict with them), the mechanism must be governed by ideal factors; while on the other, because this action is 'in' a portion of nature, the mechanism must be implicated in natural phenomena. Now the crucial question is whether such a double determination can be reconciled, for it does appear to present 'rationalist' positions with a mixture of two conflicting types of causal determinacy, each of equal importance.[9] In fact, there is only one way in which this can be achieved, and this is by the further conception of a form of *pre-given* harmony between them: either nature is granted a pre-given capacity to realise ideas, or ideas are regarded as governed wholly by nature (as the epiphenomena of natural processes). Whichever is postulated, however, the same difficulty is generated: nature itself must be presented (in a manner contradicting its original definition) as possessing the immanent purpose to produce at some stage of its development an apparatus (the brain, the 'symbolic mechanism', etc.) to express ideas. To be consistent, that is to say, 'rationalist' positions must have recourse to a concept of a teleological continuity between organic and cultural evolution. However, because this thesis – as recent work suggests[10] – implies a theoretical reductionism which cannot appeal to biological evolutionary theory (which claims no such continuity), it would seem necessary to conclude that all 'rationalist' theories of the social are inherently without foundation and cannot be rationally supported.

Now, if these arguments are accepted, there would seem to be a strong case against any utilisation of linguistic theory for the purpose of supporting a 'rationalist' type of theory of social action and culture. Indeed, it would be necessary to subject the appropriation by social theory of linguistic concepts such as 'meaning' and 'competence/performance' to an extensive criticism, so that a rigorous distinction could be maintained between on the one hand what was valid from the point of view of modes of proof and demonstration internal to linguistics, and on the other what there was within this material having specifiable implications for a social theory avoiding the difficulties mentioned above. This is clearly an enormous problem, and the author only dimly perceives certain of its defining characteristics. However, it does seem clear that general utilisations of linguistic categories as exemplified in semiology and in extrapolations from Chomsky's work on generative grammars[11] must be attacked in those areas where conclusions are drawn about the general structure of social action and about the inevitable primacy within it of a specifically human mental faculty (free will, mind), which hide the type of position we have discussed behind a thin veneer of scientific linguistics.

If, as Bachelard was probably the first to emphasise,[12] philosophy and social theory often lag behind developments in the sciences and ossify where the latter constantly develop, there would seem to be good reason for guarding against precipitate exhortations to develop general positions in social theory by means of partisan appropriations of linguistic concepts.

THE POSITIVE CONTRIBUTION OF LÉVI-STRAUSS'S SOCIAL THEORY

This brings us to a final set of comments, this time on the question of the enduring value of Lévi-Strauss's contribution to social theory. In our substantive discussions of his analyses of social organisation and of ideology we have already tried to emphasise – despite an overall critical orientation – the specific character of what remains positive and valuable within them. These comments can be briefly consolidated if we recall how we emphasised the importance of a 'de-construction' of the achievements of structural anthropology and the necessity of their reinsertion into a more adequate overall set of concepts.[13] Where the forms of causality and explanation Lévi-Strauss provides for the interpretation of the results of his major analyses were found inadequate, the task would have to be undertaken to develop more rigorous concepts suggesting precisely those specifications obliterated or neglected by them.

There is some indication that this task has already been faced in certain directions, although the results are rather uneven, and in this respect the work of Godelier in specific theoretical areas deserves special mention.[14] In both Parts Two and Three above we have already signalled the importance of his interventions in the analysis of primitive social organisation and ideology, but it should also be recalled that we have stressed the limitations of the particular way they propose an 'incorporation' of Lévi-Strauss's concepts into a Marxist framework. In tackling the problem of the articulation of the 'restricted and generalised exchange' kinship mechanisms with other characteristics of primitive societies, for example, we have seen both Godelier and his follower Friedman accept at face-value the adequacy of the general morphology of systems of which they are a part,[15] and it can be further seen in a particular paper by the latter[16] how impetuous attempts to integrate structural anthropology with Marxism before this body of theory has been able to generate a conception of what is *specific* to the modes of production of specific types of primitive society lead into an inadequate formalism. Here a preliminary abstract model of 'the general mode of production'[17] is stated at the outset and an attempt is made to interrelate its somewhat arbitrarily selected features for primitive societies with 'the kinship level' defined in advance according to the (wholly accepted) protocols of Lévi-Strauss. The result is that, instead of a detailed investigation of the concepts of primitive modes of production followed *then* by a discussion of the role of kinship within them, we are given a schematic neo-Marxist 'model' of all societies and an immediate attempt to utilise Lévi-Strauss's mechanisms of kinship exchange by positing their somewhat dubious interconnection with a set of forces of production. Now all this is not to denigrate important pioneering work into the possibility of a Marxist anthropology, but to stress that more caution and patience in the development of basic concepts is needed before precipitate attempts are made to 'incorporate' structuralism. That there is need for their development is plain when one considers the *variety* of neo-Marxisms which are beginning to develop in these areas[18] and the extent of their disagreement over basic principles.

But, if caution is required in the analysis of primitive social organisation before Lévi-Strauss's comparative work in this area can be given the body of supporting concepts it clearly needs, this is even more important for his work on ideological representation, where the kinds of problems we have outlined in Part Three confront existing schemes of interpretation with very great difficulties. Our understanding of the complexities of the processes of ideological production and reception seems at a very limited level, and as yet the status of recent attempts[19] to avoid the 'classical' mode of treatment of ideology as a distorted expression of social reality is uncertain. At this stage we can only reiterate what we said at the end of Part Three about the crucial nature of Lévi-Strauss's specification of certain types of organisation of ideological material: it represents an interpretative theoretical challenge of the highest order, but one should not shirk from the most important preliminary issue: the formulation of the correct *questions* to be answered and problems to be confronted in the *general* examination of ideology before the assumption that existing empirical work on specific systems, in specifying their 'underlying order', gives a scientific representation of their mechanisms. It is hoped that the kinds of criticisms established in Part Three at least lay a foundation for such a formulation in the context of Lévi-Strauss's important analytical advances.

Having made these brief points, it is time to bring this book to a close and to end, appropriately, with a comment from Lévi-Strauss himself which offers stern advice to a social thought bedevilled with subjectivism and theoretical uncertainty:

A la suite des sciences physiques, les sciences humaines doivent se convaincre que la réalité de leur objet d'étude n'est pas tout entière cantonnée au niveau où le sujet la perçoit [*L'Homme nu*, p. 570].

Notes

INTRODUCTION

1 Following, undoubtedly, the pioneering work of Barthes. Among many texts see J. Culler (1975) and P. Pettit (1975).

2 See E. Leach (1976) for an 'undergraduate textbook' in structuralist social anthropology.

3 See M. Sahlins (1966), E. R. Leach (1965), M. Harris (1968), H. S. Hughes (1968) and C. R. Badcock (1976), Chapter 1.

4 B. Scholte (1973), I. Rossi (1973).

5 See M. Glucksmann (1973).

6 On the theory of discourse see the beginning of Part One, below.

7 This is because of the relatively low level of rigour in the interconnection between Lévi-Strauss's major concepts. Talcott Parsons's sociological theory affords a distinct contrast. For an attempt to analyse his discourse in the way we have mentioned see B. Hindess and S. Savage (1977).

8 For the original concept see L. Althusser and E. Balibar (1970) and the discussion in K. Williams (1974).

PART ONE: ANTHROPOLOGY AS A SEMIOLOGY: LÉVI-STRAUSS'S METHODOLOGICAL PROTOCOLS

1 For five different perspectives see R. Jakobson (1973), T. Parsons (1967), A. Wilden (1968) L. Von Bertalanffy (1974), J. Derrida (1970).

2 See R. Barthes (1967) and (1972), E. Benveniste (1971), U. Eco (1973), P. Guiraud (1975), J. Kristeva (1973), among countless others.

3 Developments in the theory of theory/discourse were forged by the work of Althusser, Foucault and Derrida in France. See in particular L. Althusser (1969), Chapter 6 and L. Althusser and E. Balibar (1970), Part I. For critical analyses of the many issues K. Williams (1974) and B. Hindess (1977), Chapter 7 are important.

4 For more detail see B. Hindess, *op. cit.*, and B. Hindess and S. Savage (1977).

5 M. Glucksmann's (1973) approach is a notable exception to this tendency. In her comparative analysis of Lévi-Strauss and Althusser she recognises the importance of a strategy for analysis of distinct conceptual levels within theory (Chapter 1). Unfortunately, however, what is actually offered in the actual analysis of Lévi-Strauss's work tends to revert back to the 'influences' approach (which I discuss in what follows), referring to the latter's own idea of his 'trois maîtresses': Marx, Freud and de Saussure (cf. op. cit. p. 55ff.).

6 See I. Rossi's own two articles in Rossi (1973), B. Scholte (1973), Part 2, and M. Glucksmann, op. cit.

7 This may be represented thus:

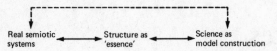

Real semiotic   Structure as   Science as
systems   'essence'   model construction

8 The famous 'linguistic analogy' over whose *precise* significance there is little agreement.

9 For the former see Lévi-Strauss (1962c), pp. 268–9 and (1961) pp. 38–42 and 153–5.

10 'Nearly' must be stressed here, as Lévi-Strauss later shows some doubt over the nature of the efficacy of the 'unconscious' in kinship. See (1963) and (1965).

11 A *methodological* role.

12 It must be noted that Freud's concept of the unconscious has a quite different theoretical specification to that of Lévi-Strauss. The former is part of a developed theory of the structures and mechanisms of the psychic apparatus. Lévi-Strauss's concept is not inserted into such a theory and he produces no real analysis of the organisational dynamics of the psyche as a complex whole.

13 The explicit *rationalism* here is prominent in Lévi-Strauss's praise of Rousseau and Bergson. See Lévi-Strauss (1962b), p. 175.

14 The following translation is that in J. M. Benoist (1973).

15 This explains why Lévi-Strauss, unlike many 'semiologists', links the existence of phonological opposites to 'cerebral mechanisms'. Barthes in *Elements of Semiology* quite correctly treats this notion with great caution (see pp. 81–2). I will say more about this shortly.

16 In this respect there is a distinct parallel between Lévi-Strauss's concept of the 'unconscious' and Durkheim's 'collective consciousness'. Both are essential in theoretical function, but at the same time empty in content. On Durkheim's concept see P. Q. Hirst (1973), Chapters 3 and 4.

17 See R. Jakobson (1967), p. 580ff.

18 On this concept see R. Jakobson (1962), p. 464ff and B. Malmberg (1963).

19 Barthes, op. cit., Malmberg, op. cit. See also D. Hymes (1964).

20 In this respect, it is just not good enough to say, as does Rossi, that for Lévi-Strauss 'The ethnographic and ethnological conclusions reached in his long career would seem to *excuse him* from supporting his basic hypothesis in terms of linguistic and . . . psychological arguments' (I. Rossi [1973], p. 37; my emphasis). On the contrary, the hypothesis of the existence and effectivity of the unconscious *grounds* a crucial aspect of Lévi-Strauss's methodological project. It is *not* enough to base this project on the *assumption* of the existence of this entity. Lévi-Strauss implicitly realises this and tries to produce evidence for its existence. Here we are questioning this attempt via an examination of the methodological function of his references to linguistics.

21 For examples see Malmberg, op. cit., pp. 121–4, Rossi, op. cit., pp. 35–8, and the papers by Mounin and Durbin in I. Rossi (1974).

22 A. Martinet (1955), p. 73ff., for example.

23 See particularly G. Mounin (1974) for a critique of Lévi-Strauss's *interpretation* of Troubetzkoy, Jakobson and De Saussure.

24 See note 16.

25 The structure of Lévi-Strauss's concept of the social commits him to what Hindess has called an anti-humanist variant of the 'rationalist theory of action' and it is therefore subject to the more general difficulties shown to be bound up with such a theory. See B. Hindess (1977b). On expressive causality see my page 54 and 167 n 18.

26 See L. Sebag (1964), Chapters 3 and 4; Barthes, op. cit and (1972); and U. Eco (1973).

27 Diagrammatically:

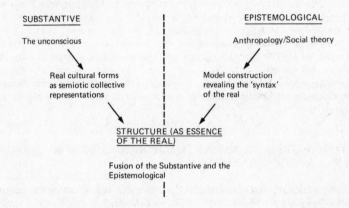

SUBSTANTIVE   EPISTEMOLOGICAL

The unconscious   Anthropology/Social theory

Real cultural forms as semiotic collective representations   Model construction revealing the 'syntax' of the real

STRUCTURE (AS ESSENCE OF THE REAL)

Fusion of the Substantive and the Epistemological

28 A. Badiou (1969); B. Hindess (1971) and (1974). Both show that the epistemology of models is a variant of the 'empiricist' conception of knowledge *as defined and criticised by Althusser*. See Althusser and Balibar, op. cit., Part I.

29 R. Carnap (1947) and (1956).

30 The appeal for syntactical rigour is mirrored in Lévi-Strauss's preoccupation with mathematisation as an ideal to be achieved in all social thought. See Lévi-Strauss (1955a) and (1964a).

31 *Viz.* the 'commutation test'. On this see R. Barthes (1967a), p. 65, 70.

32 Lévi-Strauss often considers the social sciences to be pre-scientific because of this.

33 The crucial issue is the *significance* and *status* of these relationships. On this see Chomsky (1968), pp. 64–6.

34 But see Nutini's demonstration of the dubious theoretical value of the distinction between conscious and unconscious models. See H. G. Nutini (1965).

35 See also Lévi-Strauss (1966), p. xxxix and (1964a), p. 541ff.

36 See F. Korn (1969), D. Schneider (1965), D. Goddard (1965) and Y. Simonis (1968), Chapter 5.

37 For example Sebag, op. cit.; Scholte, op. cit.; R. Boudon (1970), P. Ricoeur (1970).
38 For example Korn, op. cit., E. Leach (1970), D. Maybury-Lewis (1968).
39 The simplistic criticisms of F. Korn and D. Goddard should be noted here. Korn's suggestions for example that 'what is meant by "structuralism" is nothing more than an admonition not to treat any element out of context' (op. cit., p. 7) effectively denegates all analysis of Lévi-Strauss forms of justification of the concept of the *semiotic* (and therefore *structured*) nature of culture which is central to his work.
40 H. G. Nutini (1970). His position here differs from that in the 1965 paper.
41 Conditions, that is, which facilitate *a demarcation between what is and what is not knowledge.*
42 See Althusser's definition and criticism of the general 'empiricist conception of knowledge' in Althusser and Balibar, op. cit., p. 34ff, but note that what Althusser means by 'empiricism' is *much wider than our conventional references* and designates a general discursive structure which has a variety of philosophical manifestations.
43 B. Hindess (1977). See particularly pp. 134–41 for an elaboration on this issue of circularity.
44 For comments on this see S. F. Nadel (1957), E. Leach (1970) and M. Godelier (1972), Introduction.
45 Op. cit.

PART TWO: STRUCTURAL ANTHROPOLOGY, PRIMITIVE SOCIAL ORGANISATION AND HISTORY

1 This 'rupture' is often specified as the creation of a new Kuhnian 'paradigm'. See P. Bonté (1976), J. Derrida (1970), B. Scholte (1968), J. Llobera (1974). On the limitations of Kuhn's concept see D. Lecourt (1975), Introduction to the English edition.
2 As Llobera notes there are a variety of adjectival labels which anthropologists use to refer to the societies they study: 'lower', 'savage', 'non-literate', 'simple', or just 'other'. Art. cit., p. 4.
3 Lévi-Strauss (1952b).
4 Lévi-Strauss (1960a), p. 46ff.
5 Lévi-Strauss (1968b), Chapter XVI.
6 M. Mauss (1967).
7 Lévi-Strauss (1944).
8 Lévi-Strauss does also seem to think that the concepts have a wider range of applicability. See Lévi-Strauss (1969), p. xxxvi.
9 See I. Buchler and H. Selby (1968), R. Fox (1970).
10 See Rossi, Scholte, Diamond and Krader in I. Rossi (1974).
11 On ethnographic inexactitude see E. Leach (1970) Chapter 6, R. Needham (1971), F. Korn (1973), for important comments.
12 Lévi-Strauss (1969) p. 490.
13 Lévi-Strauss, op. cit., pp. 220, 440, 464.
14 I. Rossi, art. cit., p. 111.
15 A. Wilden (1968), p. 243.

16 But see *also* Lévi-Strauss (1968b), pp. 22–3.

17 It makes possible the formation of the 'kinship atom', op. cit., p. 46.

18 This mode of causality 'presupposes in principle that the whole in question be reducible to an *inner essence*, of which the elements of the whole are then no more than the phenomenal forms of expression, the inner principle of the essence being present at each point in the whole, but such that at each moment it is possible to write the immediate adequate equation: *such and such an element . . . = the inner essence of the whole*' [Althusser and Balibar (1970), pp. 186–7]. Korn, op. cit., fails to see the operation of this causality in Lévi-Strauss. Rossi on the other hand sees it, implicitly at least (I. Rossi, art. cit).

19 This typifies Lévi-Strauss's opposition to evolutionism and diffusionism.

20 Dual organisation places cross- and parallel cousins along with other individuals in separate moieties but does not specify why a *cross-cousin* is preferred specifically.

21 For an exemplary statement see Lévi-Strauss (1969), p. 136. Here 'duality, alternation, opposition and symmetry . . . ' are described as 'basic and immediate data of mental and social reality', linked to a 'recognition structure' capable of grasping and discerning the differences between types of relation.

22 Thus the Murngin tribe (and others of Arnhem Island) for the first type, and the Kariera (four class) and Aranda (eight class) for the second.

23 Lévi-Strauss, op. cit., pp. 106, 156.

24 For the three types of inter-class relation ('pair', 'couple' and 'cycle') and their cyclical and oscillatory structures see Lévi-Strauss, op. cit., p. 179.

25 Lévi-Strauss also considers tribes from North India and other areas of Australia.

26 This produces the situation in the diagram on page 215, Lévi-Strauss, op. cit.

27 In contrast to restricted exchange systems which function as though divided into compartments between which reciprocity takes place.

28 'Better' in the sense that it provides a more effective *integration* network.

29 E. Leach, op. cit.; F. Korn, op. cit.; R. Needham, Introduction to (1971a), pp. xci–c.

30 B. Scholte (1966) and (973) I. Rossi, art. cit.; A. Wilden (1968), Chapters I and IX.

31 See E. Leach, op. cit., p. 117 and a complementary position in his (1965a), pp. 776–80.

32 The causal relation is:

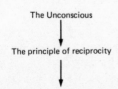

The Unconscious

↓

The principle of reciprocity

↓

Diverse exchange phenomena. Principle of reciprocity expressed within 'contingent institutional material'.

33 H. Gardner (1972), pp. 182–3 and (1973).

34 See note 18.

35 Lévi-Strauss's position can be compared with the social theories of Durkheim and Parsons in this respect. It is subject to similar difficulties. See Hindess (1977b), Part I.

36 For example, see J. A. Barnes (1971), Part Two, D. M. Schneider (1965), J. Friedman (1974). Lévi-Strauss's concepts are not 'models' nor are they 'ideal types' (see Buchler and Selby, op. cit., p. 116ff.).

37 See above for the incommensurability of substantive and epistemological concepts.

38 M. Godelier (1972a), (1973), pp. 58–65, (1975) and J. Friedman (1974) and (1975). I shall say more about their assessments of Lévi-Strauss shortly.

39 This is quite clear in M. Godelier (1973), p. 61.

40 See P. Ekeh (1974) for a clear example.

41 These concepts depend for their content on theoretical interconnection with Durkheim's *social morphology*. See Durkheim (1938), Chapter 3, and (1933), Book 1, Chapter 3, and Book 2, Chapter 2.

42 This is manifest in his concept of a 'regime'.

43 Art. cit.

44 M. Gaboriau (1970).

45 Lévi-Strauss's anti-humanist and anti-historicist remarks coincide in part with those of Althusser and Balibar, who delineate the general weaknesses of historicism in Marxist theory (Sartre, Gramsci, Colletti). See L. Althusser and E. Balibar (1970) Chapters 3 and 4. Unfortunately most of the commentators on Lévi-Strauss's 'debate with Sartre' do not see how these criticisms are crucial and *how they dominate the terms of this debate* – see L. Abel (1970), L. Rosen (1974), L. Krader (1974) and C. R. Badcock (1976), for examples.

46 Note that the point of reference is to different *histories* as being conceived by reference to different orders or scales of time. This does not eliminate the problem of how the 'objects' of different histories might be interconnected (for example the economy of a specific society and its dependancy on changes in the polity) and faces the general issue of the historical transition of *whole societies*. This is always change of a complex totality of structures and it cannot be *assumed* that transition in one type of structure can be demarcated simply by abstracting it from its position within the whole.

47 For a logical extension of Lévi-Strauss's position on this see L. Sebag (1964) Chapter 3.

48 Gaboriau, art. cit., p. 162ff.

49 Lévi-Strauss (1963).

50 See Part One.

PART THREE:– IDEOLOGY AND 'MYTHIC THOUGHT': THE STRUCTURAL INTERPRETATION OF SYMBOLIC REPRESEN-TATIONS

1 For general discussion see R. Firth (1973), Part One, G. Gurvitch (1971), J. Willer (1971). The *broad* notion of 'ideology' adopted in what follows is similar to that of Geertz in his 'Ideology as a cultural system': see Geertz (1973).

2 It is essential to note that this type of thought – the realisation of what Lévi-

Strauss calls 'mind in its untamed state' – is not *confined* to primitive societies although it is there that it is dominant. It appears in other guises in other types of social form, as Lévi-Strauss suggests in *The Savage Mind* (cf. p. 219). Here he castigates Comte for suggesting that this mode of knowledge is *historically prior* to other forms. For Lévi-Strauss no such temporal priority can be established: it is merely possible to contend that this type of thought has a particular constitution and that it is dominant in some societies and subordinate in others (like our own) where other forms of representation are favoured. 'Mind in its untamed state' (mythic thought) and 'mind cultivated for the purpose of yielding a return' can co-exist within one society, despite their differences of constitution (cf. ibid., pp. 219–22). This crucial point is often missed: see for example P. Cohen (1969).

3 Lévi-Strauss's work should in this respect be placed on a par with that of Foucault, whose main ambition is to discern the rhythms and breaks in 'societal discourse'. See Foucault (1970) and (1972) and J. J. Macquet (1974).

4 A. R. Radcliffe-Brown, 'The Sociological Theory of Totemism', in (1952) (hereafter his first theory, in this text, will be referred to as (A), the second as (B)); B. Malinowski (1948), E. Durkheim (1915).

5 S. Freud (1925), R. Firth (1939).

6 A. R. Radcliffe-Brown (1958), Chapter V (B).

7 E. E. Evans-Pritchard (1956).

8 Lévi-Strauss sees these mechanisms as basic to all symbolism and as analogous to Jakobson and Halles's *linguistic* mechanisms (see their 1956 text). Much use has also been made of the latter by the Lacanian school of psychoanalysis (with reference to Freud's 'displacement' and 'condensation' of the contents of the unconscious). See J. Lacan (1966), J. Laplanche and S. Leclaire (1972).

9 And secondarily *affective*. See Lévi-Strauss (1962b), pp. 174, 177, and (1962c), pp. 37–9. He does not ignore affectivity, as P. Worsley thinks (1967, pp. 155–6).

10 Totemism, sexual prohibitions and institutional prohibitions are therefore *paradigmatically* or *metaphorically* related. See Lévi-Strauss (1962c), p. 104.

11 For important diagrams expressing this see Lévi-Strauss (1962c), p. 115.

12 Here 'culture is thought of as a projection or reflection of nature' (ibid.).

13. Their contrariety or inversion can be understood if we set them out diagrammatically as follows:

	Totemism	Caste organisation
Conceptual model	Natural analogy	Cultural analogy
Entities exchanged	Natural (women)	Cultural (commodities)
Conceptualisation of prohibited entities	Cultural (species homogenised with respect to order of beliefs)	Natural (women regarded as non-exchangeable as are species mates)

		Totemism	Caste organisation
Social	{ Function	Homogeneous	Heterogeneous
Organisation	{ Structure	Heterogeneous	Homogeneous

INVERSION

14 Lévi-Strauss's reference to *perception* is very important. It implies the constant presence of a perceiving agent endowed with a faculty of recognition; that is to say, of a *subject*. As we shall see later, despite Lévi-Strauss's constant anti-humanism he continually reintroduces subjectivity through trying to ground ideological discursive orders (particularly structures internal to spheres of representation) in the psychological (a human faculty or mental capacity).

15 Lévi-Strauss (1962c), p. 172ff.

16 See Lévi-Strauss (1962c), pp. 153–4.

17 Op.cit., p. 165.

18 For a logical interconnection between myth and ritual see 'Structure and Dialectics' in Lévi-Strauss (1968b).

19 And also, for that matter, of those of *biology* which to Lévi-Strauss are not fundamentally different. See Lévi-Strauss (1962c), pp. 1–13.

20 This is to say that systems of knowledge and of social representations are never *reducible* to the experiences of knowing subjects (however defined), of given real phenomena.

21 (1962b), pp. 165–177, and (1962c), pp. 136–7.

22 Art. cit.

23 For a clear account see L. Dumont (1972) p. 133ff.

24 From now on the following abbreviations will be used in the notes that follow: I *The Raw and the Cooked – RC*; II *From Honey to Ashes – HA*; III *L'Origine des manières de table – OM*; IV *L'Homme nu – HN*.

25 In Lévi-Strauss (1968b), Chaper XI, (1960b) and (1960c).

26 See E. Leach (1970), Chapter 4, P. Pettit (1975), p. 82, C. R. Badcock (1976).

27 As Kirk notes (1970, p. 83, n46) Lévi-Strauss's discussion is erratic and offered 'simply as an illustration of a technique'.

28 This ordering is the setting out of the unfolding narrative in columns, bringing together elements with a specific common feature. The standard example is the organisation of a sequence of numbers (1, 2, 4, 7, 2, 8, 4, 1...) into spaced columns See Lévi-Strauss (1968b), p. 213, and for extensive discussion D. M. Segal (1969).

29 Thus for Lévi-Strauss the Oedipus myth attempts to resolve the contradiction between the primitive *belief* in the autochthony of man and the *knowledge* of his birth from the union of woman and man.

30 See Lévi-Strauss (1968b), p. 216.

31 See *HA*, pp. 248–9.

32 Clearly shown in the analysis of Winnebago myths in Lévi-Strauss (1960b).

33 M. Douglas (1967), p. 60.

34 See Lévi-Strauss (1960c), pp. 19–21.

35 Both commentators re-analyse the versions to show that their meaning need not necessarily be considered as *totally* bound up with reflections on kinship.

36 This is elaborated upon in *The Savage Mind*.

37 We cannot hope to do justice to the tetralogy here. What follows is an attempt to provide a critical consideration of certain of its major statements of principle.

38 It must be noted that there is a certain *discontinuity in analysis* in the tetralogy as a whole caused by 'un infléchissement de la méthode' in *OM*. In this text there is a concentration on a small number of specific myths (e.g. M_{354}, the 'key myth') which are illuminated using only *sequences* from many other myths. A return to the usual comparison of whole narratives is effected in *HN*, however. On this change see *OM*, p. 14.

39 See the table in *RC*, p. 77.

40 Thus '...meat had to exist before man could cook it; this meat, which occurs in the myths in the superior form of the queixada, was cooked for the first time with the help of fire obtained from the jaguar, presented in the myths as the hunter of pigs' (*HA*, p. 22).

41 For a definition see *RC*, p. 199.

42 It is important to note the way Lévi-Strauss sets out the full details of this transformation in diagrammatic form. See *HA*. This type of representation of transforms becomes less frequent in the later volumes. On the reason for this see *HN*, p. 566.

43 Using the last two results Lévi-Strauss establishes a variety of 'patterns of features' relating to $[M_{16}]$, $[M_{20}]$ and $[M_{21}]$. See *RC*, pp. 96–7.

44 *Kinship*: The Ge jaguar is the (adopted) father of the hero, whereas the Bororo hero, congruous with the jaguar, is a (real) son of a human father. *Family attitudes*: The Ge adopted father is 'close' to the child and against the mother, who is 'remote', whereas the Bororo mother is 'close' (incestuous) and the father 'remote' (murderous).

45 That is, the purely formal relations of logical affinity between myths – whether as inversion or isomorphism of themes and sequences – which Lévi-Strauss sketches (illustrated above). It must be repeated that the author recognises the great analytical potential of such demonstrations: their 'suggestiveness'. What is really important however is *what it is that they* (remembering that there are different modes of comparison) *can be considered to show*.

46 It is interesting to note that Leach seems quite uncertain about *how* to interpret his own demonstrations of structural patterns in the material he studies. This is indicative of his failure to develop strong theoretical supports – unlike Lévi-Strauss – for his own neo-structuralism. In the 'Legitimacy of Solomon' he asks: 'But what . . . is the merit of such a structural comparison? . . . I can offer no simple answer. To some extent the pleasure which can be derived from structural analysis is aesthetic. Just as a mathematician feels that an elegant solution is "better" than a clumsy solution to the same problem, so the merit of structuralism cannot be judged by such a practical criterion as: "Does this line of investigation lead to any useful result?" A demonstration of the "unconscious operation of the human mind" has merit in itself, even if some of us may feel uncertain as to just what kind of operating agent this human mind may be' [Leach (1969a), pp. 40–1].

47 This thesis is reaffirmed in 1971 in *HN*. see pp. 566 and 578ff.

48 See F. de Saussure (1959), p. 122ff and R. Barthes (1967), p. 58ff.

49 For examples see *RC*, pp. 253–4, 306; *HA*, pp. 127–8, 194; *OM*, pp. 11–13, 27–8, 124–5, 163–4.

50 Naturally there is no guarantee that the intuitions produced will be as fecund as those of a Lévi-Strauss.

51 The problem is *not* (as Pettit thinks – see his text of 1975, p. 88ff) that Lévi-Strauss's comparative procedures are not 'falsifiable'. The difficulties with them do not stem from the fact that they fail to measure up to an external epistemological standard for what is scientific – decreed by Popper or any other epistemologist. On the contrary they are bound up with the level of rigour contained in the set of concepts which 'support' them. It is important to point this out so that the right types of criticism are not made for the wrong reasons.

52 See D. Sperber (1968), pp. 67–9. This author is quite correct to say that Lévi-Strauss' concept of myth ' . . . a peu à voir, en effet, avec le modele structuraliste du langage' [op.cit., p. 69].

53 This *accounts for* the vagueness in the specification of 'mythological paradigms' to which we have just referred.

54 Pettit, op. cit., pp. 81–2.

55 See *HN*, pp. 590–6.

56 See 'Structuralism and Ecology', pp. 9–11, for a clear discussion.

57 See *HN*, p. 604 and *OM*, pp. 92–106.

58 This applies particularly of course to the idea (sketched above) that the versions of a myth can all be ordered into a kind of 'permutation group' governed by a 'formula' expressing the common law of their interrelation.

59 See *RC*, pp. 9–12; *HA*, p. 473; 'Structuralism and Ecology', p. 10.

60 See 'Structuralism and Ecology', p. 9ff.

61 K. Burridge (1967), pp. 92ff; D. Sperber (1975), p. 72; K. Ruthven (1976), p. 42.

62 *HA*, pp. 89–90.

63 E. Leach (1969), pp. 28ff.

64 See note 2 above.

65 Lévi-Strauss uses 'mythic thought' and 'the science of the concrete' almost interchangeably. Hereafter we shall refer to the latter.

66 Good examples are R. Horton (1970) and J. Willer (1971), Chapter 1.

67 M. Godelier (1971), p. 11.

68 L. Sebag (1964), Chapter 3; M. Godelier, art. cit., p. 9ff.

69 Godelier makes the link quite explicit. See art.cit., pp. 13, 19.

70 This is perfectly expressed in the following passage: 'Marxism, if not Marx himself, has too commonly reasoned as though practices followed directly from *praxis*. Without questioning the undoubted primacy of infrastructures, I believe that there is always a mediator between *praxis* and practices, namely the conceptual scheme by the operation of which matter and form, neither with any independent existence, are realised as structures, that is as entities both empirical and intelligible. It is to this theory of superstructures, scarcely touch on by Marx, that I hope to make a contribution' [*The Savage Mind*, p. 130].

71 For Althusser's general rejection of the classical notion of ideological

representation see his 'Ideology and Ideological State Apparatuses' in *Lenin and Philosophy* (1971).

72 See J. Goody (1973), p. 3ff, for example.

CONCLUSION

1 The whole of the 'finale' of *HN* for example is evidence of this constant anti-humanism. However, the discussion with Ricoeur in 'Confrontation over Myths' (1970) is also exemplary, as is the 'Overture' in *RC*.

2 See J. J. Katz (1972).

3 See J. J. Katz (1971a).

4 This is exemplified admirably in Pettit's discussion of semiology where he regards the content of a sentence and the state of mind of a speaker as more or less identical: 'The meaning of a speech act – the intention it exhibits – can be taken as the message which the sentence carries in a particular case. Also, correlatively, the meaning of the sentence is equivalent to the set of possible speech act intentions which it can be used to exhibit or express' [P. Pettit (1975), pp. 34–5].

5 See for example its utilisation by 'critical theory' in J. Habermas (1970) and by 'existential phenomenology' in J. B. O'Malley (1975).

6 The dominant one here is, of course, that inspired by Chomsky. See for example his (1966) and (1968).

7 B. Hindess (1977b).What follows relies heavily on Hindess's arguments in this paper.

8 The characteristics which for many social theorists, require it to be 'understood' by specific modes of interpretation or *'verstehen'*.

9 Again the example of Lévi-Strauss is instructive. His concept of unconscious structuring, as we noted in Part One, Section I, postulates both a natural physiological determinacy (the unconscious has its basis in the brain) *and* an ideal determinacy (a susceptibility to 'meanings') at the same time.

10 See Hindess, art. cit., and P. Q. Hirst (1976).

11 For Chomsky's own discussion of such extrapolations see N. Chomsky (1968), Part 3. Here the basis of his well-known rationalism is quite explicit.

12 See Lecourt's commentary in (1975), p. 32ff.

13 While certain of the concepts developed by Marx in his later works offer the elements of a theory of social relations denying the primacy of individual will, intersubjectivity and 'expressivism' (see Althusser and Balibar, op. cit., Parts II and III; B. Hindess and P. Q. Hirst [1975]) the Lacanian school in French psychoanalysis suggests that in parts of Freud's work we have a systematic critique of 'ego psychology' and phenomenological theories (see J. Laplanche and S. Leclaire [1972]).

14 M. Godelier (1972) and (1973).

15 See above, p. 83.

16 J. Friedman (1974) and (1975). Unfortunately these papers cannot be fully analysed here.

17 The idea that Marxism should be concerned with such a concept of 'the general mode of production' has been challenged strongly by Hindess and Hirst (1975), Introduction and Chapter Six.

18 Each of the authors – Dupré, Rey, Terray, Meillassoux, Godelier and Coquery-Vidrovitch – has a differing conception of the precise determination and interconnection between the elements of primitive modes of production.

19 Specifically by Althusser in 'Ideology and Ideological State Apparatuses' in Althusser (1971). See also P. Q. Hirst 'Althusser and the Theory of Ideology'.

Bibliography

Where dates are given in both square brackets and parentheses, the date in square brackets is that of the original, the one in parentheses that of the translation or later edition.

L. Abel, 'Sartre v. Lévi-Strauss', in N. and T. Hayes (eds) (1970).

D. F. Aberle, 'The Influence of Linguistics on Early Culture and Personality Theory, in R. Manners and D. Kaplan (eds) (1969).

L. Althusser, *For Marx* (London: Allen Lane, 1969).

L. Althusser, *Lenin and Philosophy* (London: New Left Books, 1971).

L. Althusser, *Politics and History* (London: New Left Books, 1972).

L. Althusser and E. Balibar, *Reading Capital* (London: New Left Books, 1970).

E. Ardener (ed.), *Social Anthropology and Language* (London: Tavistock, 1971).

J. M. Auzias, *Clefs pour le structuralisme* (Paris: Seghers, 1968).

C. R. Badcock, *Lévi-Strauss, Structuralism and Sociological Theory* (London: Hutchinson, 1976).

A. Badiou, *Le Concept de modèle* (Paris: Maspero, 1969).

G. Balandier, *Political Anthropology* (Harmondsworth: Penguin, 1972).

J. Banaji, 'The Crisis of British Anthropology', *New Left Review*, no. 64 (1970).

M. Banton (ed.), *The Relevance of Models for Social Anthropology* (London: Tavistock, 1965).

J. A. Barnes, *Three Styles in the Study of Kinship* (London: Tavistock, 1971).

R. Barthes, 'Sociologie et socio-logique', *Social Science Information*, vol. 1, no. 4 (1962).

R. Barthes, 'Les Sciences humaines et l'ouevre de Lévi-Strauss', *Annales*, no. 6 (1964).

R. Barthes, *Elements of Semiology* (London: Cape, 1967a).

R. Barthes [1967b], 'The Structuralist Activity', in F. and R. de George (eds) (1972).

R. Barthes, 'Historical Discourse', in M. Lane (ed.) (1970).

R. Barthes, *Mythologies* (London: Paladin, 1973).

R. Bastide (ed.), *Sens et usages du terme structure dans les sciences humaines* (The Hague: Mouton, 1962).

Z. Bauman, *Culture as Praxis* (London: Routledge, 1973).

T. Beidelman (ed.), *The Translation of Culture* (London: Tavistock, 1971).

J-M. Benoist, 'The Art of the Fugue', in *The Human Context*, vol. 5, no. 1 (1973).

E. Benveniste, *Problèmes de linguistique générale* (Paris: Gallimard, 1939).

H. J. Bershady, *Ideology and Social Knowledge* (Oxford: Blackwell, 1973).

L. Von Bertalanffy, *General System Theory* (Harmondsworth: Penguin, 1968).

R. Blackburn (ed.), *Ideology in Social Science* (London: Pan, 1972).

M. Bloch (ed.), *Marxist Analyses and Social Anthropology* (London: Malady, 1975).

M. Bloch, Review of *Anthropologie Structurale Deux, Man*, vol. 10, no. 2 (1975).

M. Bloch, Review of D. Sperber, *Rethinking Symbolism, Man*, vol. 11, no. 1 (1976).

P. Bohannan, *Social Anthropology* (London: Holt, Rinehart & Winston, 1969).

P. Bonte, 'From Ethnology to Anthropology', *Critique of Anthropology*, nos. 2 and 3 (1976).

R. Boudon, *The Uses of Structuralism* (London: Heinemann, 1970).

I. Buchler and H. Selby (eds), *Kinship and Social Organisation* (London: MacMillan, 1968).

O. Burgelin, 'Structural Analysis and Mass Communication', in D. McQuail (ed.) (1972).

K. Burridge, 'Lévi-Strauss and Myth', in E. R. Leach (ed.) (1967).

G. Canguilhem, 'The Role of Analogies and Metaphors in Biological Discovery', in A. C. Crombie (1963).

R. Carnap, *Meaning and Necessity* (Chicago: University Press, 1947).

R. Carnap, 'Methodological Character of Theoretical Concepts', *Minnesota Studies in the Philosophy of Science*, vol. 1 (1956).

E. Cassirer, *The Logic of the Humanities* (London: Yale University Press, 1966).

G. Charbonnier, *Conversations with Claude Lévi-Strauss* (London: Cape, 1969).

N. Chomsky, *Cartesian Linguistics* (London, Harper & Row, 1966).

N. Chomsky, *Language and Mind* (New York, Harcourt Brace, 1968).

M. Cohen, 'Quelques notations historiques et critiques autour de strucuralisme en linguistique', *La Pensée* no. 135 (1967).

P. Cohen, 'Theories of Myth', *Man* no. 4 (1969).

A. C. Crombie, *Scientific Change* (London: Heinemann, 1963).

J. Cuisenier, 'Formes de la parenté et formes de la pensée', *Esprit*, no. 322 (1963).

J. Culler, *Structuralist Poetics* (London: Routledge, 1975)

A. Cutler, 'Letter to Balibar' and 'Response', *Theoretical Practice*, no. 7/8 (1972).

J. Derrida, 'Structure, Sign and Play', in R. Macksey and E. Donato (eds) (1970).

M. Douglas, (1963) 'The Meaning of Myth', in E. R. Leach (ed.) (1967).

M. Douglas, *Natural Symbols* (Harmondsworth: Penguin, 1967).

J. Dubois, 'Structuralisme en linguistique', *La Pensée*, no. 135 (1967).

O. Ducrot (ed.), *Qu'est-ce que le structuralisme?* (Paris: Du Seuil, 1968).

L. Dumont, 'Descent or Intermarriage?', *South Western Journal of Anthropology*, vol. 22 (1966).

L. Dumont, *Homo Hierarchicus* (London: Paladin, 1972).

E. Durkheim, 'La Prohibition de l'inceste et ses origines', *Annee Sociologique*, I (1896).

E. Durkheim, *The Elementary Forms of the Religious Life* (London Allen & Unwin, 1915).

E. Durkheim, *The Division of Labour in Society* (Chicago: Free Press, 1933).

E. Durkheim, *The Rules of Sociological Method* (Chicago: Free Press, 1938).

E. Durkheim, *Sociology and Philosophy* (Glencoe: Free Press, 1974).

E. Durkheim and M. Mauss, *Primitive Classification* (London: Cohen & West, 1963).

U. Eco, 'Social Life as a Sign System', in D. Robey (ed.) (1972).

J. Ehrmann, 'Structures of Exchange in Cinna' in M. Lane (970).

P. Ekeh, *Social Exchange Theory* (London: Heinemann, 1974).

E. E. Evans-Pritchard, *Social Anthropology* (London: Cohen & West, 1951).

E. E. Evans-Pritchard, *Nuer Religion* (London: Oxford University Press, 1956).

A. Fabian, 'On Professional Ethics and Epistemological Foundations', *Current Anthropology*, no. 12 (1971).

L. C. Faron, Review of *L'Origine des manières de table*', *Man*, no. 4 (1969).

S. Feuchtwang, 'Investigating Religion', in M. Bloch (ed.) (1975).

M. Fichant, 'The Idea of a History of the Sciences', *Theoretical Practice*, no. 3/4 (1971).

R. Firth, *Elements of Social Organisation* (London: Watts, 1951).

R. Firth, *We, The Tikopia* (London: Allen & Unwin, 1957).

R. Firth, *Primitive Polynesian Economy* (London: Routledge, 1966).

R. Firth, *Symbols: Public and Private* (London: Allen & Unwin, 1973).

R. Firth, *Themes in Economic Anthropology* (London: Tavistock, 1967).

M. Foucault, *The Order of Things* (New York: Random House, 1970).

M. Foucault, *The Archaeology of Knowledge* (London: Tavistock, 1972).

R. Fox, *Kinship and Marriage* (Harmondsworth: Penguin, 1967).

J. G. Frazer, *Folklore in the Old Testament*, vol. II (London: Macmillan, 1919).

J. G. Frazer, *Totemism and Exogamy* (London: Macmillan, 1923).

J. G. Frazer, *The Golden Bough*, abridged edn, (London: Macmillan, 1947).

S. Freud, *On Dreams* (London: Hogarth Press, 1952).

S. Freud, *Totem and Taboo* (London: Hogarth Press, 1950).

J. Friedman, 'Marxism, Structuralism and Vulgar Materialism', *Man*, no. 9 (1974).

J. Friedman, 'Tribes, States and Transformations', in M. Bloch (ed.) (1975).

E. C. Fudge (ed.), *Phonology* (Harmondsworth: Penguin, 1973).

M. Gaboriau, 'Structural Anthropology and History', in M. Lane (ed.) (1970).

H. Gardner, *The Quest for Mind* (London: Coventure Press, 1972).

H. Gardner, 'Structure and Development', *The Human Context*, vol. V., no. 1 (1973).

C. Geertz, *The Interpretation of Culture* (New York: Basic Books, 1973).

R. and F. de George, (eds), *The Structuralists from Marx to Lévi-Strauss* (New York: Anchor, 1972).

F. C. Gimeno, 'The Structuralist Approach in Psychiatry', *The Human Context*, vol. V, no. 1 (1973).

A. Glucksmann, 'A Ventriloquial Structuralism', *New Left Review*, no. 72 (1972).

M. Glucksmann, *Structuralist Analysis in Contemporary Social Thought* (London: Routledge, 1973).

D. Goddard, 'Conceptions of Structure in Lévi-Strauss and in British Anthropology', *Social Research*, 32, no. 4 (1965).

D. Goddard, 'Anthropology: The Limits of Functionalism', in R. Blackburn (ed.) (1972).

M. Godelier, 'Myth and History', *New Left Review*, no. 69 (1971).

M. Godelier, (1972a), 'System, Structure and Contradiction in "Capital"', in R. Blackburn (ed.) (1972).

M. Godelier, *Rationality and Irrationality in Economics* (London: New Left Books, 1972b).

M. Godelier, *Horizon, trajets marxistes en anthropologie* (Paris: Maspero, 1973).

M. Godelier, 'On the Definition of a Social Formation', *Critique of Anthropology*, no. 1 (1974).

J. Goody, 'Evolution and Communication – the Domestication of the Savage Mind', *British Journal of Sociology*, vol. 24 (1973).

A. J. Greimas, *Structural Semantics* (Paris: Larousse, 1966a).

A. J. Greimas, 'Structure et histoire', *Les Temps Modernes*, no. 246 (1966b).

A. J. Greimas, 'Comparative Mythology', in P. Maranda (ed.) (1972).

P. Guiraud, *Semiology* (London: Routledge, 1975).

G. Gurvitch, *The Social Frameworks of Knowledge* (Oxford: Blackwell, 1971).

G. Gurvitch and W. E. Moore (eds), *Twentieth Century Sociology* (New York: Philosophical Library, 1952).

J. Habermas, 'Towards a Theory of Communicative Competence', *Recent Sociology*, no. 2 (1970).

M. Harris, *The Rise of Anthropological Theory* (New York: Crowell, 1968).

N. Harris, *Beliefs in Society: the Problem of Ideology* (Harmondsworth: Penguin, 1971).

E. and T. Hayes (eds), *Claude Lévi-Strauss: The Anthropologist as Hero* (Cambridge, Mass.: MIT Press, 1970).

G. W. F. Hegel, *The Philosophy of History* (London: Dover, 1972).

B. Hindess, 'Materialist Mathematics', *Theoretical Practice*, no. 3/4 (1971).

B. Hindess, *The Use of Official Statistics in Sociology* (London: Macmillan, 1973).

B. Hindess, 'Models and Masks', *Economy and Society*, vol. 2, no. 2 (1974).

B. Hindess, *Philosophy and Methodology in the Social Sciences* (Brighton: Harvester Press, 1977a).

B. Hindess, 'Humanism and Teleology in Sociological Theory' in B. Hindess (ed.) (1977b).

B. Hindess (ed.), *Sociological Theories of the Economy* (London: Macmillan, 1977c).

B. Hindess and P. Q. Hirst *Pre-Capitalist Modes of Production* (London: Routledge, 1975).

B. Hindess and S. Savage, 'Parsons and the Three Systems of Action', in H. Martins (ed.) (1977).

P. Q. Hirst, *Durkheim, Bernard and Epistemology* (London: Routledge, 1975).

P. Q. Hirst, Review of M. Sahlins, *Stone Age Economics. Journal of Peasant Studies*, vol. 2, no. 2 (1976).

P. Q. Hirst, *Social Evolution and Sociological Categories* (London: Macmillan, 1976).

P. Q. Hirst, 'Althusser and the Theory of Ideology', *Economy and Society*, no. 5 (1976).

L. Hjelmslev, *Prolegomena to a Theory of Language* (New York: Madison, 1961).

G. C. Homans, and R. Schneider, *Marriage, Authority and Final Causes* (London: Routledge, 1955).

R. Horton, 'Traditional African Thought and Western Science' in B. Wilson (ed.) (1970).

H. Hubert and M. Mauss, *Sacrifice* (London: Cohen & West, 1964).

H. Hubert and M. Mauss, *A General Theory of Magic* (London: Cohen & West, 1966).

H. S. Hughes, *The Obstructed Path* (New York: Harper & Row, 1968).

D. Hymes, 'Directions in Ethno-Linguistic Theory', *American Anthropologist*, no. 66 (1964).

W. Isajiw, *Causation and Functionalism in Sociology* (London: Routledge, 1968).

R. Jakobson, *Selected Writings*, vol. 1 (The Hague: Mouton, 1962).

R. Jakobson, *Selected Writings*, vol. 2 (The Hague: Mouton, 1967).

R. Jakobson, *Main Trends in the Science of Language* (London: Macmillan, 1973).

R. Jakobson and M. Halle, *Fundamentals of Language* (The Hague: Mouton, 1956).

H. Jalley-Crampe, 'La Notion de structure mentale dans les travaux de Lévi-Strauss', *La Pensée*, no. 135 (1967).

I. C. Jarvie, 'Reply to Fabian', *Current Anthropology*, no. 12 (1971). J. J. Katz (1971a), 'The Philosophical Relevance of Linguistic Theory', in J. R. Searle (ed.) (1971).

J. J. Katz, *Linguistic Philosophy* (London: Allen & Unwin, 1971b).

J. J. Katz, *Semantic Theory* (New York: Harper & Row, 1972).

G. Kirk, *Myth: Its Meaning and Functions* (London: Cambridge University Press, 1970).

G. Kirk, *The Nature of Greek Myths* (Harmondsworth: Penguin, 1974).

F. Korn, 'An Analysis of the Use of the term "Model" in some of Lévi-Strauss's works', *Bijdragen*, no. 125 (1969).

F. Korn, *Elementary Structures Reconsidered* (London: Tavistock, 1973).

L. Krader, 'Beyond Structuralism: The Dialectics of the Diachronic and Synchronic Methods in the Human Sciences', in I. Rossi (ed.) (1974).

J. Kristeva, 'The Semiotic Activity', *Screen*, vol. 4 1/2 (1973).

T. S. Kuhn, *The Structure of Scientific Revolutions* (Chicago: University Press, 1962).

J. Lacan, 'The Mirror Phase', *New Left Review*, no. 51 (1968).

J. Lacan, 'The Insistence of the Letter in the Unconscious', in R. and F. de George (eds) (1972).

M. Lane, *Structuralism: A Reader* (London: Cape, 1970).

J. Laplanche and S. Leclaire, 'The Unconscious: A Psychoanalytic Study', *Yale French Studies*, no. 48 (1972).

E. R. Leach, *Political Systems of Higland Burma* (London: London School of Economics, 1954).

E. R. Leach, *Rethinking Anthropology* (London: Athlone, 1961a).

E. R. Leach, 'Lévi-Strauss in the Garden of Eden', *Trans. N.Y. Acad. Sci.*, no. 23 (1961b).

E. R. Leach, 'Telstar et les aborigènes ou la pensée sauvage', *Annales*, no. 6 (1964a).

E. R. Leach (1964b), 'Anthropological Aspects of Language' in P. Maranda (ed.) (1972).

E. R. Leach, Review of *Le Cru et le cuit*, *American Anthropologist*, vol. 67 (1965a).

E. R. Leach, 'Claude Lévi-Strauss: Anthropologist and Philosopher', *New Left Review*, no. 34 (1965b).

E. R. Leach (ed.), *The Structural Study of Myth and Totemism* (London: Tavistock, 1967).

E. R. Leach, *Genesis as Myth and Other Essays* (London: Cape, 1969a).

E. R. Leach, ' "Kachin" and "Haka-Chin": a Rejoinder to Lévi-Strauss', *Man*, no. 4 (1969b).

E. R. Leach, *Lévi-Strauss* (London: Fontana, 1970).

E. R. Leach, *Aspects of Caste in India, Ceylon and N.W. Pakistan* (Cambridge: University Press, 1971).

E. R. Leach, *Culture and Communication* (London: Cambridge University Press, 1976).

D. Lecourt, *Marxism and Epistemology* (London: New Left Books, 1973).

C. Lévi-Strauss, 'Social and Psychological aspects of Chieftainship', *Trans. N.Y. Acad. Sci.* (October 1944).

C. Lévi-Strauss [1946], 'French Sociology' in Gurvitch and Moore (eds) (1952).

C. Lévi-Strauss, *La Vie familiale et social des indiens Nambikwara* (Paris: Société des Americanistes, 1948).

C. Lévi-Strauss, *Les Structures elementaires de la parenté* (Paris: P.U.F., 1949).

C. Lévi-Strauss, 'Introduction à l'oeuvre de M. Mauss', in M. Mauss (1950).

C. Lévi-Strauss, 'Contribution to Conference on Anthropology and Linguistics' (Bloomington: Indiana University, 1952a).

C. Lévi-Strauss [1952b], *Race and History* (Paris, UNESCO: 1958).

C. Lévi-Strauss, 'The Mathematics of Man', *International Social Science Bulletin* (1955a).

C. Lévi-Strauss, 'Diogène couché', *Les Temps Modernes*, vol. 6, no. 10 (1955b).

C. Lévi-Strauss [1956a], 'The Family' in H. L. Shapiro, (ed.) (1956).

C. Lévi-Strauss [1956b], 'The Sex of the Heavenly Bodies', in M. Lane, (ed.) (1970).

C. Lévi-Strauss, *Anthropologie structurale* (Paris: Plon, 1958).

C. Lévi-Strauss [1960a], *The Scope of Anthropology* (London: Cape, 1967).

C. Lévi-Strauss [1960b], 'Four Winnebago Myths: A Structural Sketch', in R. and F. de George (eds) (1972).

C. Lévi-Strauss [1960c], 'The Story of Asdiwal' in E. R. Leach (ed.) (1967).

C. Lévi-Strauss, 'On Manipulated Sociological Models', *Bijdragen*, no. 116 (1960d).

C. Lévi-Strauss, 'Le Structure et la forme', *Cahiers de l'Institute de Science Économique Appliqué*, 99, no. 7 (1960e).

C. Lévi-Strauss [1961], *Conversations with Lévi-Strauss* (with G. Charbonnier) (London: Cape, 1969).

C. Lévi-Strauss, 'Rousseau: The Father of Anthropology', *UNESCO Courier*, no. 16 (1962a).

C. Lévi-Strauss [1962b], *Totemism* (Harmondsworth: Penguin, 1964).

C. Lévi-Strauss [1962c], *The Savage Mind* (London: Weidenfield & Nicholson, 1966).

C. Lévi-Strauss, 'The Bear and the Barber', *Journal of the Royal Anthropological Institute*, no. 93 (1962d).

C. Lévi-Strauss [1962e], 'Les Limites de la notion de structure en ethnologie', in R. Bastide (ed.) (1962).

C. Lévi-Strauss [1963], 'Confrontation over Myths', *New Left Review*, no. 62 (1970).

C. Lévi-Strauss [1964a], 'Criteria of Science in the Social and Human Disciplines', *International Social Science Journal*, vol. XVI (1964).

C. Lévi-Strauss [1964b], *Mythologiques I: The Raw and the Cooked* (London: Cape, 1969).

C. Lévi-Strauss, 'The Future of Kinship Studies', *Proceedings of the Royal Anthropological Institute* (1965).

C. Lévi-Strauss [1966a], *Mythologiques II: From Honey to Ashes* (London: Cape, 1973).

C. Lévi-Strauss [1966b], 'The Culinary Triangle', *New Society*, no. 22 (1966).

C. Lévi-Strauss, *Mythologiques III: L'Origine des manières de table* (Paris: Plon, 1968a).

C. Lévi-Strauss, *Structural Anthropology* (London: Allen Lane, 1968b).

C. Lévi-Strauss, *The Elementary Structures of Kinship* (London: Eyre & Spottiswoode, 1969).

C. Lévi-Strauss, *Mythologiques IV: L'Homme nu* (Paris: Plon, 1971a).

C. Lévi-Strauss [1971b], 'Rapports de symétrie entre rites et mythes de peuples voisins', in T. Beidelman (ed.) (1971).

C. Lévi-Strauss, 'Structuralism and Ecology', *Social Science Information* (1972).

C. Lévi-Strauss, *Anthropologie structurale deux* (Paris: Plon, 1973).

J. R. Llobera, 'Some Provisional Theses on the Nature of Anthropology', *Critique of Anthropology*, no. 1 (1974).

F. G. Lounsbury, Review of R. Needham *Structure and Sentiment*, *American Anthropologist*, vol. 64 (1962).

S. Lukes, *Emile Durkheim* (London: Allen Lane, 1973).

J. F. Lyotard, 'Les Indiens ne cueillent pas les fleurs'., *Annales*, vol. 20, no. 1 (1965).

R. Macksey and E. Donato (eds), *The Languages of Criticism and the Sciences of Man* (Baltimore: John Hopkins, 1970).

J. J. Macquet, 'Isomorphism and Symbolism', in I. Rossi (ed.) (1974).

B. Malinowski, *A Scientific Theory of Culture and other Essays* (Chapel Hill: North Carolina University Press, 1944).

B. Malinowski, *Magic, Science and Religion and Other Essays* (Glencoe: Free Press, 1948).

B. Malmberg, *Structural Linguistics and Human Communication* (Berlin: Springer-Verlag, 1963).

B. Malmberg, *New Trends in Linguistics* (Stockholm: Lund University Press, 1964).

R. Manners and D. Kaplan (eds), *Theory in Anthropology* (Chicago: Aldine Press, 1969).

P. Maranda (ed.), *Mythology* (Harmondsworth: Penguin, 1972).

A. Martinet, *Economie des changements phonétiques* (Berne: A. Francke, 1955).

A. Martinet, *Elements of General Linguistics* (London: Faber & Faber, 1964).

H. Martins (ed.), *Structural Functionalism: A Reappraisal* (London: Macmillan, 1977).

M. Mauss, *Sociologie et anthropologie* (Paris: P.U.F., 1950).

M. Mauss, *The Gift* (London: Cohen & West, 1967).

M. Mauss, *A General Theory of Magic* (London: Routledge 1972).

M. Mauss and H. Hubert, *Sacrifice: Its Nature and Function* (London: Cohen & West, 1964).

D. Maybury-Lewis, 'The Analysis of Dual Organisations', *Bijdragen*, no. 116 (1960).

D. Maybury-Lewis, 'Science by Association', in N. and T. Hayes (eds) (1970).

D. Maybury-Lewis, 'Review of *Du miel aux cendres*', *American Anthropologist*, no. 71 (1969).

D. McQuail (ed.) *Sociology of Mass Communications* (Harmondsworth: Penguin, 1972).

C. Meillassoux, *Anthropologie economique des Gouro de Côte d'Ivoire* (Paris: Mouton, 1964).

C. Meillassoux, 'From Reproduction to Production', *Economy and Society*, vol. 1, no. 1 (1972).

J. Mepham, 'The Structuralist Sciences and Philosophy', in D. Robey (ed.) (1972).

M. Merleu-Ponty, *Signs* (Evanston: Northwestern University Press, 1964).

G. Mounin, 'Lévi-Strauss's use of linguistics', in I. Rossi (ed.) (1974).

S. F. Nadel, *The Theory of Social Structure* (Glencoe: Free Press, 1957).

E. Nagel, *The Structure of Science* (London: Routledge, 1961).

R. Needham, *Structure and Sentiment* (Chicago: University Press, 1962).

R. Needham, Review of *The Savage Mind*, *Man*, vol. II, no. 2 (1967).

R. Needham (ed.), *Rethinking Kinship and Marriage* (London: Tavistock, 1971a).

R. Needham (ed.) [1971b], 'Remarks on the Analysis of Kinship and Marriage' in R. Needham (1971a).

R. Needham (ed.), *Belief, Language and Experience* (Oxford: Blackwell, 1972).

H. G. Nutini [1970a], 'Some Considerations on the Nature of Social Structure and Model Building', in N. and T. Hayes (eds) (1970).

H. G. Nutini [1970b], 'Lévi-Strauss's Conception of Science', in J. Pouillon and P. Maranda (1970).

J. B. O'Malley, *Sociology of Meaning* (London: Human Context Books, 1972).

T. Parsons *et al.*, *Theories of Society* (Glencoe: Free Press, 1961).

T. Parsons, *Sociological Theory and Modern Society* (Glencoe: Free Press, 1967).

C. S. Peirce, *Philosophical Writings* (New York: Dover, 1955).

P. Pettit, *The Concept of Structuralism: A Critical Analysis* (Dublin: Gill & Macmillan, 1975).

J. Piaget, *Structuralism* (London: Routledge, 1971).

J. C. Piguet, 'Peut-on acclimatiser *La Pensée sauvage?*' *Annales*, vol. 20 (1965).

J. Pouillon and P. Maranda, *Échanges et communications*, 2 vols (Paris: du Seuil, 1970).

A. R. Radcliffe-Brown, *The Social Organisation of Australian Tribes* (London: Macmillan, 1931).

A. R. Radcliffe-Brown, *Structure and Function in Primitive Society* (London: Cohen & West, 1952).

A. R. Radcliffe-Brown, *Method in Social Anthropology* (Chicago: University Press, 1958).

P. Ricoeur, 'Structure et hermeneutique', *Esprit*, no. 322 (1963).

P. Ricoeur, 'Le Structure, le mot, l'évènement', *Esprit*, no. 350 (1967).

P. Ricoeur, *Freud and Philosophy* (Yale: University Press, 1970).

D. Robey (ed.), *Structuralism: An Introduction* (Oxford: Clarendon Press, 1973).

L. Rosen, 'Language, History and the Logic of Inquiry in the works of Lévi-Strauss and Sartre', in I. Rossi (ed.) (1974).

I. Rossi, 'The Unconscious in Lévi-Strauss Anthropology', *American Anthropologist*, no. 75 (1973).

I. Rossi (ed.), *The Unconscious in Culture* (New York: Dutton, 1974).

K. Ruthven, *Myth* (London: Methuen, 1976).

M. Sahlins, *Stone Age Economics* (London: Tavistock, 1974).

M. Sahlins, 'On the Delphic Writings of Lévi-Strauss', *Scientific American*, no. 214 (1966).

F. de Saussure, *Course in General Linguistics* (Glasgow: Collins, 1974).

A. Schaff, *Introduction to Semantics* (London: Pergamon, 1962).

D. Schneider, 'Some Muddles in the Models', in M. Banton (ed.) (1965).

D. Schneider and L. Bonjean, *The Idea of Culture in the Social Sciences* (Cambridge: University Press, 1974).

B. Scholte, 'Epistemic Paradigms . . .', *American Anthropologist*, vol. 68 (1966a).

B. Scholte, Review of L. Sebag, *Marxisme et structuralisme, American Anthropologist*, vol. 68 (1966b).

B. Scholte, 'Lévi-Strauss's Unfinished Symphony: The Analysis of Myth', in E. and T. Hayes (eds) (1970).

B. Scholte, 'The Structural Anthropology of C. Lévi-Strauss', in B. Scholte and J. Honigmann (eds) (1973).

B. Scholte and J. Honigmann, *Handbook of Social and Cultural Anthropology* (Chicago: Rand and McNally, 1973).

J. R. Searle, *The Philosophy of Language* (London: Oxford University Press, 1971).

L. Sebag, *Marxisme et structuralisme* (Paris: Payot, 1964).

D. M. Segal [1969], 'The Connection between the Semantics and the Formal Structure of a Text', in P. Maranda (ed.) (1972).

H. L. Shapiro (ed.), *Man, Culture and Society* (London: Oxford University Press, 1956).

Y. Simonis, *C. Lévi-Strauss ou la passion de l'inceste* (Paris: Aubier Montaigne, 1968).

D. Sperber, *Le Structuralisme en anthropologie* (Paris: du Seuil, 1968).

D. Sperber, 'Postface' to D. Sperber (1968) (Paris: du Seuil, 1972).

D. Sperber, *Rethinking Symbolism* (London: Cambridge University Press, 1976).

J. Suret-Canale, 'Structuralisme et anthropologie economique', *La Pensée*, no. 135 (1967).

E. Terray, *Marxism and Primitive Societies* (London: *Monthly Review*, 1972).

N. S. Trubetzkoy, *Principles of Phonology* (Berkeley and Los Angeles: University of California Press, 1960).

I. Vallier (ed.), *Comparative Methods in Sociology* (Berkeley: University of California Press, 1971).

V. Volosinov, *Marxism and the Philosophy of Language* (New York: Seminar Press, 1973).

A. Wilden, *System and Structure* (London: Tavistock, 1968).

J. Willer, *The Social Determination of Knowledge* (New Jersey: Prentice-Hall, 1971).

D. and J. Willer, *Systematic Empiricism: Critique of a Pseudoscience* (New Jersey: Prentice-Hall, 1973).

K. Williams, 'Unproblematic Archaeology', *Economy and Society*, vol. 3, no. 1 (1974).

B. Wilson (ed.), *Rationality* (Oxford: Blackwell, 1970).

P. Worsley, 'Groote Eylandt Totemism and "Le Totemisme aujourd'hui"', in E. R. Leach (ed.) (1967).

N. Yalman, Review of *The Savage Mind*, *American Anthropologist*, vol. 66 (1964).

N. Yalman, 'The Raw: The Cooked:: Nature: Culture', in E. R. Leach (ed.) (1967).

Index

Page references to Lévi-Strauss are limited to citation of main themes and of books and articles when mentioned by name in the text.

Abel, L., 168
Althusser, L., 5, 33, 54, 112, 153, 163, 165, 167–8, 172, 174
Analogy, 95, 98, 150–2
Anthropology, object of, 8ff, 39, 156ff
  neo-Marxist, 83, 86–8, 166
  'symbolic', 94–6

Bachelard, G., 160
Badcock, C. R., 163, 168, 170
Badiou, A., 25, 35, 165
Balibar, E., 54, 163, 165, 167–8
Barnes, J. A., 80, 82, 168
Barthes, R., 19, 22, 164–5, 172
Benoiste, J-M., 164
Benveniste, E., 163
Bergson, H., 113, 164
Bertalanffy, L. Von, 163
Biology, 170
Boas, F., 97, 122
Bonté, P., 166
Boudon, R., 75, 166
Bricolage, 149
Buchler, H., 45, 166, 168
Burridge, K., 172

Carnap, R., 25, 33, 34, 165
Caste, compared with totemism, 104–6, 114–16
Causality, see Contingency, Expressivism
  in production of myth, 143
Chomsky, N., 160, 165, 173
Codes, see Myth
Cohen, P., 169
Collective consciousness, 147, 164

Collective representations, 9ff, 94, 136, 148, 156–7
Colletti, L., 168
Communication, 4, 44, 50
Comte, A., 169
Consciousness, 151, 158–9
Contingency, 54, 79, 91, 93, 101
Coquery-Vidrovitch, C., 174
Correspondence rules, 33, 34
Critical theory, 173
Cross-cousin marriage, see Kinship
Culler, J., 163
Culture, 9ff, 46, 88, 166
  and nature, 46, 49–50, 79, 99, 152–7
Cybernetics, 4, 9

Derrida, J., 163, 166
Diachrony, 85, 90–3, 101, 114
Diamond, S., 166
Diffusionism, 89
Distinctive features, in Language, 18
Douglas, M., 121, 122, 170
Dual Organisation, see Kinship
Dumont, L., 170
Dupré, P., 174
Durbin, M., 164
Durkheim, E., 9, 40, 84–5, 87, 94, 97, 164, 168–9

Eco, U., 4, 22, 163, 165
Ekeh, P., 168
Elementary structures, see Kinship
Epistemology, 6, 31, 172
  empiricist, 25, 33–7, 112, 153, 166
  of models in Lévi-Strauss, 8, 21ff

Epistemology, (*contd.*)
of models in neo-positivism, 33ff
Evans-Pritchard, E. E., 97–8, 112, 169
Evolutionism, 89, 148, 167
Exchange, 43ff, 48–53, 76ff
social exchange theory, 84
Exogamy, *see* Kinship
Expressive causality, expressivism, 21, 54, 78, 80, 167, 173

Falsifiability, 172
Firth, R., 97, 168, 169
Fortes, M.,97
Foucault, M., 5, 163, 169
Fox, R., 45, 57
Frazer, J. G., 43, 57
Freud, S., 2, 7, 14, 97, 164, 169
Friedman, J., 83, 86, 88, 161, 168, 173
Fugue, 140

Gaboriau, M., 90–2, 168
Gardner, H., 77, 167
Geertz, C., 168
Glucksmann, M., 163–4
Goddard, D., 166
Godelier, M., 36, 83, 86–8, 92, 151–2, 161, 166, 168, 172–4
Goody, J., 173
Gramsci, A., 168
Guiaud, P., 163
Gurvitch, G., 168

Habermas, J., 173
Halle, M., 169
Harris, M., 2, 163
Hegel, G. W. F., 90
Hindess, B., 25, 33, 163, 166, 168, 173
Hirst, P. Q., 164, 173, 174
Historicism, 90, 168
History, 54, 88–93, 168
philosophy of, 89–90
History of ideas, 1
Hjelmslev, L., 5
Horton, R., 172
Hughes, H. S., 2, 163
Humanism, 90, 157, 168, 170
Hymes, D., 164

Ideology, 94ff, 111, 122, 151

mode of representation in, 122, 144, 151–4, 162, 172–3
myth as, 122, 144
primitive, 148ff
Incest, prohibition of, *see* Kinship
Infant thought, 51–2
Information theory, 4, 10
Intentionality, 158
Isaacs, S., 17, 51, 52, 77

Jakobson, R., 17ff, 163–5, 169

Kant, I., 2
Katz, J. J., 158, 173
Kinship,
alliance as exchange, 44ff
Aranda system, 61, 64, 82, 167
'atom', 167
Australian class systems, 58ff
bride-purchase, 69
Chinese, Indian systems, 67ff
cross-cousin marriage, 48–9, 54ff
matrilateral and patrilateral, 69ff
descent and, 45, 58ff, 65ff
dual organisation, 48–9, 53ff, 167
elementary structures, 45, 53, 80
exogamy, 48–9, 53ff
generalised or directional exchange, 45ff, 58ff
Gilyak system, 67, 69
in 'primitive' societies, 39ff, 83ff
integration and solidarity of, 66ff, 83ff
inter-class structures, 63, 64
Kachin system, 67, 69
Kariera system, 60, 61, 63–4, 82, 167
Murngin system, 40, 63–4, 167
prohibition of incest, 48–9, 53ff
régime, harmonic and disharmonic, 45–9, 65–6
residence and, 45, 58ff, 65ff, 81–2
restricted or reciprocal exchange, 45ff, 58ff
social function, 66ff, 83ff
Kirk, G. S., 122, 170
Korn, F., 75, 82, 165–7
Krader, L., 166, 168
Kristeva, J., 163

Kroeber, L., 97

Lacan, J., 169
Language, 9ff, 48, 102, 118, 133ff, 157ff
 action and, 158ff, 173
 binarism in, 17ff
Laplanche, J., 169, 173
Lawrence, W. E., 58
Leach, E. R., 2, 75, 76, 80, 146, 163, 166–7, 170, 171
Leclaire, S., 169, 173
Lecourt, D., 166, 173
Lévi-Strauss, C.,
 'Confrontation over myths', 173
 Elementary Structures of Kinship, The, 44ff
 epistemology in, *see* Epistemology of Models
 'Four Winnebago Myths', 120
 From Honey to Ashes, 128, 132, 135, 171–2
 'influences', 2, 40
 linguistics and, 17ff
 L'Homme Nu, 97, 137, 139, 140, 171–2, 173
 Linguistics, use of, 17ff
 L'Origine de manières de table, 171–2
 Methodological protocols, 4ff
 Mythologiques, 123ff
 Race and History, 90
 Society and primitive society, concepts of, 41ff
 Structural Anthropology, 90
 'Structuralism and Ecology', 16, 172
 Theory of Kinship, 44ff
 Theory of myth, 116ff
 Theory of Totemism, 97ff
 The Raw and the Cooked, 127–33, 138, 142, 146, 121–2
 The Savage Mind, 90, 95, 101, 148, 169, 171
 The Scope of Anthropology, 91
 'The Story of Asdiwal', 120–1, 141
 'The Structural Study of myth', 118ff
 Totemism, 82, 97

Tristes Tropiques, 2
Linguistics, 4, 7, 9ff, 31
 meaning in, 158, 173
 phonology, 17–21, 26, 136–7
 Saussurian, 157
Literary criticism, 1
Llobera, J. R., 166
Locke, J., 4
Lowie, R., 2, 97

Macquet, J. J., 169
Malinowski, B., 43, 94, 97, 169
Malmberg, B., 19, 164
Martinet, A., 19, 164
Marx, K., 2, 7, 152, 172, 173
Marxism, 83, 86–8, 161–2, 168, 172, 173
Mathematics, 4
Mauss, M., 2, 9, 40, 43, 48, 75–6, 94, 166
Maybury-Lewis, D., 166
Meillassoux, C., 174
Memory, 'collective', 147
Metaphor, 98, 100–1, 112, 149–53, 169
Methodology, analysis of, 5, 9
 in Lévi-Strauss, 4ff, 156
Metonymy, 100–1, 112, 149–53, 169
Mind, in Lévi-Strauss's theory, *see* Unconscious
Mode of production, 161–2, 173, 174
Models, *see* Epistemology
Morgenstern, D., 25
Mounin, G., 164
Myth, 91, 116ff
 armature, 130, 134–5, 146
 codes or schemata, 121, 125, 130, 134ff, 146
 gross constituent units/mythemes, 27, 118–20
 internal analysis of, 118ff, 125ff
 language and, 133ff
 meaning in, 118–19, 121–2, 133–4
 messages in, 118–22, 125, 130, 134–5, 139–40, 146, 154
 mythic 'speech' and 'language', 137–8, 142
 mythology as 'web', 123ff
 'reality' and, 122, 144, 151

Myth, (*contd.*)
  ritual and, 124–5
  sets of myths, 118–21, 127ff
  structural law of, 119–20
  syntagms and paradigms, 133ff, 172
  transformation, 117, 119ff, 171
  transmission, reception and effects, 141ff
  versions of, 118–21

Nadel, S. F., 166
Nagel, E., 2
Needham, R., 75, 80, 166, 167
Neumann O, Von, 4
Normative order, 5
Northrop, F. C., 33
Novel, 140
Nutini, H. G., 32, 35, 165–6

Observation,
  and epistemology, 30, 34, 37, 93, 153
  in ideological representation, 152–3
O'Malley, J. B., 173
Oral tradition, 142
'Order of orders', 42

Parsons, T., 163, 168
Pettit, P., 138, 163, 170, 172
Phenomenology, 169, 173
Philosophy of history, 89–90
Piaget, J., 17, 51
Pierce, C. S., 4
Popper, K. R., 172
Positivism, 32ff
Praxis, 172
Primitive society
  contrasted with 'modern' societies, 41–2
  economy in, 45
  exchange in, 43
  politics in, 43
Principle of parsimony, 28–9
Psychoanalysis, 169, 173
Psychology, 51–2, 77

Radcliffe-Brown, A. R., 58, 97–8, 112
Rationalism, 164

Rationalist theory of social action, 79, 159, 165
Ravel, M., 141
Reciprocity, principle of, 44ff, 48ff, 76ff
Regime, *see* Kinship
Representation, ideological, 9, 95–6, 122, 144, 150ff, 162
Residence, *see* Kinship
Rey, P. P., 173
Ricoeur, P., 166, 173
Ritual, 96, 103
Rivers, W. H. R., 56
Rosen, L., 168
Rossi, I., 2, 45, 48, 75, 163–4, 167
Rousseau, J-J., 2, 107, 113, 164
Ruthven, K., 172

Sahlins, M., 2, 163
Sartre, J-P., 90, 168
Saussure, F. de, 4, 157, 172
Savage, S., 163
Schneider, D. M., 165, 168
Scholte, B., 2, 75, 163–4, 166–7
Science, of the concrete, 95, 101, 111, 116, 136, 148ff, 169
  of the 'abstract', 148ff
Sebag, L., 12, 33, 152, 165–6, 168, 172
Segal, D. M., 170
Selby, N., 45, 168
Semiology/Semiotics, 4ff, 91, 94, 149, 156ff
Signification, 9, 50, *see also* symbolism
Simonis, Y., 165
Social Action, 156ff
Social, the, as object of knowledge, 8ff, 40, 91, 157ff
Social change, 88–93
Social solidarity, 66–72, 83–7
Society, concept of, 39, 42
Species, concept of, 101, 106–9, 112
Sperber, D., 137, 147–8, 172
Structure, concept of 8–9, 11, 22, 32, 35–6, 91–3
Subject, epistemological, 23, 25, 112–13
Superstructure, theory of, 115, 172
Symbolism, 9, 47, 50–1; *see also* Semiology

Synchrony, 73, 90–3, 114
Syntax, of models, 26
Systems theory, 4, 10

Teleology, 54, 73, 78, 88, 113, 154
Terray, E., 174
Theoretical discourse, analysis of,
    1–3, 5ff, 74–5, 163
Thurnwald, R. C., 43
Total social facts, 43, 51, 54, 76
Totemism, 26, 96ff, 107
    caste and, 104–6, 114–16, 169–70
    equilibration in, 101ff
    Functionalist theory of, 97
    social function of, 97, 101, 111ff
    totemic logic, 100, 103, 106ff
    totemic operator, 101, 107–13
    transformations and, 101ff, 107–10
Troubetzkoy, N. S., 17
Tylor, E. B., 56
Typology, of societies, 93

Unconscious, the concept of, in Lévi-
    Strauss 2, 10, 11, 12ff, 136, 147
    binarism in, 16, 18–19
    brain and, 15, 18–19, 159–60
    double determination in, 16, 159–
        60, 173
    intellection in, 14–15
    methodological function of, 13–21,
        164
    perception and, 16, 88, 112–13
    recognition structure in, 16, 79, 88,
        112–13, 159–60, 167
Unconscious, the concept of, in
    Freud, 164

'Verstehen', method of, 173
Voluntarism, 88, 160–2

Wilden, A., 49, 51, 75, 163, 166–7
Willer, J., 168, 172
Williams, K., 163
Worsley, P., 169